TRIP ARRIVES

A Rob Mathews Sports Season
Book 5

Mac McGowan

CV-LW Books

Copyright © 2023 by Terry McGowan

All rights reserved.

No part of this publication may be reproduced, distributed, or transmitted in any form or by any means, including photocopying, recording, or other electronic or mechanical methods, without the prior written permission of the publisher, except as permitted by U.S. copyright law. For permission requests, please contact Terry McGowan at mac.mcgowan23@gmail.com

The story, all names, characters, and incidents portrayed in this production are fictitious. No identification with actual persons (living or deceased), places, buildings, and products is intended or should be inferred.

Book Cover by 100 Covers

Published by CV-LW Books 1st edition 2023

ISBN# 978-1-962126-17-5   Paperback version

DEDICATION

The Rob Mathews Sports Series is dedicated first to three of our 13 grandchildren. Our oldest, JT, began reading the series as a ten-year-old. He was patient, as there were only two completed books when he started, and so he read the first few books several times. His enthusiasm pushed me to continue writing. Dean and Gavin were next, beginning to read them when they were 12 and ten. They started the series as I was working on Book 11, and again, their enthusiasm and enjoyment of the books drove me to the finish line. The series is also dedicated to my wonderful wife, Suzy, who put up with my countless hours on the computer, writing, editing, editing, and editing! Her positive comments after helping edit the first three books also pushed me to finish. Many thanks to you all!

Preface

A few words about this book and the Rob Mathews Sports Series. While each book could certainly be read "on its own," I think readers will find the series a much more enjoyable experience if starting with Book One (Fresh Start) and reading them in order until completion. This series was written in many ways as one long, gigantic book. Plot lines are established in Book One (Fresh Start) that run through the entire series, and several main characters are added as the series progresses, most notably in Book Four (Last Chance), Book Eight (New Normal), and Book Nine (Best Case). Reading the books out of order might cause you to scratch your head about who a character is or why they are doing this or that.

In addition, many character traits and attitudes are established early and subtly change as young kids mature into young adults. Since the series travels from the beginning of 9th grade to the end of 12th grade, some behavior needs to mature slowly over time as it would in the real world. Some issues simply would not change over the course of three months, the rough time span of each book. For instance, the main character's and his male friend's obsession with appearance gradually changes, showing positive improvement as early as Book Two (Game Plan) and Book Three (Team Players), and fully changes by Book Six (Missed Chances). However, please note that both teenage boys and girls do, in real life, have and express opinions about the appearance of the opposite sex.

Finally, should some of the sports action described be hard to believe, I assure you I have personally experienced or seen everything described actually happen!

Enjoy the series, and thank you for reading!

CHAPTER 1
NOVEMBER-SOPHOMORE YEAR

*E*MILY Mathews brushed back her long, auburn hair and gazed again at the November 1st edition of the *Hillsdale Express*. She smiled at the banner headline. *How could one headline make me so happy... make the whole town of Hillsdale so happy?*

HILLSDALE-PINE BLUFF GET 2 MORE GAMES

SCHEDULE APPROVED-PB TO HOST NEXT YEAR

Two more games, Emily thought happily. *Two more chances to win back the "Pick." Of course, we have to win both, or it doesn't matter.*

Since losing last Saturday, in what they thought was their last chance, Hillsdale had been a most unhappy place to reside. But the announcement that the Pine Bluff merger had been delayed had caused an immediate about-face. After a collective sigh of relief, the citizens of Hillsdale began dreaming again of bringing the "Pick" back to Hillsdale for all time.

The "Pick," a gold-plated miner's pick, had served as the symbol of victory in the Hillsdale-Pine Bluff football game since 1966. The overall series began in the 1920s and had been tied at the time of the "Pick's" inception, and Pine Bluff now led by one slim game. The "Reprieve" gave Hillsdale a chance to steal it back forever with wins in the next two games.

Hillsdale, a charming village of about 10,000 people, is nestled in the Sierra Nevada foothills above Sacramento. It is a tight-knit community that is rabid about Hillsdale High School sports ... and especially about the "Pick!" The tree-lined streets surrounding downtown are picture-perfect, as is the old-time business district, still populated by family-owned shops and restaurants. Downtown also boasted a two-block-square Main Street Park, where the community gathered for significant events.

Emily, an early widow for over a year, moved toward the stove to check the bacon she was frying. Clad in warm jogging pants and a floppy sweatshirt, she looked nothing like the stylish, almost 40-year-old she was. Standing about five-foot-six, with a slender, shapely figure, her son Rob's friends thought she was a knockout!

Moving back to the kitchen island, she thumbed through the pages of the *Hillsdale Express* to Dan Mercer's "Old Grump" column in the sports section. Her eyes darted over the words until she came to the part of the article she wanted to read again.

"The Pine Bluff merger being delayed ... "The Reprieve," as it's being called in Hillsdale ... is the best thing to happen in a while. Not only do we have a shot the next two years to beat Pine Bluff and reclaim the "Pick" for all time ... but with Rob Mathews, we have a great chance at success. If Bill McHenry sticks around Hillsdale ... that just might clinch it. That happens, and I'm officially on board the Pirate football Bandwagon."

Emily smiled and instinctively looked at the landing leading up to the upstairs bedrooms. Rob Mathews and Bill "Trip" McHenry were both in bed upstairs. *Those two goofs are Hillsdale's best chance of beating Pine Bluff,* she thought. *My son and Chuck McHenry's grandson. And ... Rick McHenry's son,* Emily realized, wrinkling her nose in distaste.

***

*U*PSTAIRS, Rob Mathews woke up with a broad smile on his face. He stretched out his still-growing, nearly six-foot-two-inch, and 200-pound body and grinned. *Basketball starts today ... all right!* Rob thought as he wiped the sleep from his eyes. *And "The Reprieve." "The Reprieve."* His grin got even bigger. *We are going to get it done!*

Rob got out of bed, placed his favorite Giants' hat over his short, brown hair... checked in the mirror for any new pimples... smiled when he didn't find any and headed downstairs.

In the bedroom next door, Trip McHenry sat up after a fitful night's sleep, trying to figure out what to do. He stretched his body out... six-foot-six and 235 pounds... and he yawned. *What am I going to do?* he thought. *Do I stay in Hillsdale or move back to L.A.? If I stay, do I go here or to Valley Christian? I really want to go back to L.A.... I think. Canyon High... now that's a basketball machine... an easy ticket to a full ride at USC.*

Trip rolled over and pulled himself off the bed. He checked himself out in the mirror, finger-combing through his dark, wavy hair, which was key to his Hollywood good looks. *That's what I want... a ride to the University of Southern California! Canyon has to be the top pick. Or Valley Christian. I've got to get that full ride to USC!*

***

NEXT door, Allison Pierce was also yawning and stretching as she clamored out of bed. She caught a look at herself in the mirror and winced. *Will I ever grow up?* she groused. In the reflection, she saw a tall, skinny, nerdy-looking girl with a mouth full of braces. Her long, jet-black hair hung halfway down her back, and her blue eyes were lost behind huge glasses. *Every boy's dream,* she reflected sarcastically.

She frowned at herself, and her mind drifted next door. *I wish I were that boy's dream,* Allison mused. *I'm so glad the Pine Bluff merger fell through... it made Rob so happy.*

***

DONNIE Fields was 30 minutes into his workout. His lean, muscled body glistened with sweat, and he wiped his bald head with a towel and thought, *this Pine Bluff deal is the best thing that ever happened. Can't waste it. We are beating Pine Bluff next year or else. I'm getting everybody on board... including Trip McHenry!*

CHAPTER 2

NOVEMBER-SOPHOMORE YEAR

"**C'MON,** McHENRY, YOU'RE LOAFING!!!!" bellowed Hillsdale High's Varsity Basketball coach Hal Bridges.

Trip McHenry shrugged his shoulders imperceptibly, rolled his eyes, and increased his effort slightly.

"NO!!!!" Coach Bridges bellowed again. "THAT'S JUST NOT GOOD ENOUGH!!!"

Coach Bridges shot a glance at Rob Mathews that said, *What the heck is going on?* Rob shrugged his shoulders and gazed at Trip to see him standing unfazed at the baseline.

"I think Coach wants you to work a little harder," Rob Mathews said under his breath.

Trip rolled his eyes at Rob and looked over at Coach Bridges, who was staring daggers at Trip. "He doesn't cut anybody any slack, does he?" Trip asked quietly.

Rob just nodded in agreement.

"TRY IT AGAIN . . . AND I WANT TO SEE EVERYONE GOING FULL OUT," boomed Coach Bridges, his eyes glued to Trip. "OK, GO!!!"

About 20 boys shot down the court at full speed, backpedaling to the far baseline. Once there, they blasted themselves full speed back to the other end of the Hillsdale High gym.

A second group took off as the first group returned, and Rob Mathews watched as the whole group strained to do their best. *I wonder what Trip will do?* Rob thought as they awaited their turn. *Is he going to dog it or show Coach what he's got?*

The answer came immediately, as Trip rocketed off the baseline with the final group and easily reached the far end first. He tapped the end line and sprinted full blast back to the starting position, a good third of the court ahead of anyone else.

"THAT'S MORE LIKE IT," Coach Bridges exploded. "THAT'S HOW IT'S DONE!!!"

The rest of the group finished, and Coach Bridges called for a water break.

"Just like his old man," Coach Bridges muttered to JV coach Bob Lucas at mid-court. "Got all the tools but is too lazy to use them unless he wants to . . ."

Coach Lucas nodded, "You'll just have to break him of that."

"If he's like his Dad, it will be easier said than done," Coach Bridges replied ruefully. "Never could get his Dad on board . . . ending up costing him at college . . . but here . . . he was good enough to get away with it. Not my best job of coaching."

***

OVER 60 boys were crowded in the gym on this first day of practice, hoping to be one of the 42 lucky souls to make one of the three Hillsdale squads.

The first hour of practice had been pure conditioning . . . drills designed to weed out the weak of mind . . . and weak of condition. Hillsdale's teams, at all three levels, had the reputation of being in shape . . . and it started on day one.

As they returned from the water break, no one had touched a ball yet, but dribbling and passing were up next and would be done at full speed.

Here is where the coaches could start to separate the real players from those guys who could just run. Here is where the cream began to rise to the top . . . and, just as importantly, where some in the group sank to the bottom.

The three head coaches, Hal Bridges, Bob Lucas, and Rick Smith, stood watching from the half-court area, barking out orders and making notes on what they saw.

Coaches Lucas and Smith looked the basketball type, tall and rangy, although Coach Smith had a bit more bulk. Both were in their early 40s, still fit and relatively trim.

Hal Bridges was over 70 . . . and, despite a slight pot belly and some creaky knees, still moved around the floor like the college point guard he once was many years ago. This was year 34 for Bridges at Hillsdale High, and 14 championship banners hung from the rafters of the Pirate's home gym . . . but none for the last 11 years.

Last year had been a killer when a missed three at the buzzer had cost Hillsdale the crown, and Coach Bridges had been bitterly disappointed.

A couple of years younger than Rob's Grandpa, Keith Russell . . . the pair were close friends. A few days ago, over coffee at Pop's Diner, Coach Bridges proclaimed to his friend, "I don't have many years left in me, but I vowed to win another title before I retired. Your grandson could make that happen real soon . . . but I'm sure we'll win at least one out of the next three!"

"He's a good one," Keith Russell said proudly, running a hand through his gray hair.

"But throw in the McHenry kid, and I think we're the favorites," Coach Bridges continued. "I only hope the kid takes after Grandpa and not Dad."

Keith Russell smiled ruefully.

"He's a good kid," Keith said as he stood, stretching out his six-foot-two, 195-pound body. "But I'm not sure yet where he falls on that count."

Coach Bridges recalled that conversation as he watched Trip sail skillfully through the ball-handling drills. *He definitely has talent . . . and raw power and speed. We need him to get his head screwed on right!*

Trip snapped a pass back hard at his partner Rob Mathews and grinned as Rob made a tough catch, whirled, and fired a perfect bounce pass back to Trip.

"Ah, "Wonder Boy" is back in town," Trip quipped, and Rob grunted out a laugh.

"Wonder Boy" was the nickname Trip stuck Rob with shortly after he moved to town about a month ago. Rob led the way on Bill's name change to "Trip." The nickname came from the hope of finding a big, tough, fast stud athlete to push the football, basketball, and baseball programs over the top. Three sports . . . triple duty . . . hence Trip. Rob and others thought Bill might be the answer.

The pair enjoyed ribbing each other, and "Wonder Boy" was Trip's favorite way of needling Rob.

"Keep dazzling me, "Wonder Boy," Trip sniped after Rob delivered another perfect pass.

Another grunt and a half-smile was the only response as Coach Bridges boomed, "LINE UP FOR SPRINTS!!! LET'S END THIS PRACTICE THE RIGHT WAY!!!!"

Rob scanned the gym, waiting his turn to run, and remembered how much fun it was to play here. His eyes went to the tall windows above the bleachers, almost reaching the high ceiling. Next, he looked lovingly at the wood parquet floor that old-timers said looked like the floor at the old Boston Garden where the Celtics played for years. Finally, he watched as the group ahead of his group dashed over the Pirates logo at mid-court.

I have some good memories of playing here, Rob thought. *The crowds are so great and they pack the place. I hope we can make some good memories here this year!*

Coach Bridges' whistle blared, and Rob's group was on the go. *This certainly is not one of the good memories,* Rob thought as he sprinted full-out down the court.

CHAPTER 3
NOVEMBER-SOPHOMORE YEAR

ROB grimaced in pain the following day as he crawled out of bed and headed for the shower. *Using different muscles than in football,* he realized as he soaked under the shower.

A few minutes later, Rob and Trip sat munching their way through cold cereal and nursing their sore muscles at the breakfast table.

"Coach Bridges always run those kinds of practices?" Trip asked, hoping it was a one-time thing.

Rob nodded and replied. "Yeah . . . probably be tough like that for the rest of this week . . . and most of next week . . . although next week he'll start letting us play basketball a little more . . . instead of just running."

"Great," Trip drawled sarcastically. "I'm ready to play now."

"Not on Coach's team," Rob said. "His teams all play full-out all the time . . . you have to be in shape, or you won't see the floor."

Trip rolled his eyes and sighed.

"Your Coach wasn't like that last year?" Rob asked.

"Nah," Trip said. "He pretty much let me skate the whole year. Kinda' did whatever I wanted and still played full-time. He knew I was the best he had . . . and he couldn't afford to sit me. It was great!"

Uh, oh, Rob thought. *This could be trouble. Coach Bridges sure isn't going to let him get away with that.*

"Yeah, I don't think Coach will go for that," Rob said. "You know I love him . . . but he's tough. Everything he does is right out there . . . if you screw up, he is yelling it for everyone to hear . . . but if you do it right, everyone knows it, too."

"Yeah, I noticed that yesterday," Trip mused.

"Don't let the negative stuff get you down . . . as long as you hustle and are a team player, you're okay," Rob advised. "But I guarantee you . . . if you don't hustle, you'll get yelled at . . . and if you're not a team player . . . well, you'll spend a lot of time on the bench."

"Can't see that happening," Trip cracked. "I'm too good for him to bench me. Can't believe he isn't smart enough to see that!"

Oh, boy, Rob groaned inside. *He's going to have to find out the hard way.*

***

*A*ND on Friday afternoon, he did!

"McHENRY, WHAT THE HECK ARE YOU DOING??!! MOVE IT!!!!" Coach Bridges bellowed. "YOU HAVE TO HUSTLE!!!!"

Trip immediately reacted with a burst of speed into another gear but eased up after Coach Bridges turned his head.

The next time down the floor, Trip had reverted to his lazy pace, and Coach Bridges exploded again.

"McHENRY!!!! ARE YOU HURT???!!! IF YOU ARE, GET OFF THE FLOOR!!! IF NOT, GET MOVING!!!!" Coach Bridges boomed.

Trip accelerated again for a moment but eased off when Coach Bridges turned to talk to Coach Lucas.

Coach Bridges was seething, and Rob was worried this would escalate into a war. *Trip needs to get with the program,* Rob thought. *If he doesn't, we lose a huge piece of our team.*

"OK, ON THE BASELINE!" Coach Bridges boomed. "WE'LL FINISH UP WITH LINES. LET'S SEE SOME HUSTLE!!!"

The 60 or so boys lined up to run in three groups, and Rob moved to the baseline with the final group that included Trip.

"ANY LAGGING AND YOU WILL ALL DO IT AGAIN," Coach Bridges warned with a tremendous roar.

Rob and Trip waited their turn, watching the other two groups do five sets of lines before pulling up, exhausted and panting.

It was the final group's turn, and they exploded off the baseline together. All 20 boys strained to do their best . . . no one wanted to have to do it again.

After the third set, though, Trip McHenry started to slow up. Rob shot him a glance that said, *come on, don't let up now.*

It didn't help.

Trip lazily completed the last two trips up and down the court, finishing half a court behind the group, and Coach Bridges boiled over.

"McHENRY, THAT WAS BULL!!! EVERYBODY . . . DO IT AGAIN!!!" Coach Bridges shrieked.

The other 59 boys groaned and stared daggers at Trip McHenry. Then the grumbling started, and Trip realized what he had done.

He's not making any friends here, Rob grimaced.

I guess the old guy is for real, Trip mused. *He is going to make us do it right . . . I thought he'd cave.*

When Group Three's turn came up, Trip led the way up and down the court and quickly finished before anyone else, then stood bent over with his hands on his knees, sucking air.

Trip looked up and saw many of the boys glaring at him as the final group finished. *Not the best way to make friends,* Trip thought. *Oh, well, I won't be here that long!*

Coach Bridges hollered out, "THAT IS THE WAY IT'S DONE!!! NICE JOB, EVERYBODY!!! HIT THE SHOWERS AND BE READY FOR MORE OF THE SAME ON MONDAY!!!"

The huge group of players grabbed their gear and headed to the locker room, but it was apparent to Rob that Coach Hal Bridges was still mad.

"YOU TWO," Coach Bridges shouted, catching Rob's eye and pointing at Rob and then Trip. "IN MY OFFICE . . . RIGHT NOW."

Uh, oh, Rob thought. *This can't be good!*

CHAPTER 4
NOVEMBER-SOPHOMORE YEAR

As Rob walked into Hal Bridges' office, he knew Trip McHenry was in for a tirade . . . but he got a surprise . . . a low-key and relatively quiet Coach Bridges.

Coach Bridges glared at Trip and motioned both boys to sit in the chairs facing his desk.

Without taking his eyes off Trip McHenry, Coach Bridges said to Rob, "You're here to listen, Mathews, not speak. Got it?"

"Got it," Rob mumbled, clearly uneasy with the situation.

"I don't want any wild stories spreading about what goes on here today," Coach Bridges continued, still glaring at Trip.

The three of them sat in silence, with Coach Bridges staring at Trip and Trip staring at his shoes. After 90 long seconds, Trip raised his head and met Coach Bridges' eyes.

They stared at each other for another 30 seconds before Coach Bridges cleared his throat and addressed Trip in the quietest voice Rob had ever heard him use.

"So, you want to explain yourself, McHenry?" Coach Bridges began.

"Explain what?" Trip replied.

"Your attitude . . . your loafing . . ." Coach Bridges answered, trying to stay patient.

"That's the way I always practice," Trip answered sulkily. "My coaches last year never cared . . . they knew I was a gamer."

"And, do you see any of your coaches from last year in this room . . . or out on that floor?" Coach Bridges asked, gesturing to the Hillsdale gym.

"No . . ." Trip answered sullenly.

"Then let's stop talking about your coaches from last year," Coach Bridges sighed.

Coach Bridges gazed at Trip, clearly trying to decide how to best handle the situation. An awkward silence pervaded the room until Coach Bridges cleared his throat again.

"Ahem," Coach Bridges began. "I knew your grandfather very well . . . good man . . . honest, ethical, a lot of integrity . . . great work ethic. I was sorry when he passed away."

Trip brightened at the mention of his grandfather.

"I coached your Dad," Coach Bridges continued. "He had great talent . . . but no work ethic . . . bad attitude . . . never really reached his potential . . ."

"I'm not my Dad," Trip flashed angrily.

There's the button, Hal Bridges thought. *Use his Dad, and we can unlock the potential.*

"I was hoping that was the case," Coach Bridges said. "I was hoping you took after your grandfather. I think you need us to help you become more like Chuck."

"I don't need you for anything," Trip flashed again. "Tiny school . . . you can't help me get my ride to USC."

Coach Bridges shook his head slowly in disbelief. *His attitude right now is just like his Dad's . . . how do we change that?* He bowed his head, took a deep breath, and thought things through as he released his breath in a heavy sigh. *His Dad's the key . . . but I need to use it the right way . . .*

CHAPTER 5
NOVEMBER-SOPHOMORE YEAR

"*YOU* sounded just like your Dad right then," Coach Bridges said with exasperation. "You've got the talent to get to USC as he did . . . but you've also got his attitude . . . and you'll end up just like he did if you don't change it . . . riding the bench and moaning about a coach that didn't like him."

"I'm not my Dad," Trip snarled.

"Prove it," Coach Bridges said sternly, his eyes boring into Trip's for what seemed like an eternity . . . at least to Rob.

Another excruciating silence ensued as Coach Bridges and Trip stared each other down. Finally, Coach Bridges took a deep breath and spoke quietly.

"McHenry . . . I am only going to say this once. The basketball program at Hillsdale High School is all mine. It's not yours, or anybody else's . . . it's mine. This is not a democracy . . . I am the king. You do things my way . . . or not at all."

Coach Bridges paused, letting his words soak in.

"My way," Coach Bridges continued, "is that nobody gets special treatment and everybody puts out their maximum effort at all times . . . or they don't get to join the club. Currently, you're not doing that . . . and it has to change . . . or you won't be out here anymore."

Trip glared back at Coach Bridges but remained silent, trying to gauge if this demanding, old coach would stick to his guns . . . or cave.

"Bottom line is," Coach Bridges said slowly, looking Trip directly in his eyes, "you've got a choice here. A choice . . . one that only you can make. And, if you make the wrong choice and don't get to join our club, it will be no one's fault but your own."

Coach Bridges paused again, choosing his words carefully.

"Your choice is to change your attitude and work hard all the time . . . or get cut at the end of next week," Coach Bridges declared.

"You're going to cut me?" Trip scoffed. "Your best player? I don't think so . . ."

"You being the best player out here is subject to debate," Coach Bridges said, glancing over at Rob for the first time. "But that's neither here nor there."

Trip looked at Coach Bridges smugly. "I doubt it. You're not going to cut me."

A small smile . . . almost a grimace instead of a smile, briefly crossed Coach Bridges' face, and he took a deep breath and let it out slowly.

"That's where your wrong, son," Coach Bridges began. "You came out of nowhere. We didn't know we might have you until a few weeks ago. We will compete for a league and sectional championship with or without you. Would you make us better . . . sure . . . if you are on board . . . but if you're not on board, you make us worse. No . . . I'm sorry, McHenry . . . but we don't need you."

I think he believes that, Trip mused. *I think he would cut me.*

"No, son, we don't need you," Coach Bridges continued. "You need us."

Trip looked at Coach Bridges with surprise. "I need you," Trip said with a snort, not quite believing what he was hearing.

"Yes, you need us," Coach Bridges said. "You need us to prove to yourself and everybody else that you aren't your Dad."

The comment took Trip by surprise and rocked him back in his seat.

"Yes," Coach Bridges said with a small smile. "You want to prove that you're better than your Dad . . . as a player and as a man."

Trip rocked back in his chair again. *How did he know? And he's right . . . I have been acting like my Dad . . . I don't want to do that!*

Coach Bridges kept a careful eye on Trip and watched as Trip's face gave away what he was thinking. *I might have him,* Coach Bridges thought, hopefully.

Rob watched in wonder . . . Coach Bridges hit on Trip's problem. *I hadn't thought of that . . . but that's what it is. It's obvious Trip doesn't respect his Dad.*

"What I teach in my program is how to become a better person . . . how to be on time, how to be a good teammate, how to work hard and work smart . . . and how to take pride in everything . . . everything you do," Coach Bridges lectured. "That's why my teams succeed . . . I get most of the kids to buy into those ideals . . . they become better people, and we become a better team. Dave Wilson coaches the same way."

Coach Bridges paused again, letting the information sink in and hoping . . . hoping that Trip McHenry was going to buy in on the concept.

"Here's the deal," Coach Bridges said. "You've got the weekend to think. Come Monday . . . you better be prepared to give 110% the whole year . . . if you're not . . . don't bother showing up."

Trip looked blankly at Coach Bridges and pondered his situation. *I don't need this team. If I lose a year now, so what?*

Trip glanced at Rob, who smiled faintly and nodded. *But I want to play here . . . want to play with Rob and the guys.*

Trip looked back at Coach Bridges and nodded, mumbling, "I'll think it over."

"Think it over hard, McHenry," Coach Bridges said earnestly. "We want you out here with us. We can do great things as a team this year. But more importantly, think about what kind of man you want to grow up to be . . . someone with a bad attitude, a loafer, an underachiever like your Dad . . . or do you want to be someone like your Grandfather?"

Trip was jolted again at the comments about his Dad, and his face clouded over a mixture of disgust and a little anger at Coach Bridges for dissing his Dad.

Coach Bridges saw the look and read it perfectly.

"Hey, I call em' like I see em'," the old coach smiled. "It's just . . . I want you to reach your potential as a player and a person. I know down deep you want to take after your Grandfather . . . this team is your first step."

Trip mumbled something, shook his head to clear the cobwebs, and hid the trace of a tear starting to trickle from the corner of his eye.

"Do some hard thinking this weekend, Bill," Coach Bridges said softly. "Think about the big picture here . . . if you do that . . . well . . . if you do that, we'll see you in the gym Monday."

With that, the two boys rose and shuffled off and out into the early evening chill, both lost in thought about what Coach Bridges said . . . and what Trip would do.

Fingers crossed, Hal Bridges mused as the boys went out the door. *Fingers crossed that he wants to take after Chuck!*

CHAPTER 6
NOVEMBER-SOPHOMORE YEAR

***T**RIP* McHenry grunted as Rob Mathews boxed him out, leaned into him, and pushed off to sky for the rebound.

Rob darted to the end of his driveway to clear the ball with Trip on his heels. A quick shoulder fake gave Rob an opening, and he exploded past Trip and sank a reverse layup, using the rim to keep Trip from blocking his shot.

"That's game," Rob crowed loudly. "One game each . . . got to play another . . . championship of the world!"

Trip grinned back at Rob. "You're on!"

The boys each picked up a large water bottle propped up against the bottom of a tree and took long, loud gulps of lukewarm water.

Rob glanced at his phone lying on the grass, stabbed at the screen, and looked at the time.

"Gotta' make it quick," Rob chirped. "Ally and her Mom will be coming over soon for "Movie Night."

"Don't worry," Trip drawled with a laugh. "I'll make quick work of you. Do or die for first outs?"

Rob nodded, and Trip launched a rainbow from where he stood and gloated as the ball seared the nets.

"Looks like I get to score first," Trip grinned.

Trip retrieved his long shot, brought the ball to mid-court, and bounced a pass to Rob to check the ball.

Rob tossed the ball lazily to Trip and bounced into a tight, aggressive defensive position right on top of Trip.

Trip gathered the ball in and shrank back from Rob's tight defense, pivoting his body to protect his dribble. He started carefully backing Rob toward the basket, with Rob begrudging every inch.

Trip maneuvered his way close, then turned to go up for a short-range fade-away when he felt his pocket being picked by Rob's quick hands.

Rob flicked the ball away from Trip, scampered after it, and retrieved it at the top of the key. Without hesitation, he turned and let fly with a three-pointer that was nothing but net.

Playing winners out, Rob had Trip check the ball, gave a quick pump fake, power-dribbled past Trip, and pulled back to swish another shot for a 5-0 lead.

Trip grimaced as the ball went through the hoop and moved closer to Rob as he checked the ball. Rob took a jab-step and pulled back to let it fly, but Trip recovered quickly and was in his face. Rob wheeled around, dribbled toward the basket, and went up for a layup with a two-foot lead on Trip. Almost from nowhere, Trip's big paw swatted the shot away toward out of bounds.

Rob raced after the ball, corralled it, and restarted his offense. A slick behind-the-back dribble gave him some room, and he roared past Trip and scooped up a quick shot off the glass for a 7-0 lead.

Trip almost seemed to lose interest at this point and gave Rob too much space after he checked the ball. Rob sized up his shot and drilled another three for a 10-0 lead.

Trip held up his hand and walked over to get a drink from his water bottle as Allison and her Mom, Linda, arrived.

"We're almost done here," Rob called out, waving to the pair. "Go ahead and go on in, Linda . . . Mom's in the kitchen."

"Thanks, Rob," Linda answered, waving as she entered the side door.

Allison moved over to a bench in the yard to watch the guys finish their game.

Rob received the ball again from Trip and launched another three, but this one misfired, and Trip nonchalantly ran the ball down, cleared it, and turned to bury a three of his own to get himself on the board.

Rob was up in Trip's face again as soon as he got the ball and was harassing Trip at every turn. Trip backed Rob down again before kissing a sweet jump hook off the glass from six feet, and the score was 10-5.

Rob again attacked defensively as Trip got the ball, and he hurried Trip into dribbling the ball off his foot and into the yard. Rob scampered after the ball, brought it back, had Trip check it, and attacked immediately.

Dribbling expertly, Rob used a crossover and blew past Trip toward the basket. Trip half-heartedly chased after Rob and watched him as he dropped in a layup.

At the top of the key, Rob received the ball from Trip and noticed he was being lazy on defense. He worked his dribble slowly, got himself set, and drained another three with no defensive effort from Trip.

"That makes it 15-5!" Rob exclaimed as he waited for the ball from Trip.

Trip's face was getting red . . . not from exertion, but frustration. *What is up with this guy? He is relentless,* Trip thought, watching Rob anxiously awaiting the ball.

Trip tossed Rob the ball and suddenly advanced on Rob, ready to play defense. Rob dribbled to the right, reversed, and pulled up for a jumper. Trip skied toward Rob, caught a piece of the shot, then turned to track it down in the middle of the key.

Trip gathered in it and coiled to go up for a dunk when he sensed a body coming at him from behind. He powered up, protecting the ball, but Rob swung mightily with his right hand and forcefully knocked the ball away as Trip tried to slam it.

The ball popped out of Trip's hands, and Rob dove to get possession first. As he did, he had to roll to stop his momentum, but he had clearly traveled. Trip's ball!

What the heck? Trip thought. *Diving on the concrete? This guy is nuts!*

Rob tossed him the ball and immediately was on top of Trip again. His hands were poking, prodding, trying to use his weight to keep Trip from backing him down.

But Trip kept moving backward, ever closer to the basket, and finally got in position for another jump hook. Rob soared to try to block it, but Trip's size and strength won out, and Trip connected for two and a 15-7 score.

Trip started the next play, and Rob was back at him, jabbing, harassing, and eventually knocking the ball away with a flick of his hand. Rob burst away after the ball and knocked Trip off his feet and onto the concrete in the process.

"Geez, man," Trip snarled as he collected himself. "Can you dial it back a notch?"

Rob checked himself and answered, "Uh, probably not . . . sorry, though, my foul. Your ball."

This guy is out of control, Trip thought.

CHAPTER 7
NOVEMBER-SOPHOMORE YEAR

*A**LLISON* had not been paying much attention, but this interaction caught her attention. *Trip's not too happy with Rob,* she thought. *Are they going to get in a fight?*

Trip got up, dusted himself off, and restarted his offense . . . and Rob was right on top of him again.

Trip's face grew dark and determined, and he foolishly tried to use his speed instead of his size and strength to get around Rob.

Rob out-positioned him, caused Trip to pick up his dribble, and then take an awkward shot with Rob draped over him. After the shot, Rob touched down first and forcefully blocked Trip out, who grunted in reaction and shoved Rob off . . . unfortunately for Trip . . . right in the direction of the ball.

Rob rocketed over, snatched it up in the corner, and turned and blasted toward the hoop. Trip, his frustration boiling over, advanced on Rob, hoping to knock his shot into Allison's yard next door!

Trip's large bulk bit on a nifty move from Rob, and he rose high to block the shot. But Rob kept his feet, pivoted, and dropped the ball in at close range after Trip flew by him.

"That's 17-7," Rob blared out as Trip checked the ball back to him.

Rob was looking for a three to end this game, and Trip knew it. Suddenly Trip was engaged . . . he was miffed . . . and wanted nothing more than to bury Rob . . . but he knew he had dug a big hole for himself.

Trip crowded Rob, and he knew immediately it was a mistake. Rob jab-stepped around him and started racing for the basket. Trip turned and roared after Rob, his long legs eating up the half-court.

Rob could feel Trip on his heels and suddenly veered off toward the corner, taking Trip by surprise. He reached the three-point line and quickly launched a three that rolled around and off.

Instead of watching, Rob followed his shot and beat Trip to the ball. He continued to the other corner with the ball, but Trip seemed to give up on the play, clearly frustrated.

Rob reached his spot . . . turned and saw he had lots of times . . . and calmly drained a three to end the game.

"Champion of the World," Rob teased Trip as the ball dropped through the net. "Two out of three . . . I'll take that every time!"

"Yeah, this win will get you a lot," Trip replied sullenly.

"Hey, I'm just kidding," Rob answered defensively.

"No, you're not," Trip replied. "You're just too gung-ho . . . you never give it a break. Geez . . . I'm just out here for some fun. I don't care if I win . . . or if you win . . . who cares?"

Rob was stung. *I don't want Trip mad at me. It was just a stupid game.*

"I'm out here for fun, too," Rob countered. "But I can't not try to do my best. I don't care about winning or losing . . . but not giving it my best shot . . . ah, I can't do that."

"Well, maybe you should try it sometime," Trip snapped. "You might enjoy the game more!"

"Nah, I can't do that," Rob answered. "I enjoy the game a ton . . . but it's called taking pride in what you do."

They stared at each other for a long moment, neither knowing what the other one was thinking . . . but both knowing they didn't want this to grow into a big deal.

Taking pride . . . what B.S., Trip thought.

Allison stood up, and the boys both noticed her, breaking the stare-down. *I thought these guys were good friends . . . I hope I don't have to get in the middle of a fight!* Allison mused.

"Oh, Allison . . . uh, yeah, we've got to get showered and stuff for "Movie Night," Rob said slowly.

"You want to go first?" Rob asked, bobbing his head at Trip.

"First?" Trip questioned. "Yeah, I'll go first. You're Champion of the World! You need to bask in the glory of your victory with Allison!"

Rob resumed staring at Trip, who stared back.

"I'll be quick," Trip barked, turning and heading for the kitchen door.

CHAPTER 8
NOVEMBER-SOPHOMORE YEAR

"*WELL,* that was a little intense," Allison said, looking at Rob as he watched Trip stride into the house.

"Yeah," Rob said, shaking his head. "Not sure what his problem is?"

Rob retrieved his water bottle, picked up Trip's too, and headed to the front porch, where he took a long swig of water sitting on the steps.

Allison followed and sat next to him.

"You think maybe you were trying a little too hard?" Allison asked quizzically.

"You, too?" Rob answered with surprise. "Kind of funny coming from the straight A+ student who overdoes everything!"

Allison paused for a moment, reflecting on what Rob had said.

"Yeah," she said with a shy smile, "I guess you're right when you put it that way."

Rob smiled back and nodded.

"But you guys . . . you were really mad at each other . . . you guys going to be all right?" Allison asked with concern.

Rob looked at her questionably.

"What . . . uh, what do you mean, all right?" Rob asked.

"You guys looked ready to fight or something," Allison continued.

"Nah, that was just playing around," Rob replied. "Just guy stuff . . . we're good."

"Why were you trying so hard?" Allison asked.

"Well," Rob said, searching for the right words. "It's a little complicated. Coach Bridges has kinda' given Trip an ultimatum . . . start hustling . . . and working harder . . . or don't bother coming back out. He has to decide this weekend."

"Oh," Allison said, surprised. "I didn't know he didn't try at practice . . . I'm kind of shocked."

"Me, too," Rob agreed. "Coach is too . . . I was trying to show him what it looks like to try all the time . . . I guess I went overboard . . . but you know my Dad . . . and Coach Wilson and Coach Bridges . . . have drummed it into me all my life . . . do your best . . . take pride in everything you're doing so you can be the best you can be . . . you know to reach my highest potential."

Allison looked at Rob with admiration, knowing he had done just that in his sports.

"You know . . . Coach Bridges just wants Trip to reach his potential because he has high hopes on a full ride to USC," Rob said. "Coach wants to see him do it . . . guess he tried to help Trip's Dad reach his potential, and it didn't work . . . he's afraid Trip's going the same route."

"What do you think Trip will do . . . will he quit?" Allison asked.

"Nah, I don't think so," Rob answered slowly. "I think the talent and will are there . . . but Trip's stubborn . . . doesn't want to be told what to do . . . but I think he'll come around."

"I hope so," Allison said, pausing and looking skyward momentarily.

"So, not to change the subject . . . but I haven't had a minute alone with you since the "Pick" game and all that happened that night . . . you doing OK?" Allison asked.

"Yeah . . . the "Reprieve" really helped . . . I'm not sure I'd be OK yet without knowing we had another chance," Rob said, shaking his head slowly. "That loss was a killer."

"How about the Carly thing . . . you OK with that?" Allison asked sympathetically.

"Yeah, I got over that real quick," Rob answered with an embarrassed smile. "I sure know how to pick em', eh, Allison?"

"You sure do," Allison replied with a light laugh.

Rob smiled sheepishly.

"Maybe next time you should actually like the girl as a person before falling in "looove," Allison teased.

"I was thinking I might just give up girls for a while," Rob answered with a smile. "And when I decide to get back into the game . . . I'll have you decide if they are right for me or not."

They laughed hard, and Allison beamed her best smile, which melted his heart and made him feel warm all over.

Rob gazed into her eyes and felt himself relax. *It feels good to be with Ally,* Rob realized. *Should I tell her that? But what would I say? Do I like her? Do I like her like that? I'm not sure . . . I should tell her . . . maybe not . . .*

Allison held her breath . . . hoping Rob would say something sweet . . .

Rob's thoughts were broken when a booming voice bellowed out, "You're up, "Wonder Boy" . . . bathroom's all yours!"

Trip stood above, grinning at them as if nothing had happened on the court ten minutes ago.

CHAPTER 9
NOVEMBER-SOPHOMORE YEAR

"*Y*OUR Mom says hustle up... dinner is almost ready," Trip added with a broad grin. "It smells fantastic."

Rob jumped up, gave Allison a quick smile, and bounded into the house and up the stairs.

Allison returned the smile, but inside she was crushed. *He was going to say something sweet right then. Doggone, Trip!*

Allison turned to Trip with a sad smile, and he knew he had come at a bad time.

"Oh, hey, did I interrupt something important?" Trip asked with embarrassment. "I'm sorry... wouldn't have expected Rob to... well... to be saying something personal-like to you, Allison... not that he shouldn't... just that he wouldn't be smart enough to do it."

Allison smiled at that, knowing Trip thought she was a good fit for Rob... and that Rob didn't know it yet. *At least that is what I hope he meant,* she mused.

"Thanks, Trip," she smiled in reply. "It was nothing important," she lied.

"So," Allison continued, changing the subject. "That was a pretty intense game you guys had... you guys OK?"

Trip looked at her quizzically.

"You're not mad at him?" Allison asked.

"Nah," Trip laughed. "Just blowing off steam. He gets pretty focused and has to be perfect out there . . . I just wanted to have some fun."

"Sounds like you might not have any fun this basketball season if you don't start to focus and try your best at practice," Allison said directly, looking Trip in the eyes.

"There's the Allison I've heard about. Bold and direct . . . don't mince words or sugarcoat anything," Trip said with a smirk.

"Guilty," Allison laughed, raising her hand.

"Why is it such a big deal to you . . . or to him?" Trip asked in bewilderment. "It's my life . . . why do you guys care so much."

"You're our friend, Trip," Allison replied sincerely, smiling into his eyes.

Trip met her eyes and her smile. *She's telling the truth,* Trip realized. *She's doesn't care about making the basketball team better . . . she said it because she really is my friend. Maybe . . . just maybe . . . Rob really is my friend, too.*

"We want you to do your best for you . . . so you reach your goals," Allison continued. "That's what Rob is talking about . . . taking pride in what you do . . . trying to do your best to get better all the time . . . so you reach your goal . . . you know, the scholarship to USC."

"Yeah . . . I get that," Trip said slowly. "But sometimes playing against some of these guys . . . you know, the younger guys . . . it just makes me lazy."

"Yeah, but if you are going to make it to USC, you've got to get into the right habits now," Allison lectured. "Playing against those guys is not going to be easy. I don't know much about sports, but I know USC is huge . . . getting a scholarship there is not going to be a sure thing . . . the competition is going be tough."

Trip nodded and reflected. *She's right . . . dorky, old Allison . . . the least athletic person I know . . . but she hit it right on the head.*

"Besides," Allison went on. "I look at it this way. You have what, maybe 16-18 weeks of basketball, right?"

Trip nodded.

"Five or six days a week. Probably three hours a day," Allison plodded on. "Let's see, that's 18 times five, that's 90 days in your season . . . at three hours a day . . . that's 270 hours of your life."

Trip marveled at Allison and saw she was passionate about the topic.

"Personally," Allison proclaimed, "if I'm spending 270 hours on something, I want to be sure it's worth my time. If I'm not doing my best . . . well, then, I've just wasted a lot of time. I don't want to spend 270 hours doing anything if it's a waste of time!"

Trip was nodding in understanding. *She's right . . . she's right.*

"But if I spent 270 hours on something that meant the world to me . . . like getting a basketball scholarship to USC . . . and I didn't get that scholarship . . . I would really be mad at myself knowing I had wasted even one of those 270 hours," Allison added.

Trip was stunned. *There it is . . . laid out in black and white. Bold and direct. Allison's specialty.*

"Yeah, I . . . I get it," Trip said shyly, looking down to meet Allison's eyes. "Thanks, Allison . . . I needed to hear it that way."

They peered into each other's eyes, and Allison broke into a smile that Trip returned. *She is my friend,* Trip thought.

"Ahem," Rob suddenly cleared his throat with a laugh. "Sorry to interrupt you guys, but dinner's ready."

Rob looked at both of them quizzically. *Is there something going on between them,* Rob thought suddenly. *I don't know how I feel about that. Weird, I guess. But why?*

Trip and Allison broke their look, and both laughed nervously . . . neither of them knowing just what, if anything, was going on.

They both stood up as Rob took a step toward the door.

"Hey, "Wonder Boy," Trip called out, stopping Rob before he went inside.

Rob paused and looked back. "Yeah?"

"Starting tomorrow," Trip said calmly, "I'm going full-out, 100 percent of the time at practice . . . I get it."

Rob turned, smiled, and raised his clenched hand for a quick fist bump.

"I'm glad, man," Rob said sincerely. "That'll get you that ride to USC. What made you decide?"

Trip glanced at Allison and nodded at her.

"She did," Trip smiled. "She just said it the right way . . . and for the right reasons."

Allison flushed, her face turning a bright red in seconds.

Rob looked back and forth between them . . . wondering.

"Yeah," Trip continued. "I just may have to start calling her "Wonder Girl!"

They all laughed hard and went through the door to dinner.

Hmmm, "Wonder Girl," Rob thought. Sounds about right.

CHAPTER 10

NOVEMBER-SOPHOMORE YEAR

"***G****REAT* JOB, McHENRY!!!!"* Coach Bridges bellowed as he watched Trip McHenry hustle his way down the floor. "THAT'S THE WAY IT'S DONE!!!"

Trip smiled slightly through gritted teeth as he pulled up on the baseline before anyone else. He was tired and panting, bent over and holding his knees, but he was satisfied with his performance during practices this week. He had laid it all out there and had been playing well, getting into better shape . . . and better habits . . . and into the good graces of Coach Bridges.

"ALL RIGHT, BRING IT IN," Coach Bridges said, and over 50 players gathered around him and Coaches Lucas and Smith at the far end of the gym.

"I'm proud of all of you for coming out and working hard since last Wednesday," Coach Bridges said in a quieter voice. "You've given it your best shot . . . and now, unfortunately, is the time for us to cut the teams down. As you know, we are keeping just 12 on Varsity and 15 on both the JV and Frosh teams . . . that means about ten of you won't be back tomorrow."

Coach Bridges paused and scanned the group, noting the reactions of the boys on the edge. A few worried faces peered back at him while some lowered their eyes to avert his gaze.

"We don't like cutting . . . but . . . you can see we just have too many," Coach Bridges continued. "We'll post the teams on my office door tonight before we leave . . . you can check the list first thing in the morning."

Several boys kept their eyes downcast . . . they knew they would be cut . . . but for some players . . . it would be a long sleepless night . . . and an even longer Friday at school if their names were not on one of the team lists.

"Again, thank you all for coming out," Coach Bridges concluded. "Remember, if you don't make it, there is always next year . . . I remember a story about Michael Jordan getting cut once in high school. Keep working at it, and next year, you might make it. OK, hit the showers!"

The large group milled around for a moment, and then big chunks of kids began heading to the locker room. Trip and Rob sauntered toward the showers, confident they would make the Varsity.

"All right, guys," Coach Bridges said to his coaches. "Give me about 15 minutes and meet me in my office, and we'll hammer this out!"

***

"I'M sorry guys . . . I'm not trying to wreck your seasons . . . but I need to bring these guys up . . . we lost nine seniors to graduation last year . . . we only have one senior in the program because of graduation and injury. I need to have the 12 best players in the program with me this year," Coach Bridges said apologetically. "This is where we have to start so you guys know who you won't have."

JV Coach Bob Lucas and Frosh Coach Rick Smith looked down at the handwritten list that Hal Bridges slid across the table. Both coaches grimaced at what they saw, immediately realizing that the cream of the freshman and sophomore classes would be playing at the Varsity level this year.

"Ugh," Bob Lucas grunted. "I understand it . . . but I don't have to like it."

Rick Smith pulled the list toward him for a better look and joined in the grunt as he read the names, classes, and positions they would play:

    1. Rob Mathews-Sophomore-1,2,3

    2. Bill McHenry-Sophomore-3,4,5

    3. Sam Jordan-Senior-2,3,4

    4. Brad Wallace-Junior-2

    5. Edgar Garcia-Sophomore-4,5

    6. Bob Johnson-Sophomore-2,3

    7. Dom Fiorenza-Sophomore-1,2

    8. Alex Cohen-Sophomore-3,4

    9. Greg Montgomery-Junior-4,5

    10. Daniel Valdez-Junior-4,5

    11. Gabe Cantor-Freshman-3,4,5

    12. Josh Lee-Freshman-1,2

"You're going to be young," Bob Lucas said as Rick Smith perused the list. "Surprised at the freshman."

Rick Smith chimed in and seconded that thought. "Those two going to get enough playing time?"

"I know what you're thinking, guys," Coach Bridges answered, clearly expecting their reactions. "Josh is the best point guard option we have if Mathews goes down . . . likewise with Gabe . . . he'll be the best choice out there if McHenry goes down . . . or if he's gone after this year."

Coach Lucas and Coach Smith looked at each other in appreciation of Coach Bridges' thought process.

"I especially need Gabe to get some real Varsity experience this year in case McHenry bolts to Valley Christian or back down south to Canyon," Coach Bridges explained. "Just the practices will be good for them . . . what better way to improve than going up against Mathews and McHenry all year?"

The two coaches listened intently and nodded in agreement.

"And, because we are so young, I might as well groom the freshmen right now . . . look at how good we'll be when Mathews is a senior with that core playing together the next two years . . . we keep McHenry, and we'll have a shot at the Sectionals . . . NorCals . . . heck, maybe even State."

"And then you ride off into the sunset," chuckled Bob Lucas.

"And then I ride off into the sunset," Coach Bridges said with a contented smile. "The perfect ending!"

***

ROB relaxed momentarily as the final group of six completed their lines, and Coach Bridges called to the Varsity to huddle up.

"That was a great first week of practice as a team," Coach Bridges said enthusiastically. You guys looked terrific out there."

The team nodded, grinned, and grunted in approval. They were all ecstatic that the grueling practices were coming to an end. It had been over two long weeks of hard-core conditioning drills with a little basketball thrown in. Next week the fun would begin.

"You guys are rounding into shape," Coach Bridges continued. "Not that we won't still be doing plenty of conditioning."

The team chuckled as a group.

"But," Coach Bridges said with a chuckle of his own, "next week, we start putting in the offense and defense and working on those individual skills a little more. Two weeks until our first game in the Valley Christian tournament."

The whole team perked up at that. Games are the best!

"Just got the draw today," Coach Bridges continued. "It will be a tough first weekend. Valley Christian has Colton the first night while we drew Blue Valley . . . we beat them in the Sectionals last year, but they have nearly everyone back this year . . . and well . . . we don't."

The team nodded and grunted some more.

"After we beat Blue Valley," Coach Bridges added, "well, you know we'll face Valley Christian."

The team groaned quietly, knowing that matchup's long and negative history.

"What can I say," Coach Bridges said with a laugh. "It will be the perfect beginning!"

CHAPTER 11
NOVEMBER-SOPHOMORE YEAR

ROB relaxed and let out a contented sigh as he pushed back from Allison's newest casserole. He glanced around and saw everyone was a member of the "Clean Plate Club"... meaning they all liked it, too!

"That was great, Ally," Rob said with a smile as he glanced around the dinner table at his Mom, Linda Pierce, Trip, and Allison. "You're becoming quite the chef!"

Ally! I love it when he calls me Ally! Allison flashed a grin full of tin around the table but settled her genuine smile on Rob, who immediately melted and tried to hide it from the others.

Why do her smiles make me feel this way? Rob puzzled.

Trip rolled his eyes at Rob and laughed, and both Moms smiled knowingly at each other. *I wonder when... or if... Rob will ever figure it out?* pondered Trip.

"You guys clear, and we'll wash while you set up the movie," Emily said cheerily. "What's on tap tonight?"

"Tonight, we're going to do, *The Princess Bride*, one of my personal favorites!" Allison beamed proudly.

Rob grimaced, Trip rolled his eyes, and Emily shot them both a dirty look that said, "Be nice ... or else!"

"Haven't you heard of *The Princess Bride,* you two?" Linda Pierce asked in disbelief. "You guys are going to love it," she continued, pushing them out of the kitchen and into the living room. "It is an all-time classic!"

"Ally, how bad is this one going to be?" Trip asked. *I wonder how I can get out of this?* he thought.

"Rob, have you hated any of my choices so far?" Allison asked in concern. "I think you guys will like this one ... it's a classic!"

"You know, she's right," Rob reluctantly agreed. "I have liked every movie she has picked."

"That's right," grinned Allison. "This will become one of your favorites ... can't believe neither one of you has seen it."

Allison awkwardly moved her gangly body around Trip so she could reach her phone and Googled the movie cover for them to see. It showed a young couple obviously in love, and they both groaned in unison.

"You'll see ... it's going to be great!" Allison said. "And I've already picked out my next two movies for the holidays ... want to hear what they are?"

Both boys glanced at the other in apprehension and nodded at Allison.

"Just for Trip, I am going to do a couple of repeats," Allison said seriously. "First, *To Kill a Mockingbird*, and two weeks later, *It's a Wonderful Life* ... just in time for the holiday season."

Trip looked tensely at Rob to see if this was good or bad news and saw Rob slowly smile ... so he relaxed a little bit.

"Good idea, Ally," Rob said in appreciation. "You'll like them both, Trip ... but they will take some explaining before, during, and after," he continued with a chuckle.

Allison was beaming with pride. *Ally . . . he called me Ally again!*

She is something, Rob thought as he watched Allison smiling. *She knows both movies will help Trip understand what is important in life. Or, at least, maybe begin to understand. I still don't quite get it all.*

"You know," Allison continued, with a sly smile, "you're going to have to start coming up with some movies after next week . . . the last segment of *Baseball* is next weekend!"

"Oh, man, I forgot about that!" Rob exclaimed. "It's been a while since I had to make a decision. Guess I better start on that now."

Allison melted Rob with another of those killer smiles, and Trip just shook his head in amazement as Emily and Linda walked into the room.

"Showtime! Anyone want Popcorn?" Emily called as she carried in two big bowls of fresh popcorn and placed them on either side of the couch where all could reach them.

It only took 15 minutes before the boys were thoroughly hooked on *The Princess Bride.* They watched, entranced, laughed uproariously, and marveled at the action as the classic film wound its way to the end.

As the credits rolled, the whole group reveled in the feel-good movie and the wonderful evening shared with good friends.

This is so cool, Trip was thinking as the film ended. *They make me feel so comfortable. They didn't have to include me in this . . . but here I am . . . I love it.*

Ah, that was awesome, Rob thought, looking directly at Allison and smiling. *She is such a goof,* he thought. *But a really nice goof.*

Allison was feeling great . . . she had made the right choice of movies. *I nailed it,* she thought. She returned Rob's smile with her best grin. *Will he ever understand how much I love him? Will he ever love me?*

The group got up, and Trip and Emily made for the front door, saying thank you for the great evening.

Rob and Allison hung back, gazing at each other, almost as if they were alone at the end of a very nice date.

Trip noticed it and saw that Emily and Linda looked on with interest. They all had smiles on their faces . . . but were on alert to look away immediately if Rob or Allison glanced their way.

"He doesn't have a clue, does he?" Trip whispered to the two Moms.

They both giggled with delight and shook their heads.

"Not a clue," Emily whispered back at Trip. "Not a clue."

With that, they looked up to see Rob and Allison staring at them quizzically. Rob glanced down at the floor, Allison quickly looked away, and Rob stumbled through the door without a goodbye.

"I'm sorry, Ally," Emily whispered. "We didn't mean to break the spell."

Allison smiled weakly back at her and nodded.

"He's still not ready for you," Emily continued. "Maybe soon."

Trip snorted in derision. "Not likely!"

"You're probably right," Emily snickered as they all laughed, and Emily and Trip strode out the door after Rob.

CHAPTER 12

NOVEMBER-SOPHOMORE YEAR

THE ball flew down the court with rapid-fire precision. After snagging the rebound, Trip McHenry snapped an outlet pass to Rob Mathews at the wing. From Rob, it advanced quickly to Brad Wallace in the middle at half-court. Wallace went to the top of the key and saw Sam Jordan and Edgar Garcia filling the lanes. Quick thinking on defense, on the part of freshmen Gabe Cantor and Josh Lee, along with junior Greg Montgomery, caused Brad Wallace to pull up and wait for McHenry and Mathews to begin the offense.

Around the horn, the ball zipped as the motion offense went into high gear. Wallace to Mathews, to Garcia, to Jordan, to McHenry. Trip soared after receiving the pass to fire a long-range jumper that seared the nets.

"NICE SHOT, McHENRY," bellowed Coach Hal Bridges. "BUT NEXT TIME, TRY PASSING IT DOWN LOW. GARCIA WAS ALL ALONE AT THE BASKET!!!"

Trip McHenry grimaced at the remark. *I just made the shot,* Trip thought. *What does he want?*

The guy just won't pass the ball, Coach Bridges pondered, watching the first-string hustle back defensively. *I know he can do it ... I've seen him do it ... and do it well. But the guy's like a black hole ... he touches it, and it's going up.*

Rob caught the look and sensed a coming storm. *At least Trip is hustling all the time now,* Rob thought. *But here comes the next thing . . . getting Trip to be a team player. That might be tough.*

"PRESSURE DEFENSE . . . LET'S GO!!!" Coach Bridges shouted.

Rob and Brad Wallace moved to double team Josh Lee, and the youngster panicked and made a sloppy pass toward the middle that Edgar Garcia picked off. With both guards out of position, Edgar snapped a pass to Trip McHenry, who dribbled quickly up the floor.

The second-stringers reacted quickly and hustled back on defense, leaving Trip in a one-on-three situation. Without waiting for help, Trip pulled up from 20 feet and launched a rainbow that nestled gently through the hoop. Trip smiled as the ball fell through, turned to go up the court, and ran into an irate Coach.

"NO, NO, NO!!!" Coach Bridges blasted into Trip's face. "THAT IS NOT THE KIND OF SHOT YOU TAKE!!! NO HELP! NO REBOUNDERS! NO NOTHING!!!!"

Trip was taken aback. *I just made another shot . . . isn't that the point?*

"HUDDLE UP . . . EVERYONE!!!" Coach Bridges roared. He stood silently seething while the Varsity players crowded around.

"That is not the type of team we are going to be," Coach Bridges said, suddenly quiet and deliberate, staring directly at Trip McHenry. "We are a team . . . not a one-man show. We will not be able to afford mistakes against the great teams . . . Valley Christian . . . Pine Bluff. We play like that and miss . . . and we've given up a possession. Made an unforced error . . . and they will PUNISH us for that!"

Coach Bridges looked around at his Varsity. *This is a good bunch . . . a great bunch,* he thought, as he looked each player in the eye.

"We have a chance to be great this year . . . a chance to beat Valley Christian . . . but only if we play as a team and limit our unforced errors," Coach Bridges continued. "We have to play hard, play tough and play smart . . . take advantage of every single possession . . . and that means we do it every day in practice . . . on every possession."

Coach Bridges paused again and scanned the young, eager faces. His eyes landed on Trip McHenry and caught his sour look.

"We will play games like we play in practice," Coach Bridges said, looking directly at Trip and holding his gaze. "You have to take pride in how you practice . . . you have to treat each day, each drill, each possession of each practice, as your opportunity to get better and to be as close to perfect as possible."

The kids looked around at each other, nodding.

"You take lousy shots . . . make bad decisions in practice . . . and you'll do it in games. You do that once too often . . . in practice or games . . . and you'll find you won't be on the floor during games very often . . . especially at crunch time," Coach Bridges finished quietly, staring straight at Trip McHenry.

Coach Bridges let his words sink in and then turned to the whole group and said, "Reminds me of a great John Wooden quote . . . "Do not confuse activity . . . with achievement."

Coach Bridges paused, seeing confused looks on the faces of most of his players.

"It means," Coach Bridges explained, "just because you are out here running around . . . it doesn't mean you are accomplishing anything. To achieve something, you have to focus, do it the right way, and do it 100%! Understand?"

The group nodded.

"Brings up another quote that fits," Coach Bridges added. "Practice does not make perfect . . . perfect practice makes perfect . . ."

The team chuckled . . . but Coach Bridges got his point across.

The team murmured in response.

"Tomorrow, we will have a short walk-thru at 9:00 am . . . be done by 10:00 so you can get back to your families for Thanksgiving," Coach Bridges said. "Let's finish with our lines. Do em' right the first time so we can get out of here!!!"

CHAPTER 13

NOVEMBER-SOPHOMORE YEAR

"**W**HY is he always on my case?" Trip McHenry lamented to Rob on their walk home.

Rob hesitated a moment forming his thoughts, and he felt Trip's stare.

"I haven't been around Coach too much," Rob began. "But this much I've learned. He's honest, he's fair, he's loyal. He preaches Team, Team, Team, and it's not just a slogan. He means it."

"So, you think he'll really bench me for being a gunner?" Trip asked incredulously. "He'll bench his best player for scoring too much?"

Rob stopped at that comment and turned to face Trip.

"Er, uh, wait . . . I didn't mean that about being the best player," Trip stammered. "One of the best . . ."

"No, wait, Trip, I don't disagree . . . you probably are the best player . . . but that's not the point," Rob said slowly and thoughtfully.

"What is the point?" Trip asked, slightly confused.

"The point is he wants the team to be the best it can be," Rob replied. "He doesn't care what your average is, what my average is . . . all he cares about is that we play to our highest potential as a team . . . in practice and games."

"You think I shoot too much?" Trip demanded, flashing a bit of anger.

"Not too much," Rob said diplomatically. "But today, you took some shots that weren't the best in the world. I think the one-on-three at the end is what really bothered Coach."

"So, you think he'll really bench me if I take that shot in games," Trip pressed.

"Again, I haven't been around Coach enough to be completely sure," Rob answered. "But . . . from what I've seen so far this season . . . and what I saw last year for a couple of weeks . . . if he says it, he means it. And, once he says it, he will follow through on it no matter what the situation. He doesn't make idle threats. He's like Norman Dale . . . the coach in *Hoosiers*!"

"Ah, *Hoosiers* . . . now there is a classic . . . I get it . . . Coach Bridges is like that . . . but you think he'd jeopardize a win by taking me off the floor?" Trip said in amazement.

Rob nodded.

"I'll have to see that to believe it," Trip said, shaking his head in disbelief.

***

THE team crowded around Coach Bridges as the short Thanksgiving morning walk-through wound down.

"Good job this morning, guys," Coach Bridges said quietly as the team huddled. "I'm pleased with the grasp of the offense you all have . . . especially you new guys. It will take some practice to refine it . . . but you are looking good!"

Coach Bridges looked directly at Trip McHenry and the freshmen Josh Lee and Gabe Cantor. "You three have picked it up quickly . . . it's a tough offense to run."

Coach Bridges scanned the group and saw eagerness, determination, and fire in their eyes. *Always good with our first game tomorrow!*

"Tomorrow, we start with a tough one," Coach Bridges continued. "Blue Valley is good! They run and gun, and we have to be able to run with them. We also have to try to slow them down by playing tough defense and smart offense."

Coach Bridges glanced Trip's way. "We have to make every possession count. Take good shots... make good passes... rebound hard. We have to control the boards... offensively and defensively. On defense, we have to get back quick... play them tough and don't give them any freebies. You'll be in a horserace from start to finish. Because of that, you'll all probably see time tomorrow... we need to keep fresh guys in there as much as possible."

Coach Bridges scanned the group again. "OK, guys... have a great Thanksgiving... but don't eat too much," he said with a broad grin.

"And, don't be late for the bus... we don't wait for anyone," Coach Bridges ended, the grin disappearing. "If you're not five minutes early... you're late!"

CHAPTER 14
NOVEMBER-SOPHOMORE YEAR

"**O**H, sorry," Trip said as he walked into the kitchen to see Emily, and Grandma and Grandpa Russell sitting at the kitchen island. "Rob's not back yet?"

"No," said Emily sorrowfully. "Rob's Grandparents will keep him out most of the afternoon . . . they don't get to see him much since we moved to Hillsdale."

Trip nodded. "How come the Mathews' don't have Thanksgiving here?"

"They did last year," Emily replied. "It was awful. A very tense afternoon."

Trip glanced around to see Grandma and Grandpa Russell nodding. "Why so tense?"

"Rob's grandparents were very involved when Rob was little . . . saw Rob all the time," Emily answered. "They were not in favor of our moving up here when Jack got sick . . . it has just made for an uncomfortable situation."

Trip nodded again.

"I get . . . so emotional around the holidays," Emily said, her eyes welling up with tears. "Holidays are for families . . . I don't have Jack . . . so I want Rob close."

Trip could feel himself choking up. "Well, uh, hey," Trip stuttered. "I . . . I can get lost and let you guys have a real family Thanksgiving . . ."

"Absolutely not," thundered Grandpa Russell, rising from his stool at the island. "You are family . . . any grandson of Chuck McHenry is a grandson of mine!"

"Really?!!!" Trip said, looking toward Emily for affirmation.

"Really," Emily said, smiling through her tears. "You know, Trip . . . I had some reservations about you moving in . . . but you are family now . . . it will be hard to go back to just Rob and me once your Aunt Barb moves in."

"When is Barbara moving in?" Grandma Russell asked.

"Middle of December," Trip answered.

"It will be nice to have her here again," Grandma Russell continued. "Are you looking forward to it?"

"Yes and no," Trip replied, looking at Emily. "I love it here. You guys have all been so nice . . . but Aunt Barb and the kids are great, too. I've spent a lot of my life with them . . . I'd go there when my folks were fighting . . . which seemed like all the time . . . or when they were both out of town."

Emily grimaced and rubbed Trip's arm as he started to well up a little.

"Yeah, I was there a lot . . . but in ways . . . I always felt like a guest . . . but here I feel . . . like a guest . . . but like a part of . . ." Trip sputtered.

"Like family," Grandpa Russell stated, with Emily nodding in agreement.

"You'll always be welcome here, Trip," Emily said. "As long as you follow the rules, that is," she added with a smile and laugh.

"Thanks, Emily," Trip replied softly.

"Hey, what do you say, Trip . . . how about we watch some football?" Grandpa Russell spouted, taking Trip by the arm and pulling him into the living room.

After settling in to watch the football game, Grandpa Russell cleared his throat.

"Ahem," Grandpa Russell began. "The girls always tend to make things so emotional."

Trip laughed in agreement. *Yeah, but I was almost crying, too!*

"But I do want you to know . . . man-to-man . . . you are a part of this family," Grandpa Russell said roughly. "You ever need anything . . . you come to Rob or Emily, or me . . . even to Grandma Russell."

"Really?" Trip asked.

"Really! You ever need a place to stay if it goes wrong at Barb's, you come back here . . . or you come to our house," Grandpa Russell said.

Trip gulped with emotion, staring over at Grandpa Russell. "You'd do that for me . . . let me live at your house?"

"You bet! I'd do anything I can do to help Chuck's grandson . . . we were like brothers, you know . . . we were like family. I can see you and Rob are going to be like that . . . you already are in ways," Grandpa Russell said, his voice breaking a little with emotion.

"Even if I end up at Valley Christian or back down in L.A.?" Trip asked.

"Yep, even if that happens. We're your family for keeps . . . Rob's your brother for life. Family doesn't care where you go to school . . . I see that bond . . . that connection between you and Rob . . . it is just like Chuck and me. You don't break that bond by going to a different school or a different job," Grandpa Russell said, gazing directly into Trip's eyes.

Trip welled up again but fought it back.

"Thanks, Mr. Russell," Trip gulped.

Grandpa Russell raised his hand to stop him.

"You are family, boy . . . you call me Grandpa!" Grandpa Russell snorted, slapping Trip gently on the shoulder.

CHAPTER 15
NOVEMBER-SOPHOMORE YEAR

"**W**HAT a good dinner, Mom," Rob sighed as he pushed his chair away from the dining room table. "Thanks!"

"Yeah, thanks, Emily," Trip said, following suit.

"Tonight, we do the dishes, right Trip?" Rob asked.

"What's this we . . .?" Trip started and then laughed, shaking his head. "Yeah, let's do the dishes . . . it's the least we can do."

The whole group cleared their stuff, and the pile of dishes was daunting. They dug in, made good progress, and began the job of handwashing and drying the pots and pans.

About halfway through, the boys heard the doorbell ring, and soon after, Allison Pierce walked in with a big, goofy smile on her face and a Thanksgiving greeting.

"Happy Holidays to the little homemakers," Allison teased.

"Yeah, grab a towel," Trip laughed, firing his dish towel at her, only to see it fall to the floor at her feet. "Good hands, Pierce!"

"Hah, I was told by the mistress of the house not to participate in any kitchen drudgery," Allison said with a flourish. "That was to be left to the kitchen maids," she laughed.

The trio laughed heartily, and the boys resumed their work while Allison deftly cut six pumpkin pie slices and put them on plates to serve after Trip and Rob completed their task.

After pie, Grandma and Grandpa Russell said their farewells. Emily graciously announced she would do the dessert dishes and scooped them up and into the kitchen, leaving the three teenagers alone in the living room.

"So, big game tomorrow?" Allison asked with a smile. "You guys excited?"

"The bigger question is, are you excited?" Trip quipped, and they all laughed.

"Are you kidding," Allison replied. "I wouldn't miss it for the world."

The boys glanced at each other.

"I mean, who could?" Allison added sarcastically. "It's every girl's dream night out on the town! Smashed in a packed gym, sitting on uncomfortable benches and watching . . . and smelling a bunch of sweaty, smelly boys run around in their shorts."

"I suppose your idea of a better night out is standing around a packed gym, dancing in a mob, inhaling perfume fumes, and making small talk?" Rob countered.

"You have me there," Allison laughed. "But I bet Trip here doesn't think the dances are so bad. What do you think, Trip?"

"Well . . . I gotta' admit I kinda' enjoy those dances," Trip smiled slowly. "But I'm more excited about the games."

"Thank goodness," Rob spouted. "I was worried there for a second!"

"So, Trip, have you found that special someone yet?" Allison queried with a smile. "Someone told me they saw you with a freshman a couple of times."

Trip's face turned slightly red in embarrassment, but he quickly found his footing and laughed with Allison.

"Yeah . . . you caught me red-handed," Trip drawled. "I have been talking to a girl for the last week or so . . . I asked her out for next weekend . . . no time this week with the night games Friday and Saturday."

"You just went up and asked her . . . with no help?" Allison asked Trip while smirking at Rob. "Imagine that."

Rob scowled good-naturedly at Allison's barb.

"Well, it doesn't matter how bad I am with girls," Rob said. "I'm off girls for a while . . . the Carly fiasco after the "Pick" game did me in . . . I need a break."

"Well, that's too bad," Trip interjected. "I think Jenny, that's her name, has a friend that just might want to date a little, handsome basketball star like you," Trip teased Rob. "Jenny likes bigger fellas like me."

Rob cracked up, laughing hard, while Allison suddenly wondered why she brought up girls.

"Well, you be my guest and date Jenny, but I'll pass for now," Rob said with a laugh. "Even if her friend does like little guys."

Whew, Allison thought. *Dodged a bullet . . . for a while anyway. Why do I ever bring up girls around Rob?*

"Right now, I'm going to focus on basketball," Rob stated with determination.

With that, Rob popped up and headed out the back door.

"Where are you going?" Trip asked.

"That reminds me . . . time to shoot some free throws," Rob said as he closed the door behind him on his way to his driveway and the basketball court.

Allison and Trip stared after him, shook their heads in amazement, and followed him out the door into the night.

CHAPTER 16
NOVEMBER-SOPHOMORE YEAR

"*FOCUS* on basketball . . . right now and for the next couple of hours," Coach Bridges implored his team as they stood around him in front of the Hillsdale bench. "You know how fast these guys are . . . how they will try to run you off the court. Be smart . . . make good decisions . . . and hustle until you drop. You get tired . . . we'll get you a blow."

Coach Bridges paused, heard the horn blow, craned his neck back into the huddle, and shouted to be heard above the growing crowd noise. "This is it . . . starters, you know your jobs . . . everybody else . . . stay ready. All right, hands in!!!"

"TEAM!!!!" they all shouted in unison as Hillsdale's starting five headed for the floor.

Rob headed toward center court and briefly shook hands with several Blue Valley players. He recognized most of the guys from facing them in last year's Sectionals.

Scanning the Valley Christian gym, he saw it was nearly full. A huge contingent of Hillsdale fans was on hand . . . all packed together like sardines in the large stands directly behind the Pirates bench.

Rob found his Mom, his Grandparents, Allison Pierce, and her folks right away, about four rows behind the bench. *Grandpa Russell always wants to sit close enough to try to hear Coach*, Rob laughed. *I'm sure he'll be able to hear him from there.*

Sitting across from the Pirates bench, Rob noticed the entire Valley Christian team was sitting with their coaching staff, with many of them glaring at Hillsdale's players ... except for Trip McHenry. Any time he looked their way, the team was all smiles. *Instructions from their coach,* Rob thought. *They are in "recruit McHenry" mode.*

Rob spotted Allison's childhood friend, Tony Russo, and the cocksure Valley Christian guard smirked at him and turned away.

"Jerk," Rob muttered, turning his attention to center court, where Trip was toeing the center court circle for the opening tip-off.

On the floor around him were Trip McHenry and Edgar Garcia playing down low and Sam Jordan and Brad Wallace on the wings. Rob expected to see a lot of Bob Johnson, filling in for Sam and Brad and the two youngsters, Josh Lee and Gabe Cantor.

Depending on the situation, Josh would spell Rob and Brad, while Gabe could fill in for Edgar or Trip and play the wing if necessary. Trip could also move up to the wing if Hillsdale wanted to go big, but against Blue Valley, speed was the premium.

Trip tapped the opening tip back to Rob behind the mid-court line, and the race was on. Rob hurried the ball up the court and dished to Sam Jordan on the wing, who swung the ball over to Trip in the corner.

Immediately, Trip turned and fired up a three and clanked it off the front iron. Blue Valley swarmed for the rebound and was off to the races. They flew down the court with precision passing, beat most of the Pirates down the floor, and converted a four-on-two with an uncontested layup.

Hillsdale went to inbound the ball after the layup, and the Lakers had thrown on a full-court press, hoping to rattle the young and inexperienced Pirates into a mistake.

It worked perfectly.

Edgar Garcia inbounded the ball with a sloppy pass to Brad Wallace. Brad got control of the ball and tried to hit Trip McHenry at half-court, who had been slow to get downcourt after his missed shot. The pass was picked off, Blue Valley pushed the ball, and converted a three-pointer for a 5-0 lead.

Edgar again tried to inbound but was having trouble finding an open man when he heard Rob call out, "TIME OUT!!!!"

"THANK YOU, ROB," Coach Bridges bellowed as the team drew near. "Now, do you guys see what I mean about speed . . . and about making every possession count!"

Four heads bobbed in agreement . . . Trip McHenry was stone-faced as the rest of the squad gathered around.

"First thing to do is relax . . . these guys are fast, but you have the size advantage. Take the time to make good passes. Don't panic . . . stay calm . . . use your size and your passing ability," Coach Bridges schooled.

Coach Bridges scanned the squad making sure everyone understood him.

"OK, here is what we do," Coach Bridges continued. "If they keep up the press, we go into press break. Edgar, you are back at mid-court. Trip, you take out the ball. You other three run the screens trying to get the ball to Rob. Trip, you are the safety valve."

Again, heads nodded in agreement.

"You two," Coach Bridges said, looking first at Rob and then at Trip. "You guys stay cool and get the ball down the floor. Once we get it down, run the offense. Good shots only. And get back on defense."

Coach Bridges let his gaze linger on Trip as the words sunk in.

The team brought their hands together, yelled "Team," and hurried back to the floor where Blue Valley was waiting with their press.

The ref handed Trip the ball, who kept his cool and waited for Rob to break free. Immediately, Sam and Brad sprinted to the wings at mid-court, and Edgar dropped deep under the Pirate's basket.

Rob surveyed the floor and saw three Lakers advancing to pounce on him, and Rob knew there had to be an open man. Using his quarterback skills, Rob found the open man was Sam Jordan at mid-court, and he rifled him a perfect pass. Brad Wallace filled the other lane, and Sam, Brad, and Edgar worked a perfect three-on-two break that resulted in an Edgar Garcia basket from two feet.

"GET BACK!!! GET BACK!!!" screamed Coach Bridges reminding the threesome to hustle back on defense.

Blue Valley advanced the ball quickly, tried one too many passes, and had it picked off by Rob at the free throw line extended.

Rob whirled and dashed up the floor, Sam Jordan and Trip McHenry filling the lanes. Rob drove the middle to the free throw line, faked to Sam on the right, and zipped a no-look pass to Trip McHenry, streaking in from the left.

Trip brought down the Hillsdale section of the stands with a resounding two-hand slam that trimmed the lead to one point.

From there, the game settled into a track meet, with both teams running and gunning. Hillsdale hung tight, but a couple more quick shots by Trip McHenry cost them a couple of possessions and Blue Valley had an 18-14 lead over the Pirates at the end of the first quarter.

Coach Bridges made his first substitutions, inserting Bob Johnson, Josh Lee, and Gabe Cantor into the game to join Edgar Garcia and Rob Mathews.

Just under six-foot, with a slightly stocky build reminiscent of Bill Tompkins, Josh looked older than his years. His sandy hair was cut relatively short, and his good looks and charm had made him a favorite of the cheerleaders.

Gabe Cantor could almost be Trip's younger and slightly smaller brother. Standing just under six-foot-four, with dark, longish hair, Gabe weighed in a good 15-20 pounds less than Trip, but you could tell he would fill out during his tenure at Hillsdale. Surprisingly strong, he was a force inside and had a nice touch.

This fivesome put together four solid minutes, working the offense beautifully, with sharp passing leading to easy baskets, and the Pirates grabbed a 25-22 lead. Josh Lee had two buckets, as did Gabe Cantor, and Bob Johnson nailed a long three-pointer.

Rob went to the bench, and Trip McHenry and Sam Jordan returned. The excellent passing continued with Josh Lee at the controls, and the offense got an easy basket for Trip, playing in Edgar's spot, down at the blocks.

These guys are good, Rob thought as he watched his teammates work together. *Gabe and Josh are the real deal.*

The three-point lead stretched to eight and then back to five when Coach Bridges tapped Rob's shoulder and sent him scurrying back in with three minutes to play.

Josh Lee stayed put, and Trip McHenry, Edgar Garcia, Sam Jordan, and Rob rounded out the team on the floor.

This group found the rhythm, and for three minutes, they put on a show of passing, shooting, defense, and rebounding, with Trip McHenry leading the way.

Trip was the beneficiary of great passing and his own good movement. He hit five wide-open shots in a row. Rob had four assists and a couple of baskets during the 14-4 run that left Blue Valley in disarray and at the wrong end of a 39-26 halftime score.

As Rob headed off to the locker room, he passed close to the Valley Christian team and could hear the comments from the coaching staff.

"I told you that McHenry kid is good . . . we have to figure out a way to get him over here next year," the head coach said.

"That's for sure," an assistant responded. "The kid would fit in just right . . . and decimate Hillsdale. What could be better."

Rob kept going but knew Trip had just heard the conversation.

We need to keep Trip at Hillsdale, Rob thought. *We just have to . . .*

CHAPTER 17
NOVEMBER-SOPHOMORE YEAR

ROB turned and listened as Coach Bridges finished his halftime comments in the locker room.

"Keep doing what you're doing," Coach Bridges said. "The passing in that second quarter is what we're after . . . that was fantastic. The first quarter not so much. All right, guys, let's head back out!"

The team jumped up and headed back for the second half. Coach Bridges touched Trip's arm and tugged Trip toward him.

"Trip, you see what I mean about the passing and good shots . . . you took some clunkers in the first quarter . . . but the last four minutes was perfection."

"Thanks, Coach!" Trip answered with a small smile.

"Be sure you remember the difference," Coach said grimly.

***

THE original starters were back on the floor to start the second half. The pace continued hot and heavy, and Blue Valley came out on fire from three-point land.

They knocked down four consecutive three-pointers while Trip launched and missed a couple of long-range duds, and all of a sudden, Hillsdale's lead was cut to 43-38.

After the second long-range miss by Trip, a seething Coach Bridges pulled McHenry, sent in Gabe Cantor for him, and Josh Lee for Brad Wallace. Coach Bridges glared at Trip until he was sure he got the message. *Stop the lousy shots,* the Coach thought!

Immediately, the moves paid dividends, as the new group, led by Rob's three driving baskets and two assists, doubled their lead back to ten at the quarter at 53-43.

Josh Lee remained on the floor to start the 4th quarter with the starters, with Brad Wallace relegated to the bench. This group solidly took control of the game, with the offense clicking on all cylinders . . . including Trip picking up a couple of nice assists on plays that he would have put up bad shots earlier in the game. The first half of the fourth quarter saw Hillsdale outscore Blue Valley 16-6 and put the game on ice with a 69-49 score with four minutes to play.

At this point, Coach Bridges emptied his bench, and Hillsdale coasted to a surprisingly easy 75-61 victory over an excellent Blue Valley team.

Hal Bridges was unexpectedly subdued in the locker room and not overly impressed with his squad's win.

"Guys, we played very well at times . . . in spurts," Coach Bridges began. "I think you would agree we could have played better."

The team nodded in agreement.

"In fact, if we play like that tomorrow night against Valley Christian, we will likely get our clocks cleaned," he added.

More agreement.

"To beat them, we will need to play a complete game," Coach Bridges said, his eyes darting around the room until they fell on Trip McHenry. "We can't afford to give away possessions with poor shot selection. Get a good night's sleep tonight . . . you'll need it.

Let's head on out to the stands . . . we'll scout Valley Christian a while before we head home."

***

THE players hurried out into the stands and were greeted by huge applause from the Hillsdale faithful.

Rob and Trip soaked up the congratulations from Rob's family and Allison before the family headed home. Rob and Trip then joined the rest of the team and watched as Valley Christian annihilated their opponents, the Colton Cowboys.

Valley Christian was big, strong, fast, and tough . . . and that was the second string. The starting five were off the charts, dominating the undermanned Cowboys from start to finish.

Trip McHenry was duly impressed. He had only seen a small sample of the team the day they played here in the early fall. *Those kids had been good,* Trip thought. *These kids are great.*

As the team left the gym at halftime, an older man approached Trip and put his hand on his shoulder.

"Say, son, I hear you might be thinking of moving to Valley Christian next year," he said softly.

Trip was taken by surprise and could only nod in agreement.

"I've got a boy on the team . . . not a member of the coaching staff or school staff," the man continued. "But I can tell you would fit in quite nicely over here. You've got the talent, the size, the grit."

Trip nodded, a faint smile on his face.

"I could help make it happen," he pressed on, shoving a business card into Trip's hand. "Think about it . . . if you're serious about playing college ball, Valley Christian is where you want to be."

Rob reached out and pulled Trip on his way.

"You don't want to get mixed up with that guy," Rob said tersely. "He's bad news. Rich guy . . . tries to kinda' bribe kids to play for them . . . you could get in trouble."

Trip nodded his thanks to Rob. *I wonder what he meant by help me,* Trip thought. *Ah, I don't need his help. If I want to go to Valley Christian, I can go . . . Rob's right . . . stay away from him.*

The bus ride home was a good one, with the team in high spirits over the solid win . . . but at the same time, there was some apprehension over the coming battle with Valley Christian.

Dylan Cobb, a slender, bespectacled, blond sophomore at Hillsdale who did Pirate sports reporting for the *Hillsdale Express,* slid in next to Trip and Rob on the bus.

Rob bobbed his head at Dylan and scooched over to give him some room. *Dyl's a good guy,* Rob thought. *Completely inept as an athlete . . . but he knows the games and does a good job as a reporter.*

"Guys," Dylan bobbed his head back at the pair. "Good game tonight for both of you."

More head bobbing and slight grins from Rob and Trip.

"You want to know your lines?" Dylan asked.

"Sure," Rob and Trip said together.

"Rob, you ended up with 15 points, eight assists, ten rebounds, four steals, and a block," Dylan said, consulting his notepad.

"Er, Trip, uh, can I call you Trip?" Trip nodded his assent. "You ended up with 24 points, four rebounds, two assists, and a block."

Dylan looked up to gauge the reactions.

"Satisfied?" Dylan asked.

"You know," Rob began, "we're never satisfied. We can always do better. Gotta' play better tomorrow if we want to have a chance at Valley Christian."

"Yeah," Dylan agreed. "How about you, uh, Trip? Satisfied?"

"No, I should have scored more. I averaged 30 a game last year . . . hopefully I'll get 36 tomorrow night . . . get my average up to speed," Trip said boastfully. "I need a career night against them . . . gotta' go big against them to have a shot at playing there next year."

Rob winced at the comments but let them pass.

The bus pulled into Hillsdale High, and the group shuffled off and milled around in the parking lot.

Rob pulled Dylan off to the side for a private word.

"Hey, Dyl," Rob started. "Do you think maybe you can not print Trip's comment about scoring 36 points on Valley Christian? Don't think it would go over too big with Valley Christian . . . you know . . . don't poke the sleeping bear."

"Yeah, I got ya'. I'll keep it out of print," Dylan said with a smirk on his face.

"What?" Rob asked, seeing Dylan's face.

"I think the sleeping bear you want to be sure not to poke is Coach Bridges," Dylan said, laughing.

"Yeah, I think you're right," Rob answered with a smile.

CHAPTER 18
NOVEMBER-SOPHOMORE YEAR

*V*ALLEY Christian's gym was standing room only. Blue Valley had just dominated Colton, and while most of their fans filed out, late-arriving fans of Valley Christian and Hillsdale were streaming in, packing the seats and lining the walls.

The local press had anointed both teams as preseason favorites to vie for the Sectional Championship along with Pine Bluff. So, not only had both schools filled the bleachers, but basketball enthusiasts from all over were here . . . including Jeb, Dirk, and Clem Danielson of Pine Bluff. Jake Gardner, now a Pine Bluff player, stood with them.

"What are they doing here?" Allison sneered to Emily.

"I don't know," Emily replied, "but I don't like it!"

"Don't worry," Grandpa Russell crowed. "He'll handle them . . . and Valley Christian!"

Emily smiled. *That's my Dad . . . believing Rob could do no wrong . . . but he's just a kid!*

***

*T*HE horn sounded, and both teams retreated to their bench for last-second instructions and encouragement.

Rob had noticed last year that the bigger the game, the quieter Coach Bridges was before tip-off, and tonight was no exception.

"You guys know the game plan," Coach Bridges said, just loud enough to be heard. "Remember, this is a big one . . . we want to do well . . . but this game does not define our season . . . it's just another step in the process. Just play your game . . . play to your potential . . . and everything else takes care of itself. READY???!!!"

"READY!!!" the team hollered back.

"TEAM!!!!!" they screamed in unison, and the starting five bounced out to mid-court.

Valley Christian's starting five sauntered out, avoiding the traditional handshakes with their opponents . . . except they all made a point of smiling at Trip McHenry and slapping his hand. *Recruiting is in full swing,* Rob thought as he watched in mild surprise.

Valley Christian was a veteran team . . . Rob smiled to see Tony Russo was riding the bench to start the game. *Nice to see him over there . . . I hope he stays there,* Rob thought.

The tip went to Valley Christian, and they smoothly worked their offense to perfection and scored on a short jumper from the block area.

Rob received the inbounds pass and was relieved to see Valley Christian was not pressing and quickly brought the ball up the court. The motion offense was flawless, and after four passes, Trip McHenry found an open seam and knocked down a 15-footer.

After both squads repeated their offense the next two times, they were tied at six, with Trip McHenry scoring all six for Hillsdale.

The pattern changed on Valley Christian's next possession as their sharpshooting off-guard nailed a three from the top of the key. Hillsdale hurried the ball up the floor, and, trying to feed the hot hand, Rob rifled a pass to Trip McHenry in the corner.

Trip caught the ball and immediately let fly with a three to tie the score. The ball clanked off the back iron. Just after he let fly, Trip noticed Edgar Garcia alone under the basket. So did Coach Bridges.

Valley Christian snagged a long rebound and raced up the court, converting a three-on-two layup for a five-point advantage.

Hillsdale again was patient and worked their offense, the ball flying around the court until it got to Trip McHenry. He immediately fired up another long three that clanked off iron . . . this time, Rob was all alone, cutting down the lane.

Another long rebound, and Valley Christian was off to the races again. This time, they converted the layup, drew a foul, hit the free throw, and the lead was 14-6.

Coach Bridges was fuming on the sidelines but chose not to call a time-out. *Let's see how they handle this. I'm going to give them a quarter.*

Rob brought the ball up slowly and worked the offense again and instead of wheeling it back to Trip the second time, he reversed the motion. It flew around the court until the ball found Trip wide open. Another 15-footer went down.

Valley Christian came down and finally missed a shot. They missed another and then outrebounded Trip and Edgar to pick up a cheap basket inside.

Down came Hillsdale again. Good ball movement. Ball to Trip. Rushed shot. No good. Sam Jordan all alone near the basket.

The Knights snatched the rebound and flew up the court. Open three. Nothing but net. Suddenly the press was on, and a bad inbounds pass led to another short-range jumper, and the lead was 21-8 Valley Christian!

Rob called a time-out, and the Pirates headed for Coach Bridges.

The crowd, especially the Hillsdale faithful behind the bench, was stunned. They had expected a tight game, win or lose, not the beginnings of a blowout.

The Danielson boys and Jake Gardner were hooting and hollering, directing most of their venom at Rob Mathews and Trip McHenry.

"Whoa, how about the two hot shots . . . forgot how to score, Mathews!!!" Jeb yelled.

Rob ignored them and ducked his head into the huddle. Coach Bridges was quiet and subdued and nodded at Rob to take charge.

"All right, guys," Rob began earnestly. "We have got to keep moving the ball . . . hit the open man. Take good shots. We have to tighten up the defense. No second chances."

The horn blared, and the quick time-out was finished.

This time down, the ball zipped back and forth perfectly, and again, Trip McHenry hit an open jumper. The defense stepped up to get a stop, Hillsdale repeated the offense, and it was Trip open again, hitting the shot. Another stop and Trip launched another quick shot . . . this one fell short . . . while Edgar Garcia stood alone under the basket.

Valley Christian went on a rampage with just 60 seconds left in the first quarter. The Knights converted three straight times down the floor while holding the Pirate's scoreless . . . in part thanks to another two missed shots by Trip McHenry . . . both shots were forced and had teammates open with much better looks.

The quarter ended with Valley Christian up 27-12 and Coach Bridges frustrated.

"Guys," Coach Bridges implored his team between quarters. "You are moving the ball well . . . but the shot selection stinks. Take good shots!!! Let's chip away and see if we can cut this lead down by halftime."

Coach Bridges scanned his squad. His eyes fell on Trip McHenry, and he was ready to explode at him. He glared at Trip for a moment, then moved on. *This game means nothing . . . and this might be the most important teaching moment I get with him this year.*

"All right, Lee, Cantor, Johnson, report in. Mathews and Garcia, you stay with them," Coach Bridges yelled.

Trip McHenry felt he had been slapped in the face, and his reaction showed it. *What the heck,* Trip thought . . . *why am I coming out if Rob is staying in the game? I've got all the points . . . I need to be in there!*

CHAPTER 19

NOVEMBER-SOPHOMORE YEAR

"**W**HY is Trip sitting down, Grandpa Russell?" Allison asked in bewilderment. "He has all the points, doesn't he?"

"Yes, he does, Allison," Grandpa Russell explained. "But he's taking bad shots!"

"Bad shots? They are going in a lot of times," Allison replied, clearly confused.

"He shot too many tough shots instead of passing to someone for an easier shot," Grandpa Russell yelled. "He's forcing them . . . you notice they were all from long-range? The offense is designed to get a lot of shots from short-range . . . he's not passing inside."

Allison nodded her head but wasn't sure she fully understood.

On the floor, Hillsdale got the ball first and promptly showed Allison what Grandpa Russell meant. The ball whirled around the court until Gabe Cantor found Josh Lee cutting through the middle, and Lee dropped home a driving layup.

Good defense earned Hillsdale a steal by Rob, and the offense clicked again when Rob found Edgar Garcia alone under the basket, and Edgar slammed one home.

Back and forth, the teams raced, with Hillsdale playing a better brand of basketball, and they continued to narrow the gap. Suddenly they were getting defensive stops, but more importantly, they were getting good shots every time down the floor.

Trip McHenry stewed on the bench, cheering on his teammates while itching to get back into the game.

Midway through the second quarter, Coach Bridges made some changes, but Trip remained firmly planted on the bench. Josh Lee and Gabe Cantor had both excelled at passing the ball, finding open teammates, and taking good shots. Gabe also hit the boards hard, collecting six rebounds in the quarter.

Rob came out for a minute, went back in, and sparked a late Hillsdale charge that cut the 15-point deficit to four as the Pirates trailed just 44-40 at the break.

***

*T*HE locker room was hushed as Coach Bridges stood before his team to speak. Trip McHenry watched petulantly as the Coach cleared his throat and began. "That was a terrific second quarter! You played Pirates basketball, and I'm proud of you. You moved the ball, took good shots, hit the boards, and played defense. You can't ask for much more."

Coach Bridges paused to let his words sink in.

"We're in a battle . . . against one of the best teams in the State. We can't let up, and we can't give anything away if we want to stay close," Coach Bridges said slowly. "Now you know the second half is usually Valley Christian's . . . in a big way."

The team murmured in agreement.

"Tonight . . . tonight we change that," Coach Bridges continued.

The team cheered.

"We're going to start the second half with the same group that started the game for us," Coach Bridges announced. "You guys on the bench . . . be ready because we are going to try to stay fresh . . . let's give it our best and make Hillsdale proud tonight."

***

*T*HE third quarter was a near-carbon copy of the first. Trip McHenry returned to his habits of forcing up shots and missing easy passes for scores. He scored another 12 points but gave away four possessions and was not a factor on the boards or on defense.

While Coach Bridges seethed and showed his exasperation at Trip's play, Trip seemed oblivious. *That's 24,* Trip thought as he hit a bucket. *One more quarter with 12, and I get my 36 points!*

The crowd, at least the Hillsdale part of the crowd, deflated as the game seemed to be slipping away as Valley Christian lengthened their lead.

"What's going on?" Allison whined to Emily.

"The talent is showing through, I'm afraid," Emily replied. "Valley Christian is so experienced . . . they are mostly seniors, I think . . . we're just babies."

"Bad shot selection," Grandpa Russell grumbled to both of them. "Going to have to talk to Trip about that at home."

"Dad . . . you stay out of it," Emily countered.

Grandpa Russell rolled his eyes at her, and Emily and Allison both howled.

Coach Bridges let Trip play the entire quarter but inserted Josh Lee for Brad Wallace halfway through the quarter and had Sam Jordan and Rob Mathews sit for Gabe Cantor and Bob Johnson with about two minutes left. The quarter ended on a long three by Valley Christian that put the deficit back to 15, with Valley Christian up 71-56.

Coach Bridges tapped Rob, Josh, Sam, Gabe, and Edgar at the quarter break to start the fourth. *Just a quick blow, then I'm back in the game,* Trip thought.

CHAPTER 20

NOVEMBER-SOPHOMORE YEAR

*T*RIP never saw the floor again. The group Coach Bridges inserted to start the fourth played their hearts out for the entire quarter. Initially, thinking the lead was safe, Valley Christian gave their still-strong second unit some action.

The Pirates blitzed that unit on a four-minute, 16-4 run that brought the Pirates to within three at 75-72. Rob had ignited the run, scoring eight, handing out four assists, and picking up two steals from Tony Russo.

Valley Christian's coach quickly called a time-out and sent his first stringers to the scorer's table to check in and finish the game.

The Hillsdale section of the bleachers had come back alive during the run and was pure pandemonium. The cheerleaders were on the floor leading the fans in rousing cheers, and Valley Christian's side would yell back in response. The result was constant noise that made it hard to think . . . hard to do anything.

"We've got them on the run," Coach Bridges screamed over the din. "Expect their starters back in the game . . . be prepared."

We've got a real shot, Rob thought, hopefully. *We need Trip back in to put us over the top.*

But Trip McHenry, languishing on the bench for those four-plus minutes, stood hovering close to Coach Bridges, expecting the call to go back in to finish off the run ... but the call never came.

Returning to the bench as the game resumed, Trip heard catcalls from the Pine Bluff contingent, and he had to admit that it stung.

As the timeout ended, Allison leaned into Grandpa Russell.

"I get what you meant about Trip . . . you know the passing and shooting and stuff," Allison said to both Emily and Grandpa Russell.

"You're a quick learner," Grandpa Russell laughed.

And a brilliant girl, Emily thought. *If you can't beat em', join em'... if you're going after Rob, you better learn to like sports... or at least understand them!*

Valley Christian had the ball, a three-point lead, and their starters on the floor. Hillsdale had two freshmen, two sophomores, and a senior ... and a whole lot of heart ... but not a lot of experience.

The Knights brought the ball calmly up the floor, swung it through their offense, got a wide-open look, and buried a jumper from the free-throw line for a five-point margin.

Hillsdale quickly retaliated on a slick pass from Josh Lee to Gabe Cantor, and Cantor banked home a soft hook for two. Valley Christian countered by working the clock down for 25 seconds before really starting their offense, and they again connected, this time powering inside over Cantor for a two-pointer.

The clock was winding down toward the two-minute mark, and the Pirates still faced a five-point deficit. Rob hurried the ball up the court, got a sweet screen from Sam Jordan, and launched a three-pointer from the wing. All net. Two-point game. Crowd on their feet. The gym bedlam.

Trip McHenry sat morosely back on the bench ... he had given up hoping to get back in the game. *What the heck is the best player on the team doing on the bench in crunch time?*

Valley Christian did not panic, even as Hillsdale applied the press. The Pirates got a little sloppy . . . a Knight leaked free. The point guard found the open man, making Hillsdale pay with a dagger three to put the lead back at five. Just 90 seconds to play.

Rob pushed the ball up the floor and swung the ball to Sam Jordan on the wing. Sam passed to the corner and set a repeat screen for Rob, who broke free, captured the pass from Gabe Cantor, and launched another three. Swish! 82-80! Just over a minute left.

Time out, Valley Christian.

Coach Bridges huddled his team and looked them up and down. There was calm on the faces of Rob and Sam and a little terror on the faces of Josh, Gabe, and Edgar. He saw Trip McHenry, and he scanned past him quickly. *He needs to be in the game,* Coach Bridges thought. *He's calm, and he's ready . . . and he's a gamer . . . no . . . I've got a lesson to teach here.* He spoke to the team.

"Guys, you've done a great job getting back into this . . . you deserve to be out there. Keep doing what you're doing, and bring us home a winner!" Coach Bridges exclaimed.

Rob glanced around the huddle and caught Trip's eye. Trip gazed at him in disbelief. Rob shrugged and looked away.

Coach Bridges caught the exchange. *Need to talk to those two after the game,* he thought.

Allison and Emily were both tense as the teams returned to the floor. Grandpa Russell was tight-lipped. He had gone from expecting a loss to a glimmer of hope of a win . . . and now he wanted the boys to win badly.

The crowd was not so tight-lipped as fans from both sides were all on their feet roaring.

Clem Danielson inched closer to the Hillsdale bench and yelled at Trip McHenry. "What's the matter, McHenry? They don't let you play crunch time? Hah! USC scholarship my foot . . . you can't even play at Hillsdale!"

For the first time in his life, Trip heard the words and really let them bother him. *What am I even doing here?* he thought ruefully. *I've got to get out of here . . .*

CHAPTER 21
NOVEMBER-SOPHOMORE YEAR

JEB Danielson lurched onto the court a few feet to yell at Rob Mathews. "Hey, Mathews . . . how you going to choke this time? You can't beat Valley Christian! Or us!!!"

The Danielson boys all hooted loudly . . . Jake Gardner hooted, too . . . but when Rob glanced over, he just stared daggers at Rob.

Whatever, Rob laughed. *We aren't choking tonight.*

Valley Christian coolly brought the ball up the floor and milked the clock. With 40 seconds left, they started the offense in earnest and worked the ball down low to the player Gabe Cantor was guarding. The heavyset senior for the Knights used his bulk to get position, received the pass, and skied for a shot just before the shot clock expired. Basket good. Foul Cantor. Only 32 ticks remaining.

The Valley Christian fans exploded as the shot fell through, and Hillsdale sagged. The free throw was good, and the Pirates were down five again.

Rob raced up court, found an opening, and started to launch a three but saw Gabe Cantor flashing to the hoop. *We need two scores,* Rob processed quickly. *Let's get the easy one first.*

He rifled the freshman a pass. Gabe caught it, went up for a two-footer . . . and bricked it off the glass. It bounced off several sets of hands and into the corner, where Valley Christian ran it down. The air left the Hillsdale section of the bleachers in one loud, long groan while the Valley Christian contingent roared with delight.

A quick foul by Josh Lee sent Valley Christian to the free throw line with a five-point lead. Gabe Cantor was near tears as he toed the key in his rebounding position. First free throw . . . good. Six-point lead. One more ices the game.

Second free throw . . . missed. Cantor muscled his way up and pulled down the rebound. Hillsdale had life . . . not much . . . but it was still a two-possession game.

A quick outlet to Josh Lee, an immediate pass to Rob, a pull-up three-pointer . . . good!!!! Three-point game with 12 seconds left. The gym was chaos, and the bleachers were shaking as fans on both sides stomped and cheered.

Valley Christian did not call time-out but hurriedly inbounded the ball and, with two quick passes, got the ball over the mid-court line. Hillsdale frantically tried for steals, double-teamed when they could, but finally had to foul before time expired.

Two perfect free throws later, the Knights were back up by five points with four seconds left, and the gift basket at the buzzer by Sam Jordan just made the final score look closer as Valley Christian held on for an 88-85 win.

Valley Christian's team and fans exploded, coming together for a mid-court celebration. Hillsdale's fans sat numb . . . again . . . watching their beloved team go down in defeat.

Allison and Emily looked on with despair. They both knew it would be a long weekend at the Mathews home . . . especially since it was both Rob and Trip . . . and Grandpa Russell.

Grandpa Russell looked as if he might cry. He stubbornly bit the inside of his mouth and shook the feeling away. But it hurt. *I thought we were going to do it,* Grandpa Russell mused . . . *but here we are again . . . it almost feels as bad as the "Pick" game . . .*

***

***R**OB* and the players on the floor felt the letdown as the horn blared when time expired. The team gathered patiently, waiting for Valley Christian's players to get lined up for the post-game handshake.

The teams went down the line slapping hands, with Valley Christian cockily acting as though they had the game all the way.

Tony Russo smirked at Rob as they passed one another and pretended to shake Rob's hand but just grazed past Rob instead.

Trip was at the end of the line . . . going through the motions when Tony and another player got to him.

"Don't think your Coach knows what he's doing," Tony said to Trip quietly . . . but loud enough for Trip to hear. "Come on over to us next year . . . a lot of these guys will graduate in June . . . we've got a spot for you . . . you won't be playing half-time with us."

Trip looked up at Tony, bobbed his head, and mumbled his thanks.

Just then, out of nowhere, Jeb Danielson was in Rob's face. "You guys are just a bunch of losers!!!" Jeb screamed. "Especially Cantor . . . you guys are a joke this year!!!"

Rob's face went dark, and Gabe Cantor looked on the verge of tears.

"Don't listen to them, Gabe . . . those guys are jerks," Rob said soothingly.

The anger Trip was feeling bubbled over when he heard Jeb's comment, and he lunged at Jeb, who stumbled backward, desperately trying to get away from the hulk of Trip McHenry.

Rob swiftly moved in front of Trip and held him back.

"Not now, Trip," Rob pleaded. "We need you to stay cool."

Edgar Garcia appeared, got a good grip on Trip, and pushed him toward the locker room.

Rob just stared at Jeb . . . waiting for Jeb to look away . . . he finally did . . . and Rob just shook his head and headed for the locker room.

CHAPTER 22
NOVEMBER-SOPHOMORE YEAR

*T*HE bus ride home was a mixed bag . . . disappointment at losing a close game . . . exultation at coming so close . . . despair for Trip, not knowing why he sat out two quarters . . . and an underlying tension that felt like an explosion was imminent . . . and the unknown of whether it would be Trip blowing up or Coach Bridges . . . or both.

The coach tapped Rob on the shoulder as Rob and Trip walked past Coach Bridges to get off the bus in the Hillsdale High parking lot.

"I want to see you two in my office," Coach Bridges said to Rob. "It won't take long."

Rob looked at Trip, and they nodded at the coach, got off the bus, and headed to the gym.

"Lecture time," Trip said snidely. "What's he gonna' lecture you about, "Wonder Boy?"

Rob shot Trip a look that told Trip to knock it off, and the pair quietly waited for Coach Bridges to arrive. Once he did, they followed along in silence as Coach Bridges opened up his office, turned on the lights, and waved his hand toward the two chairs facing his desk . . . chairs the duo had spent time in not long ago to talk about Trip's lackadaisical efforts in practice.

"So, a very interesting game," Coach Bridges began after they all had settled in their seats. His look was stern but not angry. *This is going to be a serious conversation,* Rob thought.

"I'm not crushed we lost," Coach Bridges continued, slowly and quietly. "It's more a matter of disappointed that we did not play to our potential as a team . . . and we still darn near pulled it off."

"Well, maybe if you had your best player, er, uh . . . I mean, one of your best players on the team . . . in the game at crunch time, we would have won," Trip flashed angrily.

"Maybe so . . . maybe so," Coach Bridges said wearily. "But tonight . . . was not an important game for us to win . . . in March . . . if we are up against Valley Christian in the Sectionals . . . well, that's a different story. At this point in time . . . we're trying to build a team."

"That's still no reason to bench me . . . I had 24 in two quarters tonight . . . Gabe blew that shot down the stretch . . ." Trip spouted loudly until he saw Coach Bridges hold up his hand to quiet him. "I'm just saying . . . I wouldn't have missed that shot."

Coach Bridges sighed, thought a moment, and then pointed to a framed quotation on the wall behind his desk.

"Read that for me, Trip, and tell me if it means anything to you," Coach Bridges said slowly.

Trip's eyes went to the wall.

"You mean the one by Knute Rockne?" Trip asked.

"That's the one," Coach Bridges replied. "Rockne is one of American history's most famous and well-thought-of college football coaches and coached Notre Dame football from 1918-1930."

"You want me to read it out loud for you?" Trip asked. Seeing Coach Bridges nod, he continued. "I play NOT my eleven best . . . I play my best eleven."

"What's it mean?" Coach Bridges asked, searching Trip's eyes, then gazing at Rob as both boys tried to figure out the meaning.

"Uh, uh . . . I'm not sure," Trip stumbled, looking at Rob for help.

Rob was confused as well.

"I'm, I'm not sure either, Coach," Rob sputtered.

"It means for this team . . . I don't just throw out my five best players in the school and let them play," Coach Bridges said. "I choose the five that will be the best TEAM I can put out there."

The light bulb went off at the same time for both boys and they looked at each other . . . Rob with a smile on his face, but Trip with a sulky scowl.

"Want proof?" Coach Bridges asked as he pulled some notes from his pocket and laid them on his desk. He adjusted his glasses and read off the page as both boys looked on and listened closely.

"Trip, you played the entire first and third quarters, correct?" Coach Bridges asked Trip.

Trip nodded.

"And you didn't play at all in the 2nd and 4th, correct?" Coach Bridges continued. "You scored 24 points, had two rebounds, one assist, one block, two turnovers, and seven forced shots, five of which could be considered turnovers."

Trip winced at hearing his line . . . *all I care about is the points,* he thought . . . *but there is more to the game than points . . .*

"Gabe played a similar amount of time," Coach Bridges added. "He scored 10 points, had eight rebounds, four assists, two blocks, two steals, and no turnovers."

Trip nodded and tried to process the information, but Coach Bridges plowed forward.

"Combining the scores in the 1st and 3rd quarters when you played . . . Valley Christian outscored us 54-28," Coach Bridges said, then paused to let those numbers sink in.

"The two quarters you did not play," Coach Bridges continued, "we outscored Valley Christian 57-34."

Coach Bridges paused again, letting the numbers sink in. Trip and Rob exchanged wide-eyed glances, and Trip lowered his eyes to stare at his feet.

Coach Bridges took a deep breath and sighed loudly.

"You tell me . . . which was the "best eleven" tonight?" Coach Bridges asked, letting the question hang in the air.

"Well, Trip?" he finally asked pointedly.

Trip was stunned by how much better the team did with him on the bench. "Well, uh, er, uh, I guess that second group," Trip finally stammered.

"You guess?" Coach Bridges asked quietly.

Trip nodded.

Coach Bridges paused again, letting the silence linger. After a long minute, Coach Bridges cleared his throat and began again.

"Trip," he started, causing Trip to jerk his eyes up from his feet. "I'm not saying Gabe is better than you . . . I'm not saying that you aren't part of our "best five." I'm saying that tonight you were not . . . tonight you played for yourself and not for the team."

Trip nodded, his demeanor a cross between anger and remorse. *I get it,* he thought. *I need to be a better team player. But I've got to get that scholarship to USC. Valley Christian or Canyon . . . that's the ticket. I've got to get out of here.*

"Now, I want to be perfectly clear here, Trip," Coach Bridges added sincerely. "I want to do all I can to help you get that ticket to USC you want so bad . . . I happen to think you will be much more likely getting that ticket if you become a multi-dimensional player . . . not just a scorer."

Trip's eyes raised again, and he looked Coach Bridges in the eye. *He means it,* Trip realized. *He wants to help me . . . but I gotta' get out of here.*

"I've seen what you can do if you put your heart into it," Coach Bridges continued. "You can be the most dominant player in the Section . . . going inside, hitting from outside, controlling the boards, passing, playing defense. You have the tools . . . you need to want to do it."

Trip stayed quiet, looking at the coach. *I'm so confused,* he thought.

"Look, Trip, I'm a big one for giving kids the weekend to think things through," Coach Bridges went on. "I'm not giving you an ultimatum as I did a few weeks ago . . . this whole thing is up to you. But remember, I'm going to play my best five . . . not my five best."

Trip nodded slowly.

"OK, you guys get home," Coach Bridges finished. "Talk it over with Rob and his Mom . . . and maybe with Dave Wilson . . . figure out what's best for you . . ."

Trip again looked Coach Bridges in the eye and nodded.

"I've gotten to know you pretty well these last few weeks," Coach Bridges added as the boys rose and headed for the door. "I think . . . I think you have it in you to take this advice and become a well-rounded player . . . it's something your Dad couldn't do."

Trip flashed his anger for a moment but quickly stifled it and nodded in agreement.

"I'm not going to make the same mistake with you I made with him," Coach Bridges said, with remorse in his voice. "You have the potential to be one of the all-time greats . . . and I really, really want it to happen for you . . . and for your grandmother . . . and grandfather."

Trip stopped short. He momentarily choked up. *He's right, you idiot . . . no . . . he's wrong . . . I'm so confused.*

"I'll think it over," Trip said as he left the room after Rob and softly shut the door.

CHAPTER 23
NOVEMBER-SOPHOMORE YEAR

ROB struggled to stay asleep while the early morning sun shone brightly through his bedroom window. But the smells of coffee and bacon wafted upstairs and drew him out of bed. He stood, stretched, threw on some clothes, used the bathroom, brushed his teeth, and headed downstairs.

As he hit the bottom stair, Trip McHenry bustled past him toward the front door.

"Mornin' Trip, where ya' headed?" Rob quipped pleasantly.

"For a walk," Trip blasted at Rob and slammed the door on his way out.

Rob stopped in his tracks. *What the heck . . . should I go after him . . . what should I do?*

Emily half ran into the entry just as the front door slammed, and she saw Rob.

"What is going on?" Rob asked, perplexed. "What set him off? Is he OK?"

Emily shrugged with a small half-smile. "The "Old Grump" column this morning . . . was . . . well . . . let's say it didn't go over too well with Trip. Come take a look at it."

Rob hustled into the kitchen, where Grandma and Grandpa Russell sat in their usual weekend morning spots, with the *Hillsdale Express* on the table in front of Grandpa.

"How bad is it?" Rob asked, holding his breath a little.

"I'll just give you the part about Trip," Grandpa Russell said. "Ahem, I quote, "The so-called savior of Hillsdale sports debuted this weekend, and I think we may have to defer judgment for a while. Let's just say Bill "Trip" McHenry did not have a promising start. While his scoring numbers were fine, he did almost nothing else at all to help the team. In fact, the team played much better without him. It's obvious he has massive talent . . . this old reporter has seen him in practice, and he should be dominating the floor, inside and out, controlling the boards and the defense. But sadly, all we know he can do so far is shoot . . . and that his shot selection is iffy at best. If this is how he intends to play . . . look for him to spend most of his time in Hillsdale riding the pine. Hal Bridges will not let young McHenry play the prima donna role. Many of us remember the last time that happened was with another McHenry . . . and that did not turn out well."

"Ouch," Rob said, shaking his head, turning, and heading toward the front door.

"Where are you going, Rob?" Emily called out.

"To see if I can find Trip," Rob yelled back as he scooted out into the cold morning air.

***

ROB trotted toward the ballpark, thinking he might find Trip sitting in a dugout. Sure enough, as he poked his head into the first base dugout, he found Trip seated on the bench, his long legs spread out toward the field and a faraway look in his eyes.

"Hey, Trip," Rob greeted his friend. "Thought you might be here."

Trip looked up, showed surprise, and then just nodded.

"What's up, man . . . you OK?" Rob asked.

"Yeah," Trip drawled. "I'm just confused . . . confused and hurt a little."

"Who hurt you, Trip . . . me?" Rob asked, worried something he had said or done had set Trip off. "I didn't mean to do . . ."

"It's not you," Trip said. "It's not any one person . . . it's my whole situation . . . I kinda' lost my parents . . . my school, my friends . . . and now I can't even do basketball right."

"Hey, I get it," Rob began.

"No, you don't . . . nobody does," Trip replied angrily but then paused, realizing that Rob, more than anyone in town, might understand what he was going through.

"I'm sorry, Rob . . . I didn't mean to snap at you . . . I know you do understand . . . at least better than most," Trip sighed heavily.

"I do, Trip . . . even though your circumstances are different . . . I get it," Rob replied softly.

They sat silently for a few moments, both friends collecting their thoughts.

Finally, Rob broke the silence.

"I just wanted to find you . . . let you know I'm here to help . . . if you need it," Rob said.

"You're not here to talk me into going along with Coach Bridges or to stay at Hillsdale?" Trip asked, turning to look Rob in the eyes.

"I'm just here to help if you want it . . . or need it. I'm here to support you," Rob answered quietly. "We all are . . . my Mom, my Grandparents . . . even goofy, old Allison will be there for you. You really can count on us . . . all you've got to do is let us help . . . if you need it."

Trip stared into space for a long minute. *Rob is right,* Trip thought. *Emily and her folks . . . Allison and Rob . . . are friends . . . maybe the best I've ever had. They'll help me.*

"No pressure, huh?" Trip asked, turning to smile at Rob.

"Not from me," Rob replied.

"Wonder Boy" strikes again," Trip said with a genuine smile. "Let's go home! What are you thinking being out here today . . . it's freezing!"

The boys laughed, popped up, and briskly walked the ten minutes home.

CHAPTER 24

NOVEMBER-SOPHOMORE YEAR

*T*HE boys walked in the front door, feeling the welcome blast of warm air, and headed for the kitchen.

Strolling in, they found Coach Dave Wilson regaling Emily, Grandma and Grandpa Russell, and Allison Pierce with the end of a story about his time at USC.

In his early 40s, Coach Wilson moved to Hillsdale the same year Rob and Emily did. He is the Varsity Football and Baseball coach and became the Athletic Director this year. Solidly built at six-foot-two and 225 pounds, he had played defensive back at USC.

Coach Wilson was easy-going most of the time . . . his "surfer-dude" good looks and easy smile made him very approachable. But he was very firm when he needed to be and stuck by his rules and philosophy no matter who was involved.

What the heck? Rob thought as he approached the group at the table. *Kinda' early to see Coach and Allison here.*

"Oh, hi, guys!" Emily said brightly. "Looks like you found him."

Emily beamed at both boys as she rose from the table. "I've got breakfast for you!"

The boys wolfed down their breakfast as Coach Wilson finished his story, added another, and then turned to Trip.

"So, I'm here to see you, Trip," Coach Wilson began. "Had a good conversation with Coach Bridges this morning . . . he asked that I pass along some of my comments to you."

"Here to talk me into being a team player and to stay at Hillsdale?" Trip said defensively.

"Well, not just that . . . kind of life in general, too," Coach Wilson replied.

"Oh, maybe we should leave," Emily said, motioning to her folks and Allison. Suddenly it felt awkward.

"No, no," Coach Wilson said quickly, waving Emily back down. "This is perfect. Trip's going through some tough issues . . . you guys are his support group here in Hillsdale . . . this will help us all know how best to support Trip."

Trip looked around the room and saw that everyone was engaged and interested. *These guys are my support system,* Trip thought. *Even Coach. But what does he have up his sleeve? And where does Coach Bridges stand?*

"Trip, you know I think . . . we all think . . . the best place for you is Hillsdale," Coach Wilson said quietly. "But, that's your decision. I want to go over things here that affect the big picture . . . and hopefully that will help you . . . you . . . make your decision."

Trip nodded apprehensively and gazed around the table. *Everyone is smiling at me,* he thought. *And they look like real smiles . . . these guys aren't being phony.*

"So, first, let's establish the situation," Coach Wilson said, launching into teacher/coach mode. "You are faced with deciding on whether to stay in Hillsdale, going to Hillsdale or Valley Christian, or going to Canyon . . . and boarding there. That sound about right?"

Trip nodded.

"Your goal is to play three sports in high school, but focus on basketball . . . and the ultimate goal is to land a full-ride scholarship to USC to play basketball. That still right so far?" Coach Wilson asked pleasantly.

Trip nodded again.

"You know my thoughts, Trip," Coach Wilson continued. "I think your best bet is to stay at Hillsdale . . . but . . . I don't think your chances of getting that scholarship revolve around which school you go to. I think the important thing will be the type of basketball player you are. You might not believe it . . . but I think you may have pretty much the same odds of winning a State Championship at Valley Christian, Canyon . . . or Hillsdale."

The room was silent . . . except for Grandpa Russell.

"Hear, hear to that," Grandpa Russell spouted, startling everyone.

"You really think so, Coach?" Rob asked.

"I do . . . if all the pieces come together . . . look how close you came last night against Valley Christian . . . that team has a legitimate shot at State this year . . . and, well, you guys could have won that game. But I'd say you guys have a real shot at being in the conversation over the next three years."

"And, we're going to win the "Pick" game the next two years, too!!!" Grandpa Russell bellowed as the rest of the group smiled in agreement.

"So, what's the right type of player?" Trip asked warily.

"Well, that's the part Coach Bridges asked me to pass along to you," Coach Wilson smiled. "But it takes a little background, so bear with me."

The group settled back in their chairs, but all were attentive.

What a great teacher Coach Wilson is, Allison thought.

This is going to be interesting, Rob thought.

Here it comes . . . be a team player, Trip figured.

"Back when I was in college, I took several coaching classes," Coach Wilson started. "On my final project for one class, I had to write a long paper and decided to write about evaluating talent and putting together the ultimate team."

The group all leaned forward. *This is really going to be interesting,* Rob thought.

"In my research, I interviewed about ten coaches... and came out of the interviews with a real consensus on the subject. Granted, these weren't all basketball coaches... but three of them were... and one of them had a system that intrigued me and made a lot of sense. It is so appropriate to our current situation with Trip that Coach Bridges thought it would be good for you to hear," Coach Wilson said.

Come on ... get to the point, Trip mused anxiously.

"This coach with the system," Coach Wilson said, "just happens to run the USC basketball program right now. I just got off the phone with him after talking to Coach Bridges ... I wanted to see if he still used the system ... or if he had updated it at all."

You could hear a pin drop in the room.

This is information worth hearing, Rob thought instantly.

Coach has an in at USC, Trip thought. *And this info is going to be good to know.*

"I thought that might interest you," Coach Wilson laughed.

Emily caught Coach Wilson's eye and gave him an extra wide smile.

Coach Wilson was taken aback by Emily's smile but regrouped quickly and continued.

"So, this coach told me that the first thing he looked at was attitude. The kid needed to have a great attitude and be coachable. Next, he had to hustle. Not only hustle up and down the floor ... but do the dirty work. Mixing it up inside ... scratching for every loose ball, every rebound, you know, playing tenacious defense."

Pretty standard stuff, Trip thought. *Been hearing that my whole life.*

"Pretty standard stuff, so far ..." Coach Wilson echoed Trip. "But here's where it gets interesting ..."

CHAPTER 25
NOVEMBER-SOPHOMORE YEAR

*T*RIP sat up straighter and was paying close attention.

"The coach said now that he was at USC, he had refined his evaluating system a little bit," Coach Wilson said. "He knew there would be tough competition for the best players at that level. And, to compete at that level, he had to not only get the best players . . . but they had to be the type of players to go the extra mile . . . take pride in what they did . . . and put the team first . . . but a strong second was to make an effort every time they set foot on the court to get better."

Coach Wilson paused and looked around the room and got nods of agreement.

Trip looked over and gazed at Rob. *"Wonder Boy" strikes again. Sounds like Rob's kind of guy. But, wait . . . if I want to go to USC, he has to be my kind of guy . . . or I have to be his kind of guy!*

Coach Wilson pressed on.

"He also tends to look at teams and players that are winners. Teams that are used to winning and strive for that. His evaluation system revolves around those goals but also goes into stats as well," Coach Wilson said, pausing to pull some papers and laying them on the table where Trip could see them.

"His initial system evaluated kids on a number basis by combining all their stats . . . for instance, let's say a guy's line . . . or a girl's line," Coach Wilson said with a nod to Allison and Emily, "consisted of 10 points, five rebounds, three assists, two steals one block and two turnovers. That line would result in a score of 19 when you add up everything except turnovers and then subtract the turnovers from the positive stuff. He'd also rate their defense from one-to-five points depending upon how good they were on the defensive end and add that to the total. Got it?"

They were all being drawn in at this point, and they all nodded . . . even Grandma Russell!

"He evaluated guys on his early high school teams by expecting or estimating about six-to-eight points from his marginal players who were on the edge of making it or not. His 'benchwarmers,' maybe 10-12 points, 6th, and 7th man would need to get 15-18, while the lower tier of the starting lineup would be at the 20-25 range."

"So, that leaves the two best players," Grandpa Russell interjected, glancing at Rob and then Trip. "What did the coach expect from them?"

Coach Wilson smiled as Grandpa Russell looked at Hillsdale's two best players.

"Around 40," Coach Wilson proclaimed.

Rob and Trip quickly did mental calculations.

That's not too hard, Trip thought quickly. *Let's say 30 points, five rebounds, two blocks and assists, and a three on defense. Leaves me room for a couple of turnovers, and I'm there.*

"A 40, with a couple of caveats," Coach Wilson said softly.

"Like what?" Trip said suspiciously.

"Well . . . now . . ." Coach Wilson continued, "when he is evaluating players for his USC program, he rarely looks at anyone under 35-40 on his scale at the high school level. But he also . . . and this is a big but . . . he does not look seriously at anyone who gets more than half his points from scoring. He says I don't want guys like that . . . I can't afford them."

"Why?" Trip asked, after quickly realizing . . . *hitting 40 is going to be a little tougher if I have to get 20 points from rebounding, blocks, steals, assists, and defense. Man . . . and if I score 30 a game, I've got to get a 60 score!*

Coach Wilson could see Trip was getting the point.

"I asked him that same question myself," Coach Wilson went on. "He said a guy who gets all or most of his points via scoring is too risky. What if he is cold that night . . . what if the other team shuts him down? If that happens . . . I have a guy on my team that contributes nothing to that game. I want a full squad of players that can do it all . . . those teams are hard to stop. No, I don't even look at those score-only guys . . . most of them can't repeat that success at the college level . . . it's a very different game. Give me the well-rounded player every time."

Coach Wilson paused, letting what he'd said so far sink in.

"Let's look at your numbers so far," Coach Wilson said, looking down at his notes. "First two games . . . you averaged 24 points, three rebounds, 1.5 assists, no steals, two blocks, and 4.5 turnovers a game. Coach Bridges gave you a two on defense. Adding those up gives you a 26.5 score. But 24 points came from scoring and only 2.5 points came from everything else combined."

Coach Wilson sat back and looked at Trip, who was mulling over the info and was clearly unhappy.

"So, what you're saying is I have no chance to play at USC," Trip flashed with a mixture of anger and sadness.

CHAPTER 26

NOVEMBER-SOPHOMORE YEAR

"I don't think he's saying that at all," Emily spoke up. "I'm sorry, Coach. Can I give an opinion?"

"I hoped you would," Coach Wilson smiled in return.

Emily returned his smile briefly and then turned to Trip, giving him a reassuring smile and speaking gently.

"I think Coach is showing you the road map to your scholarship. You have the talent to play at USC . . . we can all see that . . . but you need to reprioritize how you play the game," Emily said.

Trip looked at her quizzically.

"You have to emphasize the other parts of your game," Emily said firmly. "Hit the boards, play good defense . . . pass the ball. You're really good at all those things . . . when you want to be."

Trip just stared at Emily, digesting what she was saying.

"And, when you do that, Coach Bridges gives you the time you deserve . . . you hit your numbers . . . and more importantly, the Hillsdale team is just that much better," Emily added with a confident smile.

Emily paused and asked, "How am I doing, Coach?"

"Just perfectly," Coach Wilson laughed.

"So, you guys are saying being a team player will give me a better chance of getting my ride to USC and make us a better team?" Trip asked.

"Yes," the entire table answered him.

"You can see it from the first two games," Coach Wilson continued. "You're at 26.5, but Valley Christian outscored Hillsdale by 26 points while you were on the floor. Gabe Cantor only scored 10 points . . . but he penciled out at a 26 when you added everything together . . . and while he was in the game . . . Hillsdale was playing great team basketball . . . you guys outscored them by 23 points!"

"Wow!" Rob exclaimed, surprising himself that he said it out loud. "That's amazing . . . stats can really tell the story sometimes!"

"He played a complete game," Allison proclaimed dramatically. The whole table turned and stared at Allison. "Hey . . . sitting next to Grandpa Russell is really paying off for me!"

The table exploded in laughter, and Allison gave Rob and Trip a broad smile tinged with just a bit of embarrassment. *I just scored some points of my own,* Allison thought happily.

As the laughter subsided, Coach Wilson spoke again. "Here is a little chart of what you have done so far and what Coach Bridges knows you are capable of. Want to hear it?"

Trip nodded, and those around the table leaned in to listen to Coach Wilson.

"OK, we know where you are . . . at 26.5 . . . Coach Bridges knows . . . really knows you can accomplish these goals and make yourself a much better player and make your team a much better team."

"OK," Trip said quickly. "Lay it on me."

"He'd like to see you step up your defense to a solid four throughout the game," Coach Wilson said. "Average 18 points, 14 rebounds, five assists, two blocks, and two steals a game . . . and limit yourself to two turnovers a game. That puts you at a 43 per game . . . he thinks those are reachable goals."

"Wow, Trip," Allison spoke again. "Good numbers."

"Yeah," Rob said swiftly. "You can make those numbers."

"Yes, Trip," Coach Wilson piped in quietly, looking Trip directly in the eye. "You can make those numbers if you put your mind to it and take pride in how you go about your preparation and your games . . . and you can do it at Hillsdale, at Canyon or Valley Christian . . . you're that good."

Trip blushed, sat back, and thought, *Wow! That was nice to hear. I think Coach Wilson . . . and Coach Bridges believe that.*

"And that question is one you have some time to answer," Coach Wilson continued. "You're here for the rest of the school year no matter what . . . you don't have to decide that one until you give it some thought . . . but . . . deciding to play basketball the right way . . . for the team and the right way for you . . . well, you need to decide that by tomorrow."

"Coach send you with an ultimatum?" Trip asked defiantly, his anger still just beneath the surface.

"No, no," Coach Wilson answered with a small smile. "But I know Coach Bridges . . . if you continue playing like you have the first two games, you're going to spend a lot of time sitting. One thing I learned very quickly with Coach Bridges is that he doesn't blow smoke . . . if he says it . . . he means it!"

"I'd agree with you there," Grandpa Russell spouted. "Hal's a stubborn old coot."

"A mean old coot," Trip said in reply. "He just hates my family . . . my Dad anyway . . . and he doesn't like me."

"Now, wait a second there, Trip," Coach Wilson said calmly. "I wouldn't say that . . . no, not at all."

Trip looked at him in confusion.

"You know, we all have our special sayings and quotes," Coach Wilson said. "Coach Bridges told you one of his favorites . . . about the "Best Eleven" . . . that's one of my favorites, too . . . and well, I've got another one that fits here. Not sure that Coach Bridges would ever say it out loud, but he lives it."

"What is it?" Emily asked as Coach Wilson paused.

"It's that the kids don't care how much you know . . . until they know how much you care," Coach Wilson said quietly.

"Huh?" Trip, Rob, and Allison all said as Emily smiled and fought a lump in her throat at the saying her husband Jack had used in his coaching.

"It means you guys don't care about all the strategy, the lessons, the fine points of the game unless you know the coach cares about you as an individual," Coach Wilson explained. "When you know the coach is more concerned about doing the right thing for you and not just about how things affect him."

Trip and Rob still looked puzzled.

"Coach Bridges, by making this stand with you, Trip . . . he is showing you that he cares about you," Coach Wilson went on. "He has kicked himself for years that he wasn't strong enough with your Dad . . . he feels he failed your Dad . . . and your Grandparents. He honestly doesn't want that to happen again."

"He's not just doing it to make me stay . . . or to get what he can out of me?" Trip asked.

"No," Coach Wilson replied sincerely. "I honestly believe Coach Bridges wants you to be the best player and the best person you can be. Does he want you to stay at Hillsdale for the next three years? Absolutely. Will he be disappointed if you go? Absolutely. If you decide to go to Valley Christian or Canyon next year as the best player you can be . . . will he be happy for you? Absolutely."

Trip looked stunned and felt the emotions bubbling up.

"You . . . you're serious," Trip sputtered. "You really think he'll be OK with it if I leave?"

"Yes, I do . . . but only if you have made the decision to be a team player," Coach Wilson emphasized. "His whole object of doing this is to have you reach the potential your Dad never reached. He's not punishing you . . . or singling you out because he doesn't like you . . . it's just the opposite. He wants you to turn out to be the best you can be . . . like your Grandfather."

A small tear . . . just one . . . slid from Trip's right eye, and he hurriedly wiped it away.

"OK," Trip said as he stood and walked toward the door.

"I'm going to do some thinking," Trip said, pausing as he went through the doorway. "And, thank you . . . thank you all for the support. I appreciate it."

The door closed softly, and everyone at the table exhaled loudly and smiled at each other.

"Fingers crossed," Rob finally said.

"Hopefully, you can help put the odds in our favor, Rob," Coach Wilson said. "We're all rooting for the same thing . . . we all want Trip to make the right decision for Trip . . . we all hope that decision is to stay at Hillsdale!"

CHAPTER 27

DECEMBER-SOPHOMORE YEAR

***T*RIP** McHenry never said a word. Not when he got home after "doing some thinking" or when he got to practice that first Monday afternoon after the Valley Christian game. He didn't talk . . . he just did . . . he let his actions speak for him.

From the first minute of the first practice, after "thinking," Trip was a player possessed. Possessed to be the best, most complete, team player he could be . . . and he was devastating.

Coach Bridges smiled as he saw the transformation clearly after that first practice ended. *Can he sustain it?* That was his only question.

He certainly could sustain it through the first non-league game against a much larger school from the Sacramento area. Trip went off statistically. He played 24 of the game's 32 minutes and tallied 25 points, 18 rebounds, three blocks, two steals, and most notably, six assists and just one turnover, with a defensive rating of a four, according to Coach Bridges . . . for a phenomenal line of 57 . . . with less than 50 percent of that number coming from his scoring.

Most importantly, the team around him responded beautifully, playing an almost perfect game, which resulted in an 83-65 win in a game that had been projected as a tossup.

After another spirited practice, the Friday night game was another tour de force for Trip, as he went for 22 points, 15 boards, four blocks, two steals, five assists, no turnovers, another four on defense . . . and a 52 on the evaluation system set up by the USC coach.

This was done in another game that had been projected as a tossup . . . but Hillsdale won going away, 87-60. Hillsdale also got great games from Rob Mathews, Sam Jordan, and Edgar Garcia to supplement Trip, as well as solid contributions from freshmen Josh Lee and Gabe Cantor . . . and sophomore Bob Johnson. It appeared those seven were going to be getting a lot of floor time and were meshing exceptionally well . . . even though Brad Wallace was still starting at the second guard spot.

"I really like what I'm seeing," Coach Bridges told Coach Wilson after running into him in downtown Hillsdale. "Thanks for talking to him last Sunday . . . he is a different player."

Coach Bridges had let Trip . . . and the team know how much he appreciated the transformation and the leaps the squad had made as a team. They were clicking on all cylinders . . . even as they learned how to play together. *We are going to be tough to beat,* Coach Bridges thought.

The following week brought more of the same, as Hillsdale pushed their winning streak to four with two convincing wins against overmatched schools. Tuesday was a blowout affair as Hillsdale cruised to a 91-45 win, while on Friday night, the Pirates dominated their opponent by an 87-55 count in a game that featured limited time for the starters.

The starters averaged only about 16 minutes of play in both games, but they still put up great numbers . . . and allowed the bench to get quality time and numbers as well.

Through the first six games of the season, Hillsdale sat at 5-1, and the dynamic duo of Trip McHenry and Rob Mathews were clearly leading the way. Trip averaged 20 points, 15 rebounds, two blocks, two steals, five assists, and one turnover, and Coach Bridges rated his overall defense at a four! This gave Trip a 47 on the USC system.

Rob's numbers were equally impressive. He was averaging 18 points, eight rebounds, one block, four steals, ten assists, two turnovers, and a defensive rating of five . . . giving him a total score of 44 points!

In the locker room, after the Friday night game, Coach Bridges had waited until all the players had showered and dressed and pulled them together for one last chat before letting them go for the night.

"OK, guys, move in a little closer," Coach Bridges called out, and the team huddled close, some sitting on benches while others leaned against the lockers behind them.

"It's about this time every year that I choose Captains for the squad," Coach Bridges began. "In the past, I sometimes let the players decide, but the past few years, I felt it best to make the decision. Being so young this year . . . I think I should continue to make the choices."

The group made noises in agreement as they exchanged glances. "Usually, I choose two captains . . . but this year," Coach Bridges said, "I have opted for three . . . because I think they are all very deserving for different reasons."

More noises in response.

"First, and I think most obvious, is Sam Jordan," Coach Bridges announced to positive comments from the team. "Sam is our only senior, a great leader both in word and by example."

"He is also a great public speaker at the rallies," Rob threw out there, remembering how much better he did than Rob during his freshman year.

The team erupted in laughter, and Coach Bridges held up a hand to quiet them down.

"Which is a real necessity," Coach Bridges said through his own laughter, "because the second captain will be Rob Mathews . . . and we have all seen him in action as a speaker!!!"

The team howled, and Rob laughed with them.

"Seriously, though," Coach Bridges continued as the laughter died. "We all know Rob is the heart and soul of this team. He's another coach out there, and you guys know you can trust him to do the right thing . . . and to help you if you need anything . . . the same can be said of Sam."

Again, the team made positive noises.

"Finally, the last captain," Coach Bridges said slowly. "This guy has turned himself around and completely committed to Hillsdale basketball. I think his ability to step up and lead by example these last two weeks has been remarkable . . . and since we are not sure he will be back with us next year . . . well, I wanted to honor him . . . and his leadership this year."

The team cheered loudly, knowing who Coach Bridges meant.

"Trip," Coach Bridges said with real feeling. "Trip . . . you have been amazing these last two weeks . . . as an individual . . . and as a team player. I'm convinced you are going to keep it up . . . and I'm convinced we are going all the way this year if you do . . . Sectional Champs!"

The team erupted again and came together in one big group hug.

Trip was stunned. *I never, ever expected this,* Trip gulped. *Captain! Oh, man!*

"OK, guys, go out and have some fun tonight," Coach Bridges shouted. "Two more games before Christmas break . . . and then we start league in January! See you Monday!"

"Hey, Trip," Coach Bridges called out, motioning Trip to him.

"You deserve it, Trip," Coach Bridges said quietly, reaching up to massage his shoulder. "You have been amazing . . . you need to stay consistent with it . . . and I think you will. I'm going out on a limb a little with this . . . and I know you won't let me down."

"I won't, Coach," Trip said, struggling to control his emotions. "I won't."

CHAPTER 28

DECEMBER-SOPHOMORE YEAR

*A*FTER the Friday night blowout win, Hillsdale High held a Christmas "Sock Hop" dance in the gym after the game. As soon as the game ended and the crowd cleared away, parent volunteers and some kids quickly transformed the gym into a dimly lit dance floor complete with refreshments and a DJ.

Allison Pierce, Stephanie Miller, Christina Craft, Tasha Phillips, and some other sophomore girls were on the crew to help decorate, and within 20 minutes of the last fan filing out of the gym, the first students were allowed back in, and the dance was on.

The dance was only about two hours long, ending at 11:00 pm, so the dancing started more quickly than usual. The kids didn't have as much time to "warm up" or "gather the courage" to ask their favorite girl to dance.

As usual, Rob stayed on the sidelines, for the most part, watching the action and joking with his friends.

"Hey, Rob!" rang out, and Rob turned to see Trip McHenry waving him over to a corner of the gym.

"Hey, Rob," Trip repeated as he drew near. "I want you to meet Jenny."

Trip was standing with an attractive girl . . . tall, slender, with curly brown hair and a twinkle in her eye. *She looks like a girl Trip would hang out with,* Rob mused. *Movie star good looks!*

Standing with them was another girl he didn't recognize. *Must be the friend Trip has talked about,* Rob thought. *She's cute. Cute . . . but not movie star looks like Jenny . . . she's the sidekick!*

Rob stole a closer look as he moved forward . . . trying to be discreet . . . and saw she was a few inches shorter than Jenny, with straight blonde hair to the middle of her back and a pleasant face and smile.

"Rob Mathews . . . this is Jenny," Trip said proudly, with a slight grin on his face.

Jenny dazzled Rob with a smile and said brightly, "Hi, Rob! Nice to meet you . . . I . . . we've heard a lot about you!"

Rob returned her smile and mumbled a hello.

"And this is her friend, Lacy," Trip added.

Rob turned to gaze directly at Lacy and saw her smiling shyly at him, so he did the same. In the background, he saw Allison Pierce smiling and giving him a thumbs-up. *Why do I always have to watch Rob with other girls?* Allison wondered.

Why is she always around? Rob thought about Allison. *I can't do anything without her around . . . but I kinda' like her being around. Why am I thinking about Allison when I'm meeting another girl? Focus, idiot!*

"Uh, hi, Lacy," was all Rob could muster, while he alternated between looking at the floor, the ceiling, his shoes . . . anywhere but at Lacy.

Trip picked up the conversational ball, and the quartet stood around talking for a while . . . well, three of them did . . . Rob was dumbstruck as usual around girls he didn't know.

A voice from across the room... Buck Buckman's silky voice... beckoned Rob and Trip over, so the boys ambled over, leaving Jenny and Lacy alone... with Allison Pierce within earshot... and listening!

"What do you think of him, Lace?" Jenny asked her friend, obviously hoping the pair hit it off so the couples could double-date.

"Well, he is good-looking," Lacy replied, laughing nervously. "But... he sure doesn't talk much. I don't think he's said a complete sentence yet!"

"No," Jenny replied. "Trip warned me about that. Said he is kind of awkward around girls he doesn't know... but that once he gets going, he's fine."

"Well, I, uh, guess," Lacy responded slowly. "It would be fun to double-date sometime."

"Yeah, we'll take it slow," Jenny said. "Let's run into him at school... you know, Lace, stuff like that. Then you can ask him to Sadie Hawkins dance, and we'll double-date... you know dinner first... then the dance... and then..."

"Then, what," Lacy laughed, embarrassed by her friend's innuendo.

"You know what I mean... just have some fun," Jenny laughed. "Oh, hush, here they come."

Allison wrinkled her nose. *They seem ok,* she thought. *But there goes my plan to ask Rob to Sadie Hawkins...*

CHAPTER 29

DECEMBER-SOPHOMORE YEAR

THE boys returned, and Trip pulled Jenny to the dance floor for a slow dance, leaving Rob and Lacy stranded on the side of the gym.

Allison watched discreetly how Rob nervously twisted in agony at being left alone with a girl he didn't know. *Oh, Rob, you don't have a clue, do you?*

Lacy tried to instigate small talk, but Rob had only one-word answers for her, and the slow dance seemed to last forever. Finally, the song ended, and Trip and Jenny returned, giving Rob an out to use the bathroom and not leave Lacy on her own.

After stalling as long as he could, Rob slowly made his way back to the corner of the gym and realized there were probably only two songs left until the dance was over. *Almost there,* he thought. *I'm ready to hit the road.*

As the last song started, Trip grabbed Jenny again for another slow dance, and they both urged Rob and Lacy to dance.

"Come on, "Wonder Boy" . . . one dance won't kill you," Trip said, pulling Rob toward the dance floor while Jenny urged Lacy along with him.

Trip and Jenny literally pushed the pair together, and Rob found himself easing into the slow dance with Lacy. *I remember this part,* he thought. *I kinda' like slow dancing. She does smell good . . . and feel good. Thank you, Mom, for teaching me how to dance . . .*

Rob wished he had done this earlier and sooner than he hoped . . . the song was over, and the lights went up.

They moved toward the doors as a group, and as they reached the parking lot, Jenny called out, "Lacy, my Dad's over there."

Lacy looked at Rob, smiled, and started moving in that direction.

"Jenny's Dad is my ride," she said with a small, nervous smile. "Maybe I'll see you at school next week."

Rob grunted and nodded in response, and his hand went up in a small wave.

Jenny reached up and gave Trip a quick kiss on the cheek, smiled at him, and waved goodbye.

The boys looked over at each other and smiled.

"Nice girl, isn't she?" Trip asked. "And . . . beautiful . . ."

"Jenny or Lacy?" Rob asked.

"Well," Trip smiled, "both, I guess."

"Yeah, yeah they're both really nice and beautiful," Allison piped in, coming up from behind them. "Nice, beautiful, whatever . . . what else would you expect from girls dating Hillsdale High's two biggest "spooorts" heroes!!!"

Allison laughed, and Trip and Rob joined in.

"So . . . can a girl get an escort home?" Allison asked playfully. "Even if she is not hot or a cheerleader!"

CHAPTER 30
DECEMBER-SOPHOMORE YEAR

*A*s usual, a large group of kids left the gym together for the short walk home, and Allison and Trip found themselves together at the back of the group.

"Congratulations on the Captain thing," Allison said sincerely.

"Uh, thanks," Trip replied with a small smile. "It's kinda' cool."

"Trip?" Allison said, unsure how to broach this new subject. "I was curious . . . Rob said you never talked to him about changing . . . you know . . . your emphasis on team and stuff. He said you never talked to Coach Bridges either . . . what made you change?"

"Well," Trip began, "it was kinda' like when you explained why I should hustle. You know, I just had to hear it the right way. I'm stubborn, you know . . . Coach Wilson made it make sense . . . you know . . . that talk about the USC system and stuff."

"That did make sense," Allison replied. "Especially for your scholarship chances . . ."

"Yeah, well, that's the thing," Trip said quietly, slowing his pace. "Yeah, I saw the benefit of changing for my scholarship chances . . . but Coach Wilson made me see . . ." Trip paused and looked around to make sure no one else could hear him.

"You gotta' promise not to tell Rob this," Trip whispered.

Allison nodded and drew closer to Trip as they continued walking.

"Coach made me realize that Coach Bridges... and Rob... have my best interests in mind ... and that made a difference... but I also realized... it's the way Rob plays..."

Trip paused again and all but stopped and whispered again.

"Don't ever tell him... promise?" Trip asked Allison, and she nodded.

"I just want to be more like Rob," Trip admitted.

Allison's eyes teared up. *Trip is so sweet,* she thought. *Rob has made a real impression.*

Trip could see her look and quickly tried to defuse the emotion.

"You know, what red-blooded American boy doesn't want to be more like "Wonder Boy," Trip said with a laugh punctuating the end of his sentence. "One of a kind!"

They both laughed, and Allison suddenly felt closer to Trip.

"That is so sweet..." Allison started.

"None of that either..." Trip said firmly. "Don't tell Rob any of this gooey stuff... it just... it is what it is."

"Got it," said Allison, smiling brightly at Trip.

The pair continued walking together, now a good ten yards behind the group, which had been cut in half by kids turning down their own streets.

"So, are you nervous about moving tomorrow?" Allison asked.

"Moving?" Trip asked quizzically. "Moving in with Aunt Barb... is that tomorrow?"

Allison laughed with him.

"Yeah, tomorrow," Allison said. "Looking forward to it?"

"Well, yes and no," Trip said. "I've spent a lot of time with Aunt Barb and the kids... my folks weren't around a lot. Aunt Barb's great... and the kids are fun... but I've... well, I've enjoyed living with Rob and Emily... and Grandma and Grandpa Russell..."

Allison looked up at Trip and started to well up again. Trip saw the look and quickly quipped sarcastically, "It's those neighbors . . . you know, the Pierce family . . . I won't miss them . . . but I will miss those great dinners and "Movie Night."

"Oh, you don't have to miss those . . ." Allison said quickly. "Rob and I talked to our Mom's about that . . . you're part of the tradition now!"

"Even if I'm at Canyon or Valley Christian?" Trip asked, suddenly a little more serious.

"Even if," Allison smiled. "Although, the commute from Canyon might be tough."

Trip snorted out a laugh.

As they reached Allison's front porch, Rob, on his front steps, saw Allison stop and face Trip in the porchlight.

"You know, I have a feeling you'll always be a part of their family," Allison said. "Even when we're old and gray and we all have grandkids running around."

"Grandkids!" Trip scoffed, trying to lighten the mood. "Did you see old "Wonder Boy" tonight with Lacy? He's never having grandkids . . . he can't even talk to a girl!"

Allison burst out laughing.

"Well, he talks to me," Allison said, lowering her eyes.

"Well, that's you . . ." Trip began.

"You mean because I don't count as a girl?" Allison asked, looking playfully offended.

But Trip knew better.

"You count as a girl, Ally . . . you're a very special girl," Trip said softly.

"Yeah, special . . . look at me," she mocked, waving her arm from head to toe.

"You're pretty . . ." Trip began.

"Trip . . . don't . . . I know I'm a geek . . . I have a mirror," Allison said quickly.

"I've seen pictures of your sisters . . . they're gorgeous," Trip countered. "You will be, too."

"They have always been gorgeous . . . they never looked like this," Allison moaned.

"Allison . . . it doesn't matter what you look like," Trip said quietly. "You are very, very special just as you are."

Allison, tears flowing freely now, waved him away.

"He knows your special, Ally," Trip said gently, nodding his head toward Rob's house.

"What?" Allison protested. "Rob? I don't . . . I . . . uh . . ."

Trip smiled and nodded, letting Allison sputter in protest.

"I know," Trip said softly. "It's pretty obvious . . . to everyone but "Wonder Boy.""

Allison looked at Trip in surprise and then welled up again.

"There's no telling when he'll realize it," Trip laughed. "But he will eventually."

Allison's eyes started dropping real tears now.

"Until then, I'll try to keep him out of trouble," Trip chuckled. "Shouldn't be too hard . . . not sure what it is you see in him . . . the guy's clueless."

"I'm not sure either," Allison said, her voice catching a bit.

"There is just something about him," Trip replied. "He is "Wonder Boy," after all."

They both burst out laughing.

"Sweet dreams," Trip said lightly as he went down the steps.

"Trip?" Allison called out. Trip stopped and faced her.

"Thanks, Trip . . ." Allison said shyly. "Thanks for calling me special."

"You are special, Allison," Trip answered. "And don't you forget it!"

CHAPTER 31
DECEMBER-SOPHOMORE YEAR

*T*HE bus ride down the hill to the Sacramento area on Wednesday was a long one as the Hillsdale Pirates ventured into the realm of "big" high school basketball. They had scheduled Braxton High, a school of nearly 3500 kids, and a powerhouse program in a division three divisions higher than Hillsdale.

Coach Bridges had a habit of scheduling at least two powerful teams . . . Valley Christian being one . . . each year to get the Pirates some experience against a prime-time team. He felt it helped point out the weaknesses in his team and made the competition back home seem much more manageable.

Rob and Trip used the time to catch up . . . with Trip now living at his Grandma's house with Aunt Barb and her kids, they hadn't had every evening together . . . and they both realized they missed it.

They had been together Sunday for "Movie Night" . . . the tradition continued . . . and that had been fun. Allison had chosen *It's a Wonderful Life* just two weeks after doing *To Kill a Mockingbird*, and Rob had marveled at how well Trip had picked up on all the nuances . . . with some help from Allison, her Mom, and Emily.

"You gotta' remember," Trip had said with a laugh. "I grew up in Hollywood . . . my Dad's in the business . . . I'm a movie junkie."

Rob had noticed Allison and Trip being extra nice to each other and remembered their long walk home after the dance. *Nah, Trip and Allison . . . never,* Rob thought.

"So, how's it going at your new place?" Rob asked shortly after they settled in on the bus.

"Eh, it's ok," Trip grunted in response. "After living with you guys, everything is going to go downhill."

The boys laughed.

"Seriously, though," Rob pressed. "It going good?"

"Yeah," Trip replied. "Aunt Barb is great . . . she's tough on me . . . but, you know, she knows she needs to be . . . she was there when the trouble hit."

"Ah," Rob nodded in response. *Yeah, I don't really know what that means,* Rob thought. *You'll tell me if you want to.*

"The kids are fun . . . but they aren't Allison and Emily . . . or "Wonder Boy," Trip joked. "I kinda' miss having you guys around . . . you know . . . my age and stuff. But I know I need to live there to stay eligible to play ball."

"Doesn't mean you can't visit any time you want," Rob answered. "We've got "Movie Night" . . . and you can stay over sometimes."

"Yeah . . . that would be good," Trip sighed in response.

"So, your Dad is coming up this weekend?" Rob asked.

"Yeah," Trip sighed again. "He's coming up Friday afternoon . . . be here for the game on Friday night . . . he's here until Sunday, but then he has to get back. Won't be here for Christmas . . . again."

"You're always welcome at our house for Christmas," Rob answered.

"Yeah, thanks, man," Trip sighed heavily again. "Aunt Barb is doing some special stuff for Grandma and us, but I know there will be some downtime."

"Well, that's when you head over to our house," Rob grinned.

***

BRAXTON was huge and tough. Speed was their issue . . . or rather, lack of speed . . . but they made up for it with a bruising inside game and a brawling defense.

It was apparent from the early minutes that if Hillsdale was going to hang with Braxton, they would have to play as big and tough as they could.

Coach Bridges hung with his starters through the first quarter, except he inserted Josh Lee for Brad Wallace about halfway through. Hillsdale held Braxton within reach, trailing only by three.

To start the second quarter, Bob Johnson and Gabe Cantor came in, and immediately, Braxton extended their lead to eight points . . . taking advantage of the slender and inexperienced pair. Three minutes into the 2nd quarter, Coach Bridges signaled a time-out, and his players huddled around.

"OK, guys, listen up," Coach Bridges squawked loudly. "I think we can play with these guys, but I think it might require the right lineup to do it . . . Rob, Trip, Sam, Josh, and Edgar. You guys will take us through to halftime, and let's see where we are at the half. We're going to go zone . . . make them beat us from outside. Run when you can . . . we're faster . . . tough, hard defense. Ready? Team!"

Hillsdale jumped back onto the court and quickly established that this fivesome could play with Braxton.

Rob nailed a quick three to cut the lead to five. A defensive stop on a great play by Trip triggered a fast break basket by Sam Jordan, and another stop led to a pretty reverse layup inside by Trip McHenry. All of a sudden, it was a one-point game . . . and Hillsdale had Braxton's attention.

The two teams battled back and forth over the first half's final three minutes. While still outsized and outmuscled, the Pirates hustled and scrapped their way to a flat-footed 30-30 halftime tie.

The crowd was buzzing in the stands as this game had been projected as a walk in the park for Braxton. The large Hillsdale contingent happily enjoyed their good fortune, while Braxton's hometown crowd wondered when their team would blow this little school out of the water.

Allison Pierce found herself in her familiar position between Emily and Grandpa Russell. But tonight, they had company . . . company that would become standard procedure. Trip's Aunt Barb was planted next to Emily, with her two kids in tow.

Allison peered at Aunt Barb and how she was enjoying the game. *She looks so much like Trip,* Allison thought. *She's tall like Trip and sturdy . . . not fat, but sturdy. Trip would make a pretty girl,* Allison mused.

"Are you enjoying the game?" Allison heard Emily ask Aunt Barb.

"Oh, yeah, we never miss seeing Billy . . . er . . . Bill . . . oh, I mean Trip play. Not sure I will ever get used to this Trip business," Aunt Barb laughed. "His game has changed," she added. "For the better . . . not so selfish."

The group smiled and turned back to the floor as both teams poured out of their locker rooms for the second half.

CHAPTER 32
DECEMBER-SOPHOMORE YEAR

"*Now*, remember what we talked about, guys," Coach Bridges said as he prepared to send the same five back on the floor. "You guys are it . . . if you stay close. Play your hearts out, and let's steal one from the big boys."

The second half picked up where the first half left off, with the teams battling through every possession. Hillsdale's plucky five held their own as the teams traded baskets and stops, and Braxton could not get more than a four-point lead . . . while the best Hillsdale could do was forge a tie.

At the end of three quarters, the score stood at 45-43, with Braxton on top. It had become apparent that Hillsdale would live and die on offense on the backs of Rob Mathews and Trip McHenry.

While the other three, Edgar, Sam, and Josh, were playing good ball, they couldn't quite get in rhythm on the scoring side. Since the 2nd quarter began, Rob and Trip had scored all of Hillsdale's points.

Both boys were everywhere on both offense and defense and if Braxton tried double-teaming one, the other found a way to pop open and score.

Coach Bridges stuck with his plan to play these five as long as they stayed close and the group performed beautifully. They were maintaining their hustle and their poise . . . and now came the big test . . . the 4th quarter.

The crowd was loud and boisterous . . . not quite Pine Bluff or Valley Christian worthy . . . these two teams had minimal history . . . so very little built-in animosity. But as the game stayed close . . . and the Braxton side sensed this was going to stay close, the decibel level in the gym picked up a notch.

Hillsdale's side, a little smaller than usual due to the long ride just a week or so before Christmas, was also loud and vocal . . . just not Pine Bluff loud.

Up and down the teams went, grinding out possessions, as the lead went from 47-43 to 47-45 to 49-45 and then 49-48 in favor of Braxton.

The clock ticked to under a minute left, and Braxton was still clinging to a two-point lead of 59-57. Both teams had substituted very little . . . Hillsdale not all in the second half, while Braxton's starting five had all played the entire second half except their two guards, who had each sat for two-minute breaks.

Both teams looked exhausted as the rugged play and tense atmosphere of the close score took their toll. The crowd was also exhausted, but they were all on their feet and screaming as the clock wound down to under 30 seconds.

Up by two, Braxton moved the ball around, probing for a weak spot, but with the shot clock running out, they passed inside to their big man for an easy layup to put the game away.

From clear across the lane, Trip saw what was happening, leaped across the key, and jumped as high as he could toward the ball as it left the Braxton player's hand. Trip swatted the shot away, and the ball caromed off the backboard to Rob Mathews.

Rob hit Josh Lee with an outlet pass and followed at a sprint. Josh moved the ball into the front court and assessed what he had. Rob and Sam Jordan filled the lanes on either side while Edgar and Trip trailed the play. Just 15 seconds remained, and Hillsdale had a three-on-two advantage.

"PUSH IT!!!" yelled Coach Bridges from the sidelines, imploring his team to strike quickly before Braxton's defense set up.

"SCORE!!!!" the Hillsdale fans shouted from the bleachers.

Get it to Rob . . . or Trip, Grandpa Russell thought. *Either one will make it.*

Allison . . . and Emily were thinking the same thing . . . as were most of the Hillsdale contingent!

Josh hit the top of the key and decided to pass to the right . . . and into the hands of Rob Mathews.

Braxton's defense was finally getting down the floor, and two defenders rushed Rob near the right side of the lane and closed the gap to the hoop.

Rob pivoted and saw Trip McHenry wide open at the free throw line extended. He rifled Trip a pass . . . and Trip gathered the ball in and, in one fluid motion, rose to fire a three-pointer.

GOOD!!! Nothing but net!

The Hillsdale crowd went bananas as Braxton frantically called at timeout. Seven seconds left. Hillsdale 60, Braxton 59.

His teammates mobbed Trip McHenry as they gathered during the timeout. Trip looked into the crowd and saw his Aunt Barb beaming at him. He looked more closely . . . and saw Allison, Emily, and Grandpa Russell beaming as well. *It can't get better than this,* Trip thought.

It couldn't get better . . . but, unfortunately, it could get worse . . . and it did . . . Hillsdale had left Braxton too much time on the clock.

Braxton inbounded the ball and quickly moved it down the court. They worked a beautiful play . . . with two perfect screens that isolated their six-foot seven-inch center on Josh Lee . . . all, maybe, six feet of Josh, down low at the blocks with two seconds left.

Seeing who was guarding him, the big man turned and kissed a short jumper off the glass at the buzzer . . . and Braxton heaved a huge sigh of relief and celebrated a hard-fought 61-60 win over Hillsdale.

All the joy of just a few moments ago was gone . . . and a feeling like you had been punched in the gut replaced it.

Grandpa Russell sank to his seat in disappointment . . . but rallied quickly as he realized a win over Braxton would have amounted to a minor miracle.

Trip and Rob exchanged glances . . . *what just happened? We had it . . . what went wrong?*

"Nobody's fault but mine," Coach Bridges roared as the team gathered before shaking hands with the Braxton team. "I should have prepared you for that play . . . they ran a good one. I should have warned you about that play . . . saw them run it a few years ago. Great game, though . . . great game!"

Josh Lee looked devastated. Trip walked over to him just as the teams started shaking hands. Josh's head was down, his shoulders were slumped and he looked to be on the verge of tears.

"Not your fault, Josh," Trip said quietly. "You played a heck of a game. Nothing you could have done on that play . . . they ran it to perfection."

Josh moved forward to get closer to the line of players from Braxton, but Trip felt a tug on his sleeve, and he turned to see Rob and Coach Bridges right behind.

"I made the right decision on you," Coach Bridges told Trip. "Yes sir, Captain McHenry . . . I made the right decision."

CHAPTER 33
DECEMBER-SOPHOMORE YEAR

"**You** want to see what the "Old Grump" had to say this morning?" Emily asked Rob as he padded into the kitchen on Friday morning. This was the last day of school before Christmas... and a game night for the Hillsdale Pirates... the last preseason game, as league would start the first week of January.

"Sure... can you read it to me?" Rob replied as he moved around the kitchen, making his breakfast.

Emily cleared her throat and affected a "Grandpa Russell" voice that cracked Rob up.

"I'm officially back on the Hillsdale Pirate basketball bandwagon... specifically because I'm back on the Bill "Trip" McHenry bandwagon. After a slow start with McHenry looking selfish on offense and lazy on rebounding and defense (does that remind you old-timers of anyone?), he has come on strong after the Valley Christian game to become a force to be reckoned with. His numbers have been fantastic in all phases of the game, and his defense has been exceptional."

"Nice," said Rob.

"There's more," Emily said.

"The Braxton game has me excited... though technically it was a loss. Hillsdale had no business being in that game, and yet it took a buzzer-beater to beat them... at Braxton!

McHenry's line was fantastic . . . 23 points, 16 rebounds, three assists, two steals, and three blocks . . . and zero, I repeat, zero turnovers! This looks like his average numbers so far this year . . . but when you account for the level of the competition . . . Braxton is one of the best high school programs in the State . . . it becomes all that much more impressive."

"Wow!" Rob said. "The "Old Grump" is on board."

"Still more," Emily smiled. "I like this part the best."

"And, lest you think we are forgetting the other key component to Hillsdale's success, think again. Rob Mathews is again proving what a stellar athlete he is for the Pirates. His line, again his average for the year, is equally impressive. Mathews matched McHenry's 23 points, added 12 assists, six rebounds, two steals, one block . . . and get this, zero turnovers . . . for a guy handling the ball as much as Mathews does . . . simply amazing."

Emily smiled broadly at Rob, who looked sheepish.

"Any more?" Rob asked.

"Just a bit," Emily replied.

"The two sophomores carried Hillsdale against Braxton, but there is potential galore. I see a solid core of players . . . Edgar Garcia, Josh Lee, Gabe Cantor, and Bob Johnson . . . these guys are going to be tough for a while. I think this group of guys . . . come Sectional time . . . after having a whole season to mesh . . . have a legitimate shot at dethroning Valley Christian. You heard it here first."

"Grandpa Russell is going to love this story," Rob said, smiling. "Have you talked with him about it yet?"

"Who do you think called at 6:30 this morning to make sure I read it?" Emily grinned.

***

***R*ICK** McHenry popped his head into the locker room about 30 minutes before game time, and he and Trip shared a hug and some small talk. He exchanged some brief stilted pleasantries with Coach Bridges and excused himself from the locker room.

He strode confidently into the gym, reveling in his old high school glories. Rick spotted his sister Barb, his nephews, and his target for the evening . . . Emily Russell Mathews.

"Hi, guys," he called out. His sister and nephews jumped up to greet him and pulled him into the stands to say hello to Emily, and her parents.

After all the hugging and small talk, Rick sat down next to Emily and turned his back on his family to focus only on her.

"Emily, you look lovely tonight," Rick began. "Of course, you always do."

Emily snorted. "Some things never change, do they, Rick," Emily said.

"Truce!" Rick said, holding his hands up defensively. "One bad night does not make a man . . . especially when he was just a kid. I'm a changed man!"

Emily looked very unconvinced.

"Look, I'm just in town until Sunday . . ." Rick started.

"Good," Emily said quickly.

"Whoa, hear me out," Rick replied. "I hoped I could take you to lunch tomorrow . . ."

"I'm not dating, Rick," Emily said icily.

"Not a date, Em . . . not a date, Emily," Rick said, correcting himself after Emily glared at him. "A thank you for what you have done for Bill . . . it means a lot that you did that for me."

"I didn't do it for you, Rick," Emily said coldly.

"Oh, come on, Em . . . Emily," Rick said jovially. "It's just a thank you lunch . . . it will give us a chance to reconnect."

Emily glared at him again.

"Please, Emily," Rick said pleadingly. "Bill asked me to do that . . . to thank you."

Emily looked at him suspiciously. *If Trip asked him to do it, well . . . maybe I better go.*

"OK . . . OK, Rick," Emily said grudgingly. "But it needs to be quick, and it's not a date."

"Agreed," Rick said. "I'll pick you up at Noon!" Smiling, he walked down the bleachers and went to watch the game with several alums . . . and Coach Dave Wilson.

A little flustered, Emily turned and saw Allison Pierce gazing at her.

"Not your favorite guy?" Allison queried.

"Not my favorite guy," Emily replied.

Both teams poured onto the court for warmups, and the crowd started to buzz.

Allison kept her eyes on Rick McHenry and saw him standing and talking with Coach Wilson. The conversation seemed to start normally . . . friendly . . . but suddenly Coach Wilson seemed to get mad.

"Emily," Allison said, "I thought Trip's Dad was old friends with Coach Wilson?"

Emily turned to Allison, nodding her head in assent, and followed her gaze to the two men.

Coach Wilson heatedly talked to Rick McHenry and poked Rick in the chest with his finger. Rick stood with a mischievous grin on his face and seemed just to let the Coach vent.

With one last poke of his finger, Coach Wilson stomped off, and Rick returned to his friends as if nothing had happened.

"That's odd," Emily said to Allison. "I wonder what that was about? That's not like Dave at all . . ."

CHAPTER 34

DECEMBER-SOPHOMORE YEAR

*A***LL** Trip McHenry could think about was impressing his old man. *I've got to have a big game tonight,* Trip thought as they ran their layup drill. *Gotta' go really big tonight . . . maybe get 40 points! That will show him.*

And, once the game started, Trip set out to make that happen . . . and all of a sudden, he was the old Trip. Selfish on offense and leaking out early on defense to try to get easy baskets . . . and it backfired completely. His overall game suffered, and he clanked six shots in the first four minutes without a score until Coach Bridges called a time-out and yanked Trip from the game. He sat dejectedly on the bench until the end of the first quarter, with Hillsdale clinging to a 16-15 lead.

As the team huddled up, Trip saw Rob Mathews speaking with Coach Bridges, and then Coach Bridges waved Trip over.

"Report in for Cantor," Coach Bridges barked. "And, listen to Mathews."

Trip looked confused, but when he turned, he saw Rob striding over to pull him aside.

"You're pressing, man," Rob whispered to Trip. "I know you want to go off in front of your Dad . . . the best way to do that is play like you did at Braxton . . . you read the "Old Grump" . . . you know what to do."

Trip gazed at Rob and immediately knew he was right.

"Just relax, Trip," Rob continued. "These guys aren't that good . . . you can dominate them if you play the game the right way."

Trip nodded, and the team broke off and hustled back to the floor.

The transformation was total and immediate.

Hillsdale came down, and Trip made a dazzling pass to Rob, cutting down the lane for a layup. At the other end, he snagged a rebound, exploded from the pack, dribbled to the top of the key, and fed Sam Jordan, filling the lane on the left for another layup.

The following three times, Hillsdale ran the offense perfectly, leaving Trip wide open . . . two three-pointers and a savage dunk later, Hillsdale's lead was up to ten.

Suddenly, Trip was everywhere, doing everything and completely dominating the game.

Trip glanced over at his Dad during a free throw and saw him grinning from ear to ear. *He's proud of me,* Trip thought.

In the 3rd quarter, it was more of the same, as Trip McHenry, with help from the whole team, put on a show. The crowd was roaring as highlight after highlight revolved around Trip, and Hillsdale pushed the lead to 22 points at the end of the quarter.

Rick McHenry, who had moved into the stands at halftime to sit with his sister, was grinning broadly and enjoying the show. *The rumors are true,* Rick thought. *Old Bridges . . . and maybe Emily's kid have gotten through to Bill. He is really something.*

With the game in hand, Coach Bridges emptied his bench to start the 4th quarter, and they played well enough to stay on the floor, even though they gave up some of the lead. All in all, it was a solid 78-62 win when the buzzer sounded to end the game.

Not counting those rough first four minutes, Trip McHenry had a complete game in just two quarters of play. He ended up with 24 points, 15 rebounds, three blocks, a steal, and five assists . . . and his three turnovers were all in the first four minutes.

"Guys, an excellent game . . . after a bit of a rough start," Coach Bridges said after the game. "You started playing like a team again . . . and look where it got you."

The team murmured in assent.

"All right . . . you guys know the Christmas practice schedule . . . we'll see you Monday," Coach Bridges said, dismissing them for Christmas vacation.

"Good job," Rob said to Trip as they made their way out into the cold winter's night.

"Thanks, you too!" Trip replied. "And, thanks for getting my head straight . . . I kinda' spaced there for a while."

"Hey, I get it," Rob responded. "Easy to get caught up in that . . . with your Dad here."

"Hey, Bill!" a voice called out from the dark. Coming toward them was Rick McHenry, with a massive grin on his face.

"Great game, son!" Rick exclaimed, reaching out and embracing Trip awkwardly.

"Hey, thanks, Dad!" Trip mumbled in reply. "Kinda' a slow start . . ."

"Not how you start," Rick spouted, "it's how you finish . . . and you finished great."

"Thanks, Dad," Trip said, embarrassed by his Dad. "You remember Rob, right?"

"Oh, yeah, Rob," Rick answered. "Yeah, you had a good game, too."

"Thanks," Rob answered.

"Let's get some food!" Rick smiled. "There is a great place down near Valley Christian."

"Well, uh, I was going to hang with Rob . . . thought you'd be busy," Trip sputtered.

"Nonsense," Rick almost shouted. "I'm here for you tonight, kid. Can't stay long this trip . . . but want this to be our night. You understand . . . right, Rob?"

"Uh, sure, of course," Rob replied.

"Great!" Rick yelled as he pulled Trip toward his car.

Trip turned and mouthed he was sorry to Rob as Rick almost shoved him into the car.

CHAPTER 35

DECEMBER-SOPHOMORE YEAR

ROB bounded to the front door on Saturday around Noon, responding to a loud knock. He swung the door open and was surprised to see Rick McHenry standing there ... a bouquet of flowers in his hand.

What the heck? Rob thought. *What is he doing here ... with flowers?*

"Good morning, Rob," Rick beamed. "I'm here to pick your Mom up for lunch!"

"What?" Rob sputtered, clearly confused.

"Oh, Emily probably forgot to mention it," Rick said as he walked into the house uninvited.

Rob closed the door behind him and turned to face Rick.

"Uh, er, I'll let her know you're here," Rob said uneasily.

Mom doesn't date ... especially not this guy, Rob mused. *She doesn't seem to like him at all. But ... maybe she's ready now ... it has been a year and a half since Dad died.*

"Uh, Mom," Rob called out as he trotted down the short hall toward Emily's bedroom. "Rick, er ... Mr. McHenry's here."

Emily came out looking flushed ... not with excitement, but embarrassment.

"This is not what it looks like, Rob," Emily whispered. "It's a thank you lunch for having Trip stay with us . . . it is definitely not a date."

"Mom," Rob whispered back. "You can date if you want . . . it's been a long time."

"Thanks, Rob," Emily replied, still whispering. "When I am ready to date, it definitely will not be Rick McHenry."

Whew, Rob thought with genuine relief.

Emily brushed past Rob and went down the stairs and into the living room to greet Rick . . . and was surprised . . . and annoyed . . . to see Rick with flowers in his hand.

"For you, Emily," Rick said, with a slight bow and big grin.

"Thank you, Rick," Emily said frostily as she went to the kitchen to put them in a vase.

"Shall we," Emily said brusquely to Rick, clearly in a hurry to get out of Rob's sight.

She walked briskly to the door and out to the street.

Rick walked to his car and went to open the door for Emily.

"I'm not getting in your car, Rick," Emily said icily.

Rick did a double-take, not believing what he heard.

"The last time I got in your car, I ended up walking home in the dark by myself," Emily continued. "I'm not a country girl just back from her first year of college anymore. If we're going to lunch, we're walking."

Emily started walking, and Rick followed, catching up quickly.

"OK, OK, I get it. I was young and dumb . . . I was hoping then, as now, that we could rekindle our relationship," Rick said, trying to sound sincere.

"Relationship??!!" Emily spat out. "One week in 7th grade does not constitute a relationship."

"C'mon, Em, uh, er, Emily, you know I always loved you growing up . . . still do," Rick said as they walked briskly toward town.

"So, your way of showing your love is to trick me into taking a car ride with you when you knew I was serious about Jack . . . and attacking me!" Emily asked incredulously.

"I had to try, Emily," Rick whined.

Emily stopped and faced Rick.

"What is it you want here today, Rick?" Emily asked, point blank.

"I want to thank you for all you've done for Bill," Rick said. "You and Rob have done a lot for him . . . you know, he's a different kid . . . he looks happy . . . and healthy . . ."

"Stable," Emily interjected.

"Yeah, OK, stable," Rick replied defensively. "I know I haven't been the best father . . . I know I haven't given him the best home . . . or stability."

"OK, so you've thanked me . . . what else do you want, Rick?" Emily questioned.

"I want you, Emily . . . we could make a great couple . . . you could be a great Mom for Bill . . . we could . . ." Rick said, talking fast.

"Stop!" Emily said, her voice quaking in anger. "Rick, we are never going to be a couple . . . I have no feelings for you . . . no warm feelings. Even if I was ready to start dating . . . and I'm not . . . you would not be on my list to ever date."

Rick looked crestfallen . . . and then a little angry. He looked up and down at Emily, and his face got red.

"You were always just a little too good for me, weren't you, Em," Rick began. "Even when we were kids. Then you met Jack, and I could never measure up."

"I'm leaving!" Emily spouted and turned to walk away.

"No!" Rick shouted. "You'll listen to me . . . now!!!!"

CHAPTER 36

DECEMBER-SOPHOMORE YEAR

*E*MILY stopped in her tracks, unsure whether to be afraid or mad . . . she chose mad!

"Your Mr. Goody Two-shoes, with his ethics and morals," Rick sneered. "Treated you like a princess, didn't he?"

Emily just stared at him in disgust.

"And you just let him do it," Rick snarled.

Emily turned and began walking home.

"Now, it's Dave Wilson's turn, I suppose," Rick called out.

Emily stopped in surprise and turned to face Rick.

"Dave Wilson . . . what's Dave got to do with this?" Emily asked in confusion.

"Ah, bingo . . . he's right up your alley, isn't he, Em," Rick said. "The perfect guy . . . nice, mellow, full of integrity . . . a good role model for your son."

"Dave and I are not a couple . . . I hardly know him," Emily said sharply.

"Well, he made it pretty clear I better keep my hands off you," Rick replied.

"What?!!! Dave Wilson and I have never even talked about dating . . ." Emily responded.

"Yeah," Rick shot back. "Well, he told me you were a nice girl . . . meaning you were too nice for me . . . and that I better stay away from you or I would have to answer to him."

Emily paused, allowing what Rick said to sink in. *That's what they talked about when Dave got so mad. What right does he have to decide who I date???? Still . . . it was sweet.*

"I'm sure Dave didn't claim we were seeing each other," Emily finally replied, "because we're not."

"No, he's too good for that," Rick sneered. "He just said you weren't dating anyone yet and wouldn't let you get tangled up with me."

"Well, I'd say Dave probably has a reason for that," Emily said knowingly.

The comment hung in the air for a long moment, and the fight seemed to go out of Rick.

"Yeah, I guess he does," Rick said sadly. "Look, Emily . . . I really want to be one of those guys . . . you know, like Dave . . . like Jack . . . but I just can't do it. I just can't be good like that . . . I try sometimes, but I can't make it stick."

"You could if you wanted . . . but you have always taken the easy way out, Rick," Emily said quietly. "That's what Coach Bridges is trying to change in Bill . . . and it's working. Dave Wilson will teach him that, too."

Rick looked at Emily and nodded. "Yeah, I get it," Rick said. "I don't like it, but I get it. I don't know if one year . . . or part of a year will be enough, but it couldn't hurt."

"What do you mean?" Emily asked, clearly puzzled.

"I doubt Bill will be at Hillsdale more than this year," Rick said. "Last night, we talked about it, and I think he's leaning toward either Canyon or Valley Christian next year."

Emily looked shocked.

"I think he's got too much of me in him," Rick said. "He's out for number one."

"I think staying at Hillsdale is what's best for him," Emily said softly.

"You think him staying at Hillsdale is best for your high school sports . . . and gives your son a chance to be a champion alongside Bill," Rick shot back.

"You're unbelievable," Emily replied, shaking her head and walking away.

"You all think you are so, so good," Rick shouted after Emily. "You're not, you know! And he's my kid, and he'll do what I say!!!"

Emily never looked back and sped up her pace until she reached her front walkway. Once there, she looked back at Rick, slowly walking toward his car in dejection.

"Mom, you OK?" Rob said as he opened the front door to see her standing there quietly, watching Rick McHenry drive away.

"Yes, honey," Emily said, close to tears. "I'm fine . . . and I'm so glad to see you and have you close . . . and so glad to know I had some great years with your Dad . . ."

"Mom, you sure you're OK?" Rob said as he hugged her close.

"Yes, Rob . . . I'm OK . . . better than OK. I love you," Emily said as she returned the hug.

"Rick and I have some history," Emily told Rob. "Not all of it good history."

Rob nodded but didn't really understand.

"He's not a class guy," Emily said, trying to put it in a way Rob would understand.

Rob just looked perplexed.

"He's not your Dad . . . he's not Coach Bridges . . . or Coach Wilson," Emily said, tearing up. "He doesn't do the right things in life . . . I hope he doesn't take Trip down."

"Me, too," Rob said, suddenly grasping the situation.

"You need to help Trip . . . we all do," Emily said sadly.

"I'm in," Rob said.

"So am I," Emily added, pulling Rob close for another hug.

CHAPTER 37
DECEMBER-SOPHOMORE YEAR

*S*UNDAY "Movie Night" held some surprises for the group.

First, Linda Pierce, Allison's Mom, would not join the group tonight. Her ever-traveling husband was home this Sunday night because of the holidays, and they were going to a Christmas party.

Second, Emily had been lobbying for the chance to pick a movie for a long time, and the kids finally agreed. Since Linda was gone, tonight was a good night for that to happen.

The final surprise was a new person at "Movie Night" . . . Coach Dave Wilson.

Coach Wilson had knocked on the door late Sunday afternoon, hoping to catch Trip and check out how his weekend went with his Dad.

"It was weird," Trip answered after Coach Wilson, Rob, Trip, and Allison were settled into seats around the dining room table. Emily was preparing a casserole for the oven in the kitchen, but she welcomed Coach Wilson warmly and was a definite part of the conversation.

"Weird?" Coach Wilson asked. "How so?"

"I don't know," Trip explained. "Friday night, he insisted we eat down near Valley Christian and some VC alumni were there . . . guys Dad played against in high school."

"Hmmm?" Coach Wilson mumbled.

"They were all pushing me to play over there next year." Trip relayed. "Dad was too, but not too hard . . . I don't know . . . maybe he was playing hard to get with them . . . didn't want those VC guys thinking I was dying to go there, you know."

The group nodded.

"But, by Saturday afternoon, he was all about getting me out of Hillsdale . . . at least out of Hillsdale High," Trip said, shaking his head in confusion. "He just seemed mad at the world . . . but maddest at Hillsdale High for some reason."

Rob shot his Mom a look, and Emily shrugged her shoulders.

"Anyway . . . it was just weird," Trip continued. "He made Aunt Barb set up a visit to Valley Christian in February. They told us February was better . . . I'll have more stats to push at them. He set up a visit to Canyon over Martin Luther King weekend. Aunt Barb is gonna' take me there, too . . . Dad's out of town . . . go figure . . ."

"Interesting," Coach Wilson said.

"Then, today, as he was leaving, he told me I should stay away from Rob and from . . . you, Coach," Trip said haltingly. "Not sure what that's about."

Rob again looked at his Mom . . . who was sharing a look with Coach Wilson. *Wait, what?* Rob thought. *What the heck is going on here?*

Allison caught the look as well and wondered. *I sure wish I knew what Coach Wilson and Trip's Dad were talking about. Has it got something to do with Emily?*

"Where do you want to go to school, Trip?" Allison blurted.

"Ah . . . I don't know yet . . ." Trip said with confusion. "I wanted to visit both those places anyway . . . I mean, they are both good options . . . it was just how my Dad was so angry about everything."

"And you should visit those schools," Emily said, walking toward the table. "You should look at all three options carefully . . . and then you should make the best decision for you."

"Agreed!" Coach Wilson added. "They're all going to give you something different . . . you have to figure out what's important to you."

"Well, Dad said that I'm his kid, and he's making the decision," Trip said dejectedly. "Of course, when he said that, Aunt Barb piped up and said, while I'm living in her house, she has a say, too! That shut Dad up."

They all smiled.

"Well, with that, I'll get out of your way," Coach Wilson announced as he stood to leave.

"Uh, Coach . . . uh, would you like to stay for "Movie Night" with us?" Emily suddenly said, surprising everyone at the table.

"Dinner is almost ready, and then we'll watch a movie," Emily said warmly.

"Oh, uh, gee," Coach Wilson stammered. "Sure, I guess. That would be nice."

Allison and Rob exchanged a look. *What the heck is going on? Coach and Mom?*

"Have you picked a movie yet, Emily?" Allison asked brightly.

For hours, Emily had been working on what to choose, and nothing seemed right. Suddenly she had an idea.

"*The Music Man*," Emily declared with a big smile.

Allison grinned, Rob and Trip looked worried, and Coach Wilson laughed.

"You want the boys to see what a "two-bit cymbal salesman" really looks like, Emily?" Coach Wilson asked with laughter, recalling the day he talked Emily into letting Trip live with them.

"You said it was one of your favorites," Emily said, smiling at Coach Wilson. "So, in honor of your being here, it seemed the perfect choice!"

CHAPTER 38
DECEMBER-SOPHOMORE YEAR

ROB and Trip groaned in despair as *The Music Man* trotted out three songs before the first actual conversation. *My worst nightmare comes true,* Rob groaned inwardly. *Think Stephanie Miller on steroids!*

But with help from Allison, Emily, and Coach Wilson, they started to enjoy the story of a "two-bit cymbal salesman" who finds himself falling in love with a small-town girl and unable to leave.

Rob and his friends laughed, thinking of Coach Wilson as the salesman . . . but Rob wondered . . . *does that make Mom the librarian?*

As the movie wound down, Rob found he had enjoyed most of the film . . . *but it is not in my top 100 . . . or top 1000!*

Rob also enjoyed watching his Mom and Coach Wilson watch the movie. *I think they really like each other,* he thought. *Maybe Mom is ready to date. But Coach?*

He glanced at Allison, who gave him her best smile, glanced at Emily, and then back to Rob with her eyebrows raised in surprise . . . and delight. *She sees it, too,* Rob thought. *I really need to talk to Allison about this . . .*

"Well, this has been wonderful," Coach Wilson said a while later as the movie ended and he rose from his chair. "But I need to get out of your hair. Thanks for a great evening!"

"Let me walk you to the door," Emily said, rising quickly and leading him to the front door.

Coach Wilson reached for the doorknob but turned as he felt Emily's hand on his shoulder.

"Dave?" she said softly.

"Yes, Emily?" Dave replied.

"First," Emily began slowly. "I wanted to thank you for what you are trying to do for Trip. You still have his best interests at heart . . . and you're not just steering him to stay at Hillsdale . . . even though we both know that's what's best for him."

They both smiled warmly, and Coach Wilson nodded.

"I . . . uh . . . also wanted to talk to you about Rick," Emily sputtered. "I know what you said to him Friday night . . ."

Coach Wilson looked down momentarily, collecting himself, then looked up and met Emily's eyes with a slight smile.

"Yeah, not my best moment . . ." Coach Wilson began.

"Yeah," Emily laughed. "I have to tell you my first reaction was how dare you meddle in my life . . . but I immediately knew you were doing it for the right reasons . . . hey, you know what Rick is like better than anyone, right?"

Coach Wilson nodded.

"I think the reason Rick is so angry is that I told him I wanted nothing to do with him ever . . . never have," Emily said, a slight tear welling up.

Emily paused and wiped away the stray tear.

"What you did was very sweet," Emily continued as Coach Wilson let her talk. "We never made it to lunch Saturday because we had it out before we got 100 yards down the street."

Coach Wilson nodded slightly and remained quiet.

"I appreciate you . . . you stepping up like that . . . talking to Rick like that . . ." Emily said. "It means a lot to me . . . that you . . . you think enough of me, to . . . to help like that."

They gazed at each other for a long moment.

"I really enjoyed tonight," Emily began again.

Coach Wilson smiled, tilted his head at her, and began to speak, but Emily held up her hand.

"But Dave, I'm not ready to date yet . . . not anybody . . . certainly not Rick . . . but not even you . . ." Emily said softly, with tears now flowing down her cheeks.

"I understand," Coach Wilson said softly. "No pressure here."

She smiled at him through her tears, and he grasped the doorknob, pulled the door open, and got halfway through when Emily reached out and tugged at his shoulder.

"Dave?" Emily began softly. "When I am ready . . . can I let you know . . . and maybe . . . will you ask me out then?"

"When you're ready, just call," Coach Wilson said, a smile breaking his face.

"You'll be the first one I call," Emily replied, drawing close and giving him a quick kiss on the cheek, before stepping back.

"Thank you, Dave Wilson . . . you're a good man," Emily said, her tears starting to flow again.

"Thanks, Emily," was all Coach Wilson could answer as he slowly shut the door, smiling all the while.

***

"So, you saw it, too?" Rob asked Allison as he stood on her front porch.

Trip and Rob had walked Allison home, and then Trip headed around the corner to his new house, leaving the pair alone.

"Oh, yeah," Allison replied. "There was definite flirting going on tonight!"

"Yeah, I thought so," Rob answered.

"How do you feel about it?" Allison asked.

"I'm not sure," Rob answered truthfully. "She said she wasn't ready . . . but I guess she will be sometime soon."

"It's been a long time," Allison agreed. "She should be close."

Rob paused a long time, mulling it over.

"I guess it could be a lot worse . . . than Coach Wilson, you know," Rob finally said. "It could be Rick McHenry!"

"Yeah, I don't think so," Allison laughed, wrinkling her nose. "Your Mom's not too fond of him."

They both laughed.

"You know that movie tonight," Rob ventured after a moment. "It reminded me of Coach and Mom . . . you know . . . small town . . . the newcomer falling in love . . ."

"Rob Mathews, my, how you have progressed," Allison shouted gleefully.

Rob blushed and waved his hand at her.

"Aw, cut it out," Rob protested.

After another pause, Rob spoke of the movie again.

"You know . . . I think Mom did it on purpose," Rob said slowly, thinking things through. "Not just her and Coach . . . but I think she wanted Trip to see it . . . you know . . . the flashy guy comes to town . . . falls in love with the townspeople . . . the kids and stuff . . . you know . . . I think she was trying to tell Trip that Hillsdale High is the place he needs to be."

Allison looked at Rob and gave him her best smile. It warmed him up to see her smile, and he returned it.

"I think you're right, Rob," Allison said quietly.

I think she sent that message to Trip, Allison thought. *But I hope she was sending you that message, too . . . I want to be your librarian.*

"Do you think Trip got the message?" Rob asked.

"I don't know," Allison pondered. "He surprises me sometimes about stuff like that . . . you know . . . he's pretty perceptive about people . . . and about himself."

Rob nodded, knowing Allison was right.

"Well, I hope it works," said Rob.

"Me, too," Allison replied, thinking again about the librarian in the movie. "Me, too."

CHAPTER 39
JANUARY-SOPHOMORE YEAR

WITH the holidays over, the students of Hillsdale High, somewhat reluctantly, started back to school after a long winter vacation.

The Winter Break had seen the formation of a tight-knit group of guys at the Mathews house. Even though Trip lived around the corner with his Aunt Barb, he was at Rob's home constantly. Buck Buckman was fast becoming close friends with Trip, as was Donnie Fields, and the quartet spent hours watching games, and movies, playing video games, and generally horsing around.

Allison Pierce was allowed in for some of those sessions, but in general, she preferred Emily's company . . . but very much liked being "around" the guys.

Sunday night continued to be "Movie Night" . . . Linda Pierce resumed her spot, while Coach Wilson was not invited again. *Maybe it was just Mom being nice to Coach,* Rob pondered. *Maybe she isn't ready to date yet.*

Occasionally, Trip would opt out of the tight group to spend a little time with Jenny.

"We need to double-date sometime," Trip would say to Rob every once in a while. "I think Lacy likes you." But neither boy ever did anything to follow through on a date. The general feeling was, *let's enjoy Winter Break.*

Of course, the basketball team had not had a complete vacation. Coach Bridges kept them busy with long, tiring practices designed to keep them sharp, in shape, and ready to attack the 16-game League schedule that began on Wednesday at Oakville. The Pirates would host Colton on Friday night.

Trip and Rob spent time after practice working on playing together. They ran phantom plays, whipping passes back and forth, learning each other's patterns and tendencies, and trying to perfect their timing. They often coerced Sam Jordan, Edgar Garcia, Josh Lee, or Gabe Cantor to stay late with them while they worked on their pick-and-roll together. Sometimes one or two would stay, and sometimes, all four.

The benefits were obvious . . . the offense was becoming a finely tuned machine, with each player learning the nuances of playing together. Rob and Trip had meshed so well that they felt confident and ready when they traveled to Oakville on Wednesday.

Oakville, never knew what hit them. The first quarter onslaught was triggered by Rob and Trip, who were unstoppable. When the first quarter ended, the score was Mathews/McHenry 31 and Oakville 9 . . . the scoreboard had Hillsdale up 35-9.

Rob and Trip had parlayed their extra hours of practice on the pick-and-roll into 24 points in the quarter. Rob had totaled 14 points and seven assists, while Trip added 17 points, three assists, and ten rebounds.

The second quarter saw the pair watching from the bench as the reserves held their own and even added slightly to the lead as Hillsdale went into the half with a 51-23 lead.

The third quarter was a replay of the first quarter for about four minutes . . . until Coach Bridges pulled the starters as a group and got the bench a good amount of playing time.

The only question left as the 4th quarter started was whether or not the Pirates could reach 100 . . . but with Rob and Trip planted on the bench, the offense slowed down . . . although, behind Josh Lee and Gabe Cantor, it was still effective.

Bob Johnson lit the gym up with an array of three-pointers, Sam Jordan was solid, and Edgar Garcia thundered home a pair of dunks. Final score . . . 91-51.

CHAPTER 40
JANUARY-SOPHOMORE YEAR

*O*N Friday night, it was Hillsdale's first home game of the League season, and the crowd was overflowing as the JV game ended, and the Varsity exploded out of the locker room and onto the floor for warmups.

There was a definite buzz in the air as the crowd was anxious to see their hometown heroes blow the Colton Cowboys off the floor. By halftime, the game was no longer in doubt.

The Pirates jumped the Cowboys like they had Oakville two nights ago, leading 54-21 at the half. Rob and Trip again combined to dominate Colton, with plenty of help from the entire roster.

In the stands, the talk at halftime had turned away from the game and veered toward the sock hop immediately following the game . . . and the Sadie Hawkins Dance, just two weeks away.

"So, are you inviting anyone to Sadie Hawkins?" Emily asked Allison Pierce during the halftime break.

"Ugh," Allison replied. "I'm not sure yet."

Emily looked at her and smiled, knowing she longed to ask Rob . . . but was afraid he'd say no or laugh at her.

"I was thinking about asking Zack . . . you know, the guy I met this summer in San Francisco . . . but I'm not sure he's going to want to travel all the way up here for that,"

Allison began, searching Emily's eyes hopefully. "Do you think if I asked Rob . . . he would go with me?"

Emily smiled a somewhat sorrowful smile, and Allison's enthusiasm dampened.

"Well, I guess there's always Evan," Allison sighed ruefully.

"He'll come around one of these days," Emily smiled brightly. "You still don't want him yet . . . way too immature!"

They both laughed at the thought.

"Besides, after Carly, I think he may want a break from girls," Emily said with a snort.

"Yeah, she was something," Allison replied with a dreamy look. "I thought after that he might start thinking about me a little . . . you know . . . he said maybe he should just date friends . . ."

"Give him time," Emily counseled. "He might not be ready until he's out of college . . . so try to be patient."

"Trip asked him the other day if he had anyone special . . . that he wanted to ask him to Sadie Hawkins," Allison said, looking dour.

"What did he say?" Emily asked.

"He didn't care if anyone asked him . . . unless it was some hot girl," Allison groaned.

"And, look at this," Allison continued, waving her hand from the top of her head to the tips of her toes. "I don't qualify for hot!"

"You will, sweetie," Emily soothed. "Just be patient."

"Yeah, well, I'm running out of patience!" Allison exclaimed, breaking into bittersweet laughter, as Emily reached over to give her a short hug.

***

***T**HE* horn sounded to bring the teams together to begin the second half. The starters retook the floor and erupted against Colton again, going on a 16-2 run in the first four minutes of the 2nd half to put the game on ice. It was a great time for Coach Bridges to tinker with combinations and to get his reserves valuable floor time.

His starting five had become Rob and Josh Lee at the guards, Sam Jordan and Trip at the wings, and Edgar Garcia down low. Brad Wallace was the number one sub for Josh or Rob, with one of those two always on the floor. Gabe Cantor was progressing and subbed in for the other three starters. Bob Johnson was getting a lot of time as a game changer . . . someone who could stretch the court and drain three-pointers, opening up the middle for the big guys.

Dom Fiorenza and Alex Cohen saw decent minutes as backups, but juniors Greg Montgomery and Daniel Valdez were reduced to mop-up minutes. Those four and Josh Lee were on the floor when Hillsdale put the final touches on a 93-56 win over Colton.

***

"**G***O* on, just ask him," Jenny said, pushing Lacy toward Rob as she grinned at Trip.

The Sock Hop in the gym was packed with happy high schoolers . . . as happy as high schoolers could get anyway. A big crowd of kids was off to the side, mainly watching the older kids dancing in the middle of the gym floor.

"Yeah, go on," Trip added. "He'll say yes . . . guaranteed!"

Lacy inched her way over to Rob, waiting for him to distance himself a little from Buck Buckman, Donnie Fields and Christina Craft, and Allison Pierce.

"Uh, hi, Rob," Lacy said, smiling at Rob and motioning him closer.

"Oh, uh, hi . . . hi, Lacy," Rob sputtered. *Oh, geez,* Rob thought. *Mr. Smooth is back. Come on, idiot. Wake up!*

"Hey, uh, Rob," Lacy said, hesitating. "I . . . I . . . uh, wondered if you would like to . . . uh . . . go to . . . uh, Sadie Hawkins with me?"

Rob flushed with embarrassment and felt his heart start racing. He glanced over and saw Allison looking at him, trying to look like she wasn't listening.

"Uh, gee, uh . . . Lacy, I uh . . ." Rob sputtered.

"Jenny and Trip said we could double with them," Lacy said quickly. "They said we could go out for dinner . . . you know and . . . and then the dance."

Lacy looked at him, imploring him to say yes with her eyes. *Oh, please don't say no*, Lacy thought. *This will be so embarrassing if you say no!*

"Yeah, uh, ok, Lacy," Rob gulped weakly. "Sounds good."

Lacy flushed with relief and smiled gaily at Rob. She turned, flashed a big grin at Jenny and Trip, and turned back to Rob.

"So, you wanna' dance," Lacy said, hearing a slow dance start.

"Uh, sure," Rob said reluctantly, letting himself be led onto the dance floor.

Once Lacy was in his arms on the dance floor, Rob relaxed and remembered the one thing he liked about dances . . . the slow songs.

Allison Pierce listened to the exchange, and her heart sank. Her head dropped, and she fought back tears. *I really need to listen to Emily*, she thought, berating herself. *Look at Lacy . . . I can't compete with her . . . she's hot! Rob will never go out with anyone that looks like I do!*

She watched the pair on the dance floor . . . with Lacy laying her head on Rob's shoulder.

Allison watched the scene for half of the song . . . then scanned the room . . . spotted Evan . . . and went over to ask him to go to Sadie Hawkins with her again.

CHAPTER 41
JANUARY-SOPHOMORE YEAR

*T*HE next week saw games on Tuesday and Thursday nights against Barker City and Cooley, and the Hillsdale Pirates continued to dominate league play.

The script was similar to last week's games, although Barker City put up a little more resistance. They were down just 12 at the half before a 3rd quarter run pushed the lead to 24 to begin the 4th quarter. The final score was 84-67.

Against Cooley, Hillsdale was lights out. Everything they did worked . . . not only worked . . . but worked perfectly. Every combination meshed together to play almost flawless basketball. You could see the confidence building with every practice and every game.

On this night, the Pirates jolted Cooley and astounded the big crowd with a 61-point first half. Even with Coach Bridges calling off the dogs and not pushing the pace or pressing, Hillsdale could not seem to miss, and as time grew short, the only drama was whether or not they could crack the 100-mark.

Dom Fiorenza turned the trick with a long three-pointer with 30 seconds to play, and the Pirates coasted to a convincing 102-47 win over the hapless Cougars.

"AWESOME GAME!!!" Coach Bridges shouted as his team gathered in the locker room after the game. "You guys were just awesome," he said proudly, smiling as he waved for quiet.

"Calm down," Coach Bridges said loudly, trying to set a more serious tone.

"Now, the easy part of the first half of league is behind us," Coach Bridges intoned deeply. "The second half won't be quite so easy."

He had their attention now.

"Foothill and Taylor will push you guys," Coach Bridges continued. "And, it's a good thing . . . because then we have Milltown and Pine Bluff . . . and we know they will push you hardest of all this year . . . except for Valley Christian, of course."

"Tomorrow we're off," Coach Bridges added. "It's a long weekend with a holiday Monday for school . . . but we will practice on Monday. We've got Foothill Wednesday, and I want two quality practices before we play them."

The team mumbled their assent.

"Enjoy your weekend!" Coach Bridges announced, and the team dispersed hurriedly.

"Hey, Trip," Coach Bridges called out, beckoning Trip to him. "I hope you have a good visit down at Canyon this weekend."

"Thanks, Coach," Trip replied.

"When are you leaving?" Coach Bridges asked gruffly.

"Flying down tonight with Aunt Barb," Trip replied.

"You'll be home in time for practice on Monday?" Coach Bridges asked.

"Yes, sir! Five minutes early . . . so I'm not late!" Trip grinned in reply.

"You know I'll give you a good . . . a great report," Coach Bridges coughed out. "You have earned it . . . and whatever I can do to help you reach your goal . . . well . . ."

Trip looked closely at Coach Bridges and saw he was filled with emotion.

"You're on the way to reaching your potential, Trip . . . you've really worked hard to change . . . to grow," Coach Bridges choked out. "I will do anything you need me to do to get into Canyon . . . or Valley Christian . . . if that's what you decide is best for you."

Now it was Trip's turn to choke up.

"Thanks, Coach," Trip managed, his lip trembling.

"You've done everything I've asked," Coach Bridges answered. "You keep doing that . . . and you can write your own ticket anywhere you want to be."

"I will, Coach . . . no matter what happens . . . I promise that this year . . . well, I'm all yours," Trip croaked out.

Coach Bridges nodded with a tight-lipped smile and turned and stalked into his office, closing the door behind him.

***

"**H**EY, Rob, it's Trip," Trip said as Rob answered the phone on Saturday afternoon.

"Hey, Trip . . . how did it go yesterday at Canyon?" Rob asked.

"It was awesome, man," Trip bubbled. "The campus is so cool . . . pretty close to the beach . . . but close to town, too. The dorm rooms are awesome . . . the gym is unreal . . . the weight room . . . the cafeteria . . . I can't stop smiling . . . it's so cool!!!"

"That's great, Trip," Rob lied, dying inside to hear his friend so enthused about Canyon. *I don't want to lose you to Canyon,* Rob thought.

"Went to their game last night, and it was unreal," Trip continued. "A huge crowd . . . way into the team . . . the team is great . . . big, strong, fast . . . they know what they're doing, Rob. I know I can hang with them. I like the coaches . . . and they seem to like me. The head coach told me he got rave reviews about me from Coach Bridges."

"How about the school?" Rob asked.

"Fantastic!" Trip answered quickly. "Lots of hot girls . . . kids all seem cool . . . got the city vibe I'm used to . . . you know . . . I really fit in."

"Great," Rob said, trying to sound enthusiastic and failing miserably . . . but Trip didn't notice.

"They offered me a full ride after the meeting yesterday," Trip blurted out, unable to contain himself any longer. "I can't believe it . . . all expenses paid . . . to Canyon!"

"That's awesome, man," Rob lied again, reeling.

"Aunt Barb and I are going to talk things over today with my Dad . . . conference call," Trip said. "Talk about the good and the bad, you know."

"What's the bad?" Rob asked hopefully.

"Oh, you know . . . having no family around . . . living in a dorm . . . big city life. Like any of those things are bad, right?!" Trip laughed.

Rob's heart sank.

"Hey, I gotta' run soon," Trip said. "Got that conference call in a few . . . and then some of the guys from the team, the sophomores, are picking me up to hang out for the night . . . they want me to see what a Saturday night looks like at Canyon!"

"Oh, you gotta' dance or something?" Rob asked.

"No, but they said it is a typical night . . . said it would be fun! Hey, here's Aunt Barb . . . gotta' go . . . see you tomorrow, Rob, and I'll tell you all about it," Trip jabbered excitedly.

"All right . . . have fun, Trip," Rob said glumly, turning to look at his Mom . . . who was frowning after hearing both sides of the conversation on the speakerphone.

CHAPTER 42

JANUARY-SOPHOMORE YEAR

"*ROB?*" The voice was a taut, hoarse whisper

"Hello . . . Trip . . . is that you?" Rob asked, his voice alarmed. *Something is wrong,* he thought.

Rob looked at the clock and saw it was 10:30 pm. He glanced over at his Mom, sitting up straight and staring at him. *Something is wrong,* Emily thought immediately.

"Put it on speaker," Emily said, walking swiftly toward Rob.

"Yeah, it's me," Trip rasped. "I'm in trouble, Rob . . . I gotta' get out of here."

Emily and Rob were frozen in their tracks momentarily.

"What's wrong, Trip," Emily said firmly. "Let us help."

"These Canyon guys are nuts," Trip said urgently. "They brought me to a party in the hills . . . it's crazy here . . . all sorts of stuff going on . . . stuff I don't want to be around."

"Like what?" Rob asked, feeling helpless.

"No need for that now," Emily said firmly. "Why don't you call your Aunt Barb?"

"I don't have my phone," Trip whispered. "I'm holed up in some bedroom on a landline . . . I only remembered your number . . . Aunt Barb's is on my speed dial on my phone."

"Why don't you have your phone?" Emily asked.

"The Canyon guys said I had to leave it at my hotel," Trip croaked. "I really want to get out of here before anyone finds me . . . or this place gets busted."

"I'm calling Barb now on my cell," Emily said, taking control. "Hang on . . . where are you . . . do you have an address?"

"No," Trip almost sobbed out.

"Barb? It's Emily," Emily barked into her cell. "Trip's in trouble and needs you to go get him before it goes too far . . . he's somewhere out in a neighborhood in the hills . . . I'll get you an address as soon as I can."

"Oh, no," Barb answered. "I'm heading to my car . . . let me know when you have an address . . . is he OK?"

"I think so . . . for now," Emily replied. "I think he's trying to get out before anything bad happens . . . before they make him do something wrong."

"Got it! Call me with an address!!!" Aunt Barb shouted.

Emily turned to see Rob hanging up the phone.

"What are you doing?" Emily said sharply. "How are we going to reach him?"

"I've got the house's phone number," Rob explained quickly. "Trip saw a window he could climb out of . . . I told him to go down the street to see if anyone will let him in and let him use their phone . . . he just had to get out of there."

The pair stood and looked at each other in concern, hoping the phone would ring soon.

One minute passed . . . two . . . three . . . five . . .

The phone's shrill ring jarred Rob and Emily as it finally sang out. Rob pounced on the phone, hit the speaker, and spat out, "Trip, Trip, you OK?"

"Yeah," Trip said breathlessly. "It took me three tries, but I got a guy to open the door."

"What's the address?" Emily shouted, and she wrote it down and then dialed Barb.

"Aunt Barb's on her way," Emily said to Trip, still on the line. "She says she'll be there in 20 minutes, Trip . . . hang on. You OK?"

"Yeah, it was nuts," Trip repeated. "I had to get out of there before they made me do anything . . . they said it was my initiation into Canyon . . . oh, geez, it was nuts. I had to get outta' there . . . all I could see was the cops showing up, and there went my season with you guys . . . I couldn't . . . I couldn't let you guys down . . . couldn't let Coach Bridges down . . ."

Rob and Emily could hear small sobs coming from Trip and the reassuring voice of an older man at the house in L.A.

"You're OK, son," the voice said. "Once you get off the phone, I'll call the cops and get them over there . . ."

"No," Trip sobbed out. "I can't get them in trouble . . . those guys will blame me . . . and I'll get dropped from my team in Hillsdale . . ."

"OK, OK, don't worry about it . . . I won't call them," the voice said quietly.

"Thank you, sir . . . for your help," Emily said to the voice.

"We've had problems with that house before . . ." the voice said, trailing off.

"We so appreciate your help," Emily said sincerely. "Trip, hang in there!"

"Yeah," Trip grunted, pulling himself together.

"We'll stay on the line with you if you want," Emily added.

"No, I'm OK . . . I'll call you once we get back to our motel," Trip said haltingly.

CHAPTER 43

JANUARY-SOPHOMORE YEAR

"TRIP... you made it home," Rob said, opening the door to let Trip in late Sunday afternoon. "Aunt Barb is OK with you coming over?"

"Hey, it's "Movie Night," man," Trip replied casually. "Like I'm going to miss that?"

Rob smiled, ushered Trip in, and closed the door just as Emily entered the room.

"Trip, I'm so glad you're home," Emily offered. "We were so worried about you all weekend!"

"I'm glad to be home, too," Trip replied with relief. "I was so happy to get away from those Canyon guys... we tried to get a flight last night... but it was too late. We had to wait until morning."

"How did your Dad take the news about your night?" Rob asked.

"He was really mad," Trip said.

"Was he going to call the school to complain?" Rob responded.

"Call the school?" Trip replied in confusion. "He was mad at Aunt Barb and me for not wanting to go there... he was so mad we had blown the deal... said that was normal for private schools in L.A."

"I hardly think so," Emily said. "I don't think that's the norm... you just got unlucky and got in with the wrong crowd."

"Is he still trying to talk you into going there?" Rob asked incredulously. "How can he want you to go someplace like that?"

"No, not anymore," Trip answered. "We . . . Aunt Barb mainly . . . talked him out of it."

Rob and Emily both nodded with relief.

"I mean . . . uh," Trip sputtered. "I don't belong there . . . I don't get that anymore . . . I just don't want to be near anything like that now!"

Trip welled up a bit, trying to push back the emotion.

"You guys . . ." Trip said, waving at Rob and Emily, "and Coach Wilson and Coach Bridges . . . Buck and Donnie . . . Allison . . . the team . . . you guys have changed me . . . for the better. I don't belong down in L.A. right now . . . I belong in Hillsdale."

It was Emily's turn to well up, and she moved forward and gave Trip a big hug. Trip held on tight . . . not wanting to let go.

Rob grinned as he watched them hug and gave Trip a high five as they broke apart.

"Hey, one thing," Trip resumed. "I was wondering if we could kinda' keep the party thing quiet . . . I feel funny about it . . . I'll tell folks I just wanted to live in Hillsdale with Aunt Barb."

"Sure . . . we get it," said Emily, nodding at Rob to include him.

"I stopped over to see Coach Wilson when we got in . . . and I saw Coach Bridges just before I came here," Trip added. "Wanted them to know the whole story . . . just in case something got back to them from the Canyon coach. They were both pretty mad . . . wanted to call Canyon and yell at them . . . but I think I talked them out of that."

"So, they're good with everything?" Rob asked. "There aren't any issues on this end, are there?"

"No . . . they're both good," Trip replied. "Except I reminded them I was still looking at Valley Christian in February."

Rob's heart dropped. *Oh yeah, I forgot about Valley Christian,* Rob thought.

"Oh," Rob replied glumly.

"Well, at least that means you'll be in Hillsdale . . . right around the corner," Emily said brightly, trying to change Rob's mood. "A whole lot better than being down in Southern California!"

"You're right, Mom," Rob said. "As long as you're in the neighborhood, I'm good!!!"

"One more thing," Trip said. "Thanks, you guys . . . thanks for helping . . . thanks for caring . . . for being there for me when I really needed you . . . I . . . I love you guys."

They all froze momentarily. Then, Rob high-fived Trip, and Emily gave him a big hug.

"We love you, too," Emily choked out.

After a long moment, Trip broke the hug, shook himself, and resumed his street-wise persona.

"So, when are we heading over to Allison's . . . I'm starved?" Trip crowed.

The trio laughed, then headed out the door for the short walk to Allison's for "Movie Night."

As they walked up Allison's front porch steps, all Rob could think of was, *one down, one to go . . . Canyon is out . . . Valley Christian has got to go next!*

CHAPTER 44
JANUARY-SOPHOMORE YEAR

"So, what's wrong with asking Allison and Evan to join you guys for dinner before the dance on Saturday?" Emily asked Rob on Tuesday night at the dinner table. "You guys are all friends..."

"Aw, Mom," Rob protested, "Allison and Evan are so..."

Rob stopped as Emily glared at him.

"You can't go there," Emily said emphatically. "Not where dating is involved... in fact, some people would say you are as geeky as they come in that department... or, maybe, more so..."

Rob scowled, knowing his Mom was kidding... but that she was serious... and right at the same time.

"Oh, OK, Mom, I'll ask Trip about it," Rob gave in. "If he's good with it... we'll ask them to come along."

Trip was all in... since he and Emily had concocted the scheme. The date was set... Jenny and Trip, Rob and Lacy... and Allison and Evan were all going to dinner together before the Sadie Hawkins Dance... one big, happy family!

***

B*UT* before that could happen, the Hillsdale Pirates had two challenging games to contend with on their schedule, and Wednesday night's game against Foothill proved to be a good test.

The game started like the previous four league games, with Hillsdale bolting out of the gates and taking a quick 21-11 lead at the end of the first quarter. The Spartans had no answer for Trip McHenry, as the big man scorched them for 13 points in the quarter while corralling six boards and dishing out a pair of assists.

The test came when Coach Bridges rested Rob and Trip to start the 2nd quarter. Foothill found they could match up much better with Josh Lee running the offense and Gabe Cantor trying to replace Trip McHenry.

The offense stalled as Gabe Cantor was stone cold, and the defense and rebounding both suffered. Midway through the quarter, the lead had been trimmed to 27-23. Gabe Cantor was clearly off his game, but to his credit, he kept battling.

Also, to Trip's credit, he pulled Gabe aside during the time-out with four minutes left in the half.

"Gabe," Trip whispered to the big freshman. "Just relax out there . . . you'll warm up . . . until you do, just keep playing defense and pounding the boards."

Coach Bridges saw the exchange, smiled tightly, and decided to stick with Gabe for the time being. *This will be a good experience for him,* the crusty old coach thought. *It will be helpful for next week's games.*

The pep talk worked, and although Gabe only scored a basket and a free throw, his defense and rebounding improved, and he tossed out a couple of great passes for assists. Hillsdale pushed the lead back to seven points, leading Foothill 38-31 at the half.

The crowd was enjoying this game almost more than the previous four blowouts, as there was actually some drama.

"I hope they don't let these guys hang around too long," Grandpa Russell spouted during halftime to all those around him. "Allison . . . what do you think?" he asked. "You ready for them to make a run?"

"You bet, Grandpa Russell," Allison beamed, enjoying being asked her opinion on sports. *What is wrong with me?* Allison pondered merrily. *Am I really getting to be a "spooorts" fan?*

"Are you looking forward to Sadie Hawkins on Saturday?" Emily asked Allison. "I heard you and Evan are triple-dating."

"Yes," Allison said, wondering what Emily had to do with that arrangement. "It should be a lot of fun."

What could be better than a triple-date? A date with Rob all alone, Allison thought wistfully. *Oh well . . . this is the next best thing . . . at least I'll be with him . . . but I hope I don't have to watch him all gooey-eyed with Lacy!*

"It was nice of Trip to suggest it," Emily added.

Trip? Hmmm, that explains it . . . maybe Trip is a better friend than I thought, Allison mused as she nodded a yes at Emily.

Allison looked down and smiled at Trip, standing in the team huddle as they readied themselves for the 3rd quarter. *Maybe a very good friend!*

***

THE 3rd quarter began, and Hillsdale's vaunted offensive attack seemed stymied. Foothill was playing an aggressive, all-out defense on Rob and Trip and daring the other three players to carry the load.

Time and time again, the Pirates worked guys open, but neither Josh, Sam, nor Edgar could connect on their shots. Foothill's confidence grew with each passing minute, and they slowly closed the gap.

Halfway through the quarter, they tied the game at 42, and the lead changed hands several times before the quarter ended, with Hillsdale clinging to a 54-52 lead. Hillsdale's offense had kept pace thanks to Bob Johnson, who had come in to nail a basket and two three-pointers.

In the 4th quarter, Coach Bridges decided to go fast . . . and he inserted Gabe Cantor for Edgar Garcia to give the offense more mobility.

The move worked to perfection, as Foothill could no longer lay off Edgar to double team Rob or Trip, and the change started opening up the floor for the whole team.

That meant the shots that weren't falling early on . . . started to fall when the shooters became Rob Mathews and Trip McHenry.

The pair put on a clinic in the 4th quarter, igniting a 21-8 run that turned a two-point lead into a 75-60 lead in five minutes. The Hillsdale crowd was on their feet screaming as the run ended with a pair of long-range threes by Rob and a thunderous two-handed slam by Trip that brought the house down . . . and had the Foothill coach screaming for a time out . . . wondering what had just run over his team!

The whole team got into the act in the final three minutes, as Coach Bridges emptied the bench, and Hillsdale cruised home to an 84-71 final score.

***

***T**AYLOR's* Tornados proved a tough test for only about two minutes. Tied at four, two minutes in, Hillsdale found their groove and ran off 16 unanswered points on four threes from Rob and two crowd-pleasing, put-back dunks by Trip McHenry.

Taylor was shell-shocked and could never get into any rhythm on offense or defense. A game that was supposed to be close became a total blowout by halftime, with Hillsdale up by a 53-22 score.

The crowd kept roaring, though, as the "M&M Boys," as the *Hillsdale Express* had dubbed the pair of Rob Mathews and Trip McHenry, kept up their incredible offense until they were pulled after three quarters with Hillsdale holding an insurmountable 81-40 lead.

Rob ended his night with a game-high 31 points and added eight rebounds, six assists, four steals, and two blocks. On the other hand, Trip had a game-high 18 rebounds, 26 points, five assists, three blocks, and a steal. Neither one had a turnover!!!

The only question was whether the rest of the Pirates would carry on with the hot shooting and break the 100-point barrier.

Bob Johnson nailed a pair of threes, Josh Lee drove the lane, scored twice, and dished off three assists to Gabe Cantor. Sam Jordan had a breakaway dunk, Brad Wallace scored ten points in the 4th quarter . . . and Hillsdale stormed to a resounding 107-54 victory!

"BEAT PINE BLUFF!!!" "BEAT PINE BLUFF!!!" was the chant from the Hillsdale faithful as the clock wound down. Next week came the real tests . . . Milltown and Pine Bluff.

CHAPTER 45

JANUARY-SOPHOMORE YEAR

ROB padded into his kitchen Saturday morning and was greeted by the broad grin of Grandpa Russell.

"Hey, guys," Rob mumbled to his Grandparents and his Mom.

He shuffled to the table and rubbed his eyes, suddenly aware that the whole family was grinning at him.

"Hey, uh, what's up?" Rob asked in wonderment.

Grandpa Russell held up the *Hillsdale Express* Sports Section and pointed to a smaller headline below and to the left of the banner shouting out Hillsdale's convincing win over Taylor.

Rob did a double-take and then moved forward and squinted at the smaller headline.

MILLTOWN UPSETS PINE BLUFF

Rob's face broke into a massive grin as he pumped his fist in delight.

"All right," he said aloud. "Love to see that!"

"You said it!" Grandpa Russell spouted. "Always a good day when Pine Bluff goes down."

Grandma Russell and Emily glanced at each other and smiled ruefully. They knew how wins and losses against Pine Bluff affected their "boys."

"I never thought they'd lose this year . . . except to us, of course," Rob quipped.

They all laughed.

"The "Old Grump" have anything of interest this morning, Grandpa?" Rob asked.

"Yes . . . a short one today," Grandpa Russell said. "Want to hear it?"

Rob nodded, and he thanked his Mom as she dropped a plateful of breakfast in front of him.

"The "M&M Boys" were at the top of their game last night in the unexpected blowout of Taylor. They are a delight to watch, and they . . . and the whole team seems to be getting better each week," Grandpa Russell read with satisfaction. "The only thing I have worried about all year is whether there will be enough competition for the Pirates in League play . . . and so far . . . there has been none to speak of . . ."

Grandpa Russell paused and looked at Rob, who nodded in assent.

"That's going to change," Rob said.

"Precisely," Grandpa Russell answered. "Listen to this."

"That will change next week," Grandpa Russell continued reading the column. "First, Milltown, who upset Pine Bluff last night in a defensive battle . . . and then Pine Bluff. They will give Hillsdale plenty of competition . . . especially Pine Bluff. You can forget that loss to Milltown . . . the Warriors will be out for blood! I'm fully on the Hillsdale bandwagon though . . . prediction . . . the Pirates beat them both!"

"Not bad," Rob said. "I'm starting to like this "Old Grump" guy!"

CHAPTER 46
JANUARY-SOPHOMORE YEAR

*L**ATE* Saturday afternoon, Trip showed up ready to roll to Sadie Hawkins. Since none of the kids could drive . . . and the weather was not horrible . . . clear and cold . . . the plan was for the six kids to meet at Rob's, and then they would walk downtown for dinner . . . walk to the school for the dance . . . and walk home afterward.

With that came the inevitable mob of six families in Rob's living room trying to get photos of the couples as they prepared to leave. After many forced smiles and wishes for a good time, the three couples disentangled from their families and escaped safely into Rob's front yard.

Being the only real "couple," Trip and Jenny separated from the other four, talking and whispering to each other five paces in front of the rest as they ambled toward downtown.

The two girls, Allison and Lacy, were in-between the other two guys, and an uneasy silence descended upon the group. *Ugh, this is awkward,* Rob thought as he walked next to Lacy. *Think of something . . . what do I say?*

Allison saved the day and started chattering about the restaurant they were headed to, and soon, all but Rob were rattling on about food, other restaurants, and the dance. Several times, Allison directed questions specifically to Rob, and he answered quickly . . . but to the point and without elaboration.

This is the way to go, Rob realized. *If I talk to Allison, maybe that will get me going with Lacy. Yeah . . . good plan.*

And that is how the night progressed, with Rob basically talking with Allison and Trip during dinner . . . masking the fact that he and Lacy were not connecting.

Rob glanced at Lacy occasionally, saw her smiling face, and figured she was enjoying herself. *Yeah, this is not bad,* Rob thought. *Spending the night with Trip and Allison talking . . . and having Lacy to slow dance with at the dance. I wonder if I should give her a goodnight kiss . . . no, yes . . . ah, too early to tell.*

After dinner, the group strolled to the school, and the couples kept a little more distance. Rob's safety net was gone and he gazed over at Lacy several times. *She is hot,* Rob thought. *Why can't I think of anything to say?*

Finally, after a virtually silent ten minutes, they arrived at the dance and joined the already bustling crowd inside the gym.

Rob and Lacy milled around in a large group of friends on the fringe of the dance floor, venturing out for a handful of slow dances. Rob gladly said yes when Lacy asked if she could fast dance with a couple of other guys and some girls, and his relief when she did was evident.

As the night wound down to the last dance, Rob was relieved nothing had gone wrong yet . . . his record at dances was not a good one. He held Lacy in his arms as they slowly moved to the final song. He looked down at her and found her gazing up at him expectantly . . . and he had nothing.

I just can't think of a thing to say to this girl, Rob thought glumly. *I'm just not cut out for this dating stuff!*

The song ended, Lacy hung her head in disappointment, and the couple slowly worked their way toward the gym doors with the rest of the crowd.

As they maneuvered through the open doors and into the night, they found Trip, Jenny, Allison, and Evan waiting for them to walk home. With shouted farewells to a lot of their friends, the group walked home, talking excitedly about the dance and how much fun they had. *Guess I was at a different dance,* Rob thought. Lacy agreed.

Evan, who lived very close to school, was the first to veer off. Rob offered to see Allison home, and since Allison and Evan weren't really a couple, Evan gladly agreed.

Trip and Jenny were next, taking the next road to the right, while Rob, Lacy, and Allison went left. A short detour after that brought the threesome to Lacy's house.

Rob timidly walked Lacy to her front porch . . . while Allison hung back on the sidewalk, about 20 feet away . . . trying not to eavesdrop . . . and not doing it well.

OK, Lacy thought as she turned to face Rob on her porch. *Here is where the big stud comes through in the clutch. He's going to say something now that's going to wow me.*

Instead, Rob stood tongue-tied and looked down at her in confusion.

"Er, good night, Lacy . . . uh . . . I had fun . . . thanks for asking me," Rob finally said.

Lacy just stared at him as he backed away and started to turn and leave.

"Wait!" Lacy exclaimed in confusion. "Is that it?"

Rob paused and looked at Lacy, not knowing what to do. Finally, he just gave a short nod and turned again to leave.

"Well, that's just great," Lacy spat out at Rob. "So, I wasted three weeks and a whole dance . . . and that's all you've got for me?"

Rob looked confused and wanted to escape, knowing this might get worse.

"Do you speak?" Lacy demanded.

"Yes, I know you do . . . you spoke to her all night," Lacy continued, pointing angrily at Allison. "But you can't say three words to me?"

Rob stayed mute. *I have no idea of what to say . . . what does she want?*

"Some big man on campus," Lacy snapped. "I'm not wasting any more time on you."

With that, Lacy stomped to her front door, strode in, and slammed the door behind her.

CHAPTER 47
JANUARY-SOPHOMORE YEAR

ROB stood for a moment in shock. *What the heck just happened?* Then, he turned and saw a forgotten Allison Pierce staring at him with her mouth hanging open in surprise.

They stood staring at each other momentarily in the street lamp's light. Both were stunned at the suddenness of Lacy's reaction . . . but both knew she was right.

Why am I such an idiot around hot girls? Rob tormented himself. *But did I even like Lacy? No! Then why do I care?*

Rob's head was down, and when he looked back up, he saw Allison smiling that smile at him. Not the one that made fun of him . . . the one that always melted him . . . the one that he knew meant she really cared about him . . . she was really his friend.

He started walking toward Allison and returned her smile with one of his own, and they both burst out laughing.

"Let's go home," Rob said to Allison, and they started their five-minute walk.

"Pretty smooth, huh?" Rob asked Allison playfully. "I sure know how to handle girls."

Allison laughed.

"Well, you know what Trip would say, don't you?" Allison asked.

"No, what?" Rob asked.

"Wonder Boy" strikes again!" Allison cackled.

The pair cracked up and continued walking.

They reached Allison's front porch, and Rob stopped at the bottom of the stairs while Allison reached the porch and turned to face him.

"Thanks for walking me home, Rob," Allison began. "You know . . . maybe you should actually try dating someone you, A, know, and B, like, and C, know you have something to talk about."

"That's your new plan for me?" Rob asked, smiling at her.

"My plan for Stephanie Miller worked, didn't it?" Allison teased.

"It did," Rob answered softly.

"So, maybe you date friends," Allison said, "and forget what they look like . . . concentrate on whether you like them . . . whether you have something in common."

"I don't have any real friends that are girls," Rob said, oblivious to the fact that he had just hurt Allison deeply.

Why won't he even consider me? she pouted.

"Sure you do," Allison said as she berated herself. *Why am I helping him find other girls all the time? That's right, remember what Emily said . . . he's not ready to date yet.*

"What about Lisa in Science . . . you guys are always talking and laughing?" Allison queried.

"She's a junior," Rob replied.

"So what?" Allison answered emphatically. "Plus, with Lisa, you still get someone really cute . . . why didn't I think of her before?"

"Ah, I don't know," Rob said sheepishly. "Why would a junior want to date me?"

"Because she likes you . . . what else?" Allison said.

"She does?" Rob asked in surprise.

"Yes!" Allison replied.

Rob paused and reflected.

"Aw, I think it's time to just give up on girls for a while," he finally stated.

"Well, just give it some thought . . . you have more friends that are girls than you think you do," Allison said softly with encouragement. "And I know some of them would love to date you."

"Thanks, Ally," Rob answered sincerely. "See you tomorrow night for "Movie Night!"

Ally! I love it when he calls me Ally! Allison thought.

He turned and headed home, turning once he reached his porch to look back at her with a wave.

"I know some of them would love to date you," Allison repeated softly to herself. "Especially me."

CHAPTER 48
JANUARY-SOPHOMORE YEAR

*T*HE aftermath of Sadie Hawkins was long forgotten by the middle of the following week. All that was on the mind of Rob Mathews was Milltown . . . and Pine Bluff!

Again, the two perennial powers in League play stood in the way of Hillsdale's hopes for that elusive League Championship. Rob wanted to be part of the team that hung that next banner in the gym.

Milltown posed a possible problem for the Pirates. They were big, tough, strong, and played tenacious defense . . . that combination had engineered a big upset of Pine Bluff just last week. It was a game Hillsdale had to shoot the ball at a high percentage from the outside . . . because second-chance rebounds would be hard to come by, and Milltown's big frontline would punish anyone driving the lane.

"You know the drill," Coach Bridges said just before leading the team onto the overflowing Milltown High School gym floor. "These guys play very tough . . . it's an extension of the football season for a lot of these guys . . . you have to play strong . . . don't be timid . . . play full-out the whole game . . . I think we can outrun them when we get the chance . . . the key will be pounding the defensive boards so we can get out and run . . . even after a made basket . . . hurry the ball up and keep moving the ball . . . they'll be in a zone . . . we need to make our shots."

The team nodded, understanding the game plan.

"The winner comes out of here in first place," Coach Bridges said as he neared the front door and halted the squad. "I'd rather be in first than second after this one, guys . . . go do your jobs!!"

The team burst through the doors and onto the court amid a thunderous ovation from the Hillsdale faithful, which had made the easy trip to Milltown.

However, their ovation paled compared to the one the Miners received as they hit the court. After their road upset of Pine Bluff last Friday, the hometown fans rewarded their squad with an enormous welcome home . . . it was their last real chance to do that tonight.

Hillsdale picked up where they left off last Friday and shot the lights out against Milltown. The Pirate's ball movement and quickness left them wide-open shots all night long as Milltown stubbornly stuck to their tight zone.

Rob, Trip, and Bob Johnson, getting a rare start instead of Josh Lee, lit up the Miners with a dazzling display of long-range shooting. Edgar Garcia and Trip controlled the defensive boards, igniting several fast breaks that led to easy baskets.

By half, the Pirates led by 15 points and, after three quarters, had pushed the lead to 23, and Coach Bridges emptied the bench. Hillsdale's second unit gave back some of the lead but played hard and showed improvement.

When the final horn sounded, the Pirates delighted in a 76-58 win, which sent the huge hometown crowd home disappointed . . . and sent the Hillsdale Pirates home alone atop the standings. Now, it was Pine Bluff's turn to face the budding juggernaut.

***

Now, it was Hillsdale's turn to have the hometown crowd cheering them on, and the Pirates fans were up to the challenge. Hillsdale's gym was jampacked, with a standing-room-only crowd that befitted the marque home game of the year . . . the Pine Bluff Warriors.

Pine Bluff had been coasting through the season, much as Hillsdale had, crushing league opponents after a successful preseason schedule. That had ended against Milltown . . . and Pine Bluff had responded by annihilating their next opponent . . . and now wanted to do the same to Hillsdale.

The Warriors were led, of course, by the Danielson boys, Jeb, Dirk, and Clem, with Jeb again vying for Most Valuable Player honors. He was the glue of Pine Bluff's program. They also boasted three football players that Rob knew well . . . they had each harassed him during the "Pick" game, and he had taken some real shots from them.

They also had Jake "The Snake" Gardner on their bench . . . he was the third guard after Jeb and Clem Danielson . . . and Jake was dying to renew his rivalry with Rob Mathews.

There was certainly no love lost between these two teams, and the players shot daggers at each other across the gym floor, all during warmups. Especially Trip McHenry . . . who had a vivid memory of an ugly Saturday morning game in Valley Christian's gym last fall.

Everybody in the gym was ready for a heated rendition of Pine Bluff-Hillsdale basketball . . . and they got what they came for.

Allison squashed tightly in the stands between Emily and her Mom, strained to hear anything. Aunt Barb and the boys were right there, too. Grandpa Russell sat behind her and tried to tell Allison something, but the noise was too loud. She smiled and nodded, which seemed to appease him, and she turned back just in time to see Trip win the center jump to begin the game.

The two teams went at each other with a real vengeance. No love was lost here, and even newcomer Trip McHenry had been around long enough to grasp the bitterness of the rivalry. His eyes bore into Jeb Danielson's whenever he could, determined that Jeb and his team were going down tonight.

Both teams came out playing full-court defense, clawing, scratching, and fighting to win each possession. The tension was palpable on the court and in the stands as the teams flew up and down the court.

Younger players like Josh Lee and Gabe Cantor were timid in their first minutes, but the pace and ferocity of the game quickly caused them to get into the flow.

The Danielson boys and Jake Gardner seemed to be at the dirtiest best . . . using any trick they could to upset the Pirates flow . . . and if they could get away with it . . . inflict a little personal pain at the same time.

The two teams traded basket after basket in the first half . . . the largest lead either team could muster was a mere three points. Rob and Trip were both playing well and carrying the load for Hillsdale. Trip was controlling the boards and already had nine defensive rebounds and three on the offensive side at the half.

The score at half was knotted at 35, and both teams were exhausted as they collapsed into their locker rooms for the quick, 15-minute half-time break.

Trip and Rob compared bruises received on their way to the locker room. "Those guys are really dirty," Trip said with a short laugh.

"Yeah . . . they might be just getting started," Rob snorted.

CHAPTER 49
JANUARY-SOPHOMORE YEAR

"*NOTHING* we need to change," Coach Bridges announced while the team rested. "Keep doing what you're doing, and we'll be fine . . . I could see them starting to falter toward the end of the half . . . keep pushing them, and we'll push the lead."

Out the Pirates flew to open the second half, and Coach Bridges' prediction came true. Hillsdale's pressure had taken a toll. With Rob's floor leadership, overall game, and Trip's dominance inside, the Pirates extended the lead bit by bit until, at the end of three quarters, the score stood at 55-48 in favor of Hillsdale.

The run was partially fueled at the free throw line as the tired Warriors began trying to play more physically to slow down the Pirates. If possible, their play became even dirtier. The lead could have been higher had Hillsdale made those free throws . . . but their 50% from the line in the 3rd quarter hurt them. Pine Bluff had repeatedly fouled the two freshmen, Josh Lee and Gabe Cantor, and the strategy was paying off.

The crowd was rocking and rolling at every play, even though the fans could barely move because there were so many people scrunched together. It was hard to breathe, and Hillsdale's fans were gearing up for a piece of revenge . . . winning this game would take a little of the sting out of losing the "Pick."

"This is our year to win the title," Grandpa Russell screamed just before the 4th quarter got underway. "I can feel it . . . Coach Bridges is going to get his title . . . but I bet he doesn't retire like he keeps saying he will once he wins another championship . . . who could leave this bunch."

The game turned on one play in the first minute of the 4th quarter.

Trip skied for a rebound and shot a quick outlet to Josh Lee, who flipped a nifty pass ahead to Rob, ahead of the pack. Rob hauled in the pass at the top of the key, took several long dribbles toward the rim, and went up for a layup.

Out of the blue, from behind came Jake Gardner. "The Snake" had seen some time in the first three quarters, hacking and hewing his way against Rob and Josh Lee, with his knees and elbows continually finding the mark without detection.

This time though, Gardner did not worry about being deceptive. He roared up behind Rob and body-blocked him to the floor. Rob was sent flying under the basket, where he lost his balance and crashed head and shoulder first into the wall.

The crowd erupted in outrage and concern, and players raced toward Rob . . . except Trip, who was after Jake Gardner . . . who retreated quickly to the safety of his football player teammates.

Edgar Garcia got in Trip's way and carted him forcefully back to the Pirate's bench. "C'mon, man," Edgar pleaded. "We can't lose you . . . especially if Rob's hurt."

Trip understood and calmed down.

In the stands, the noise was unbelievable, as fans were screaming for Jake Gardner's blood . . . except for three people sitting above the Pirates bench in shock and concern.

Emily stood with her eyes on Rob under the basket, spread-eagled on the floor with Doc Barber, Coach Bridges, and Coach Dave Wilson hovering over him. She saw him hit the wall. *He's not moving . . .* she thought . . . *please move something . . . please . . .*

Grandpa Russell stood . . . pale and breathing hard . . . staring at Rob on the floor. "C'mon, son, get up, get up," Grandpa Russell prayed softly.

Allison Pierce was crying. *Please be OK. Please be OK . . . you've got to be OK.*

"I better get down there," Emily said in a panic.

"Wait a second," Grandpa Russell said as the crowd was suddenly hushed, all eyes on Rob.

They all watched as one, as Rob moved his arm, rolled his neck, and sat slowly upright with help from Coach Wilson and Coach Bridges. They helped Rob to his feet, but instead of heading back to the floor, Rob was led off under his own power to the locker room by Doc Barber and Coach Wilson.

The crowd erupted in cheers as Rob ducked into the locker room. The cheers soon turned into loud boos as Jake Gardner was ejected from the game and escorted into his locker room through some unruly fans who had moved onto the floor, out for Jake's blood.

Coach Bridges tried to rally his team, but their concentration was shot. They could be seen watching the locker room door in hopes of seeing Rob emerging and in good shape ... but that didn't happen.

With Rob gone, Pine Bluff took advantage and double-teamed Trip while continually harassing Josh Lee, Brad Wallace, and Gabe Cantor into numerous mistakes.

The lead that was at ten after Jake Gardner's foul was slowly chipped away until Pine Bluff took a 2-point lead with under a minute to play.

A steal by Clem Danielson led to a three-pointer from brother Jeb that sealed the deal. Final score ... Pine Bluff 74, Hillsdale 69 ... a three-way tie for first place ... and an unknown future for Rob Mathews ... who had never emerged from the locker room.

CHAPTER 50

FEBRUARY-SOPHOMORE YEAR

ROB and Emily slowly exited Doc Barber's office on Monday afternoon in relief. Emily's relief was complete . . . Rob was OK . . . no concussion . . . just a shoulder bruise and a stiff neck.

Rob was relieved . . . but disappointed he would be missing tomorrow night's game on doctor's orders.

"Just a precaution, Rob," Doc Barber had said. "With your concussion history from the "Pick" game last year . . . well, I just want to give you a couple more days . . . let's take another look Wednesday morning . . . you should be good to go to practice that afternoon."

Rob hated to miss a practice . . . let alone a game. *Good thing this is not a tough game I'm missing,* Rob thought as he walked toward school with his Mom. *And, there are two more games this week . . . I need to be healthy.*

Coach Bridges was disappointed . . . but he had expected Rob to sit out a little . . . and he agreed if Rob had to sit, this was the best week to do it.

The team was disappointed. It had lost a chance to sit in first place alone and a chance to prove to everyone . . . including themselves, that they were the best in the league.

Instead, youthful mistakes and the lack of floor leadership with Rob being gone let the seeds of doubt creep in for the Pirates. They also realized their slim margin for error was gone . . . another loss and their title hopes would almost certainly evaporate.

The next two weeks had Hillsdale playing three times each week. Games this week would be Tuesday, Thursday, and Saturday nights. The following week was unusual, Tuesday, Wednesday, and Friday night games, before playing Milltown and Pine Bluff again the last week of the season on Wednesday and Friday nights.

***

ON Tuesday, Oakville came to Hillsdale, and the Pirates were out to convince themselves they were still good. They started slowly, feeling Rob's absence, but once they got comfortable, the talent took over, and Hillsdale pulled away.

Trip McHenry was everywhere, controlling the boards on both ends of the floor, draining three-pointers, doling out assists, blocking shots . . . a man on a mission!

Rob was on the bench cheering on the team and amazed at Trip's play. At the final horn, the scoreboard read Hillsdale 81 and Oakville 47, and Trip had set the single-game scoring record at Hillsdale High of 40 points . . . while adding 20 rebounds, five blocks, three steals, and five assists. The crowd rose to give him a sustained standing ovation when Gabe Cantor tapped him out with four minutes to play.

"Nice job, "Wonder Boy!" Rob teased Trip as he sat on the bench, drenched with sweat.

"No way!" Trip scoffed. "You're not getting rid of that nickname!"

After the game, Trip put up with the adulation from the crowd and the press but clearly didn't love it.

"Hey," Trip said quietly to Rob as they walked home. "Don't ever do this again . . . you being hurt doesn't work for me."

"Me, either," Rob chuckled.

***

C*OLTON* and Barker City were next on the schedule for Hillsdale, and both teams paid the price of the Pirates being back at full strength. Rob was back at practice on Wednesday and appeared to have not skipped a beat . . . and Colton was the first team to see that firsthand.

Rob and Trip dazzled the Cowboys and broke the game open immediately, going on a 23-6 run in the 1st quarter. The team fed off Rob's joy for being back on the floor, and at the half, Hillsdale was in command at 48-16.

As a precaution, Coach Bridges sat Rob the entire second half, but Hillsdale still walked away with an easy 88-48 win.

When the Pirates came home on Saturday night to face Barker City, the word was out on what a show the Pirates were putting on, and people from all over were showing up to watch. The gym was bulging with people . . . including Valley Christian's entire Varsity coaching staff . . . and several college scouts.

Hillsdale, led as usual by Rob and Trip, did not disappoint. Straight out the gate, Hillsdale went on a 10-0 run before Barker City called a timeout. Back on the floor, the Pirates added another 13 points before Barker City finally managed to score.

By halftime, the score stood at 51-22, and at the end of three quarters, when Coach Bridges emptied the bench for the remainder of the game, it was 79-45. The benches played an even 4th quarter giving Hillsdale a 91-57 victory.

The whole team got into the act and played well, but Rob and Trip gave the college scouts and the Valley Christian coaches something to consider. Rob's final line was 25 points, 12 assists, eight rebounds, four steals, and a block, while Trip went off for 23 points, 21 rebounds, four blocks, a steal, and four assists! Both players had just one turnover each!

Trip was very aware of the Valley Christian coaches in attendance . . . his visit to the VC campus with Aunt Barb was scheduled for next Saturday morning. His Dad was pushing Valley Christian hard . . . and the visit was all-important. *I have to keep impressing,* Trip thought. *Valley Christian could make me a shoo-in at USC!*

***

*T*HE next week Trip kept on impressing, and so did the Pirates, running off three lopsided victories in a row. Trip was outstanding in all three games, averaging 22 points, 17 rebounds, three blocks, two steals, four assists, one turnover, and a four as a defender . . . for a 49 on the USC scale!

Hillsdale coasted against Cooley, beating the Cougars 88-50 on the road. Back home against Foothill, the Spartans again gave them a short test before Hillsdale took control for an 81-65 victory. Friday night in Taylor, they got a much better game from the Tornados but still breezed to an 88-66 win.

The teams' reputation kept growing stronger locally and regionally . . . and rightfully so . . . as it was not just Rob and Trip that were carrying this team . . . the whole squad was maturing and improving. The amount of playing time for all had been high, and the minutes were paying off . . . the question was would they pay off at crunch time . . . against Milltown, Pine Bluff . . . and hopefully, against Valley Christian in the Sectionals.

Hillsdale's record stood at 19-3, with their only losses coming to Valley Christian, Braxton, and Pine Bluff . . . and the Pirates sorely wanted revenge for two of those losses . . . Valley Christian and Pine Bluff. They knew they wouldn't face Braxton in the Sectionals . . . they were too big a school . . . but the other two . . . different story.

"Listen up, guys," Coach Bridges said, quieting down his team in the locker room after the Taylor win. "We have had a hectic two weeks . . . six games . . . six wins . . . have a restful weekend . . . we have only two games next week . . . but you know how big they are. By the way, I just heard . . . Pine Bluff beat Milltown . . . the two of us now have the best shot at winning the title by ourselves!"

Coach Bridges paused, letting that soak in.

"Relax . . . enjoy . . . and come back ready to win the League Championship next week," Coach Bridges said quietly and then turned and walked into his office.

CHAPTER 51

FEBRUARY-SOPHOMORE YEAR

ROB Mathews, Donnie Fields, and Buck Buckman sat on Aunt Barb's front porch with Trip McHenry, listening with mixed emotions about Trip's visit to Valley Christian earlier this rainy winter Saturday.

"So, what did you think of it?" Buck asked Trip, with the guys all ears.

"It's amazing," Trip answered with a broad smile. "You guys just don't know . . . it is much better than Canyon . . . the whole place looks new . . . the kids are great . . . Tony Russo led me around with this beautiful girl . . . Sabrina . . . ah, Sabrina . . ."

The guys all laughed hard as Trip went on and on about Sabrina.

"I thought you had a girlfriend?" Donnie asked.

"Yeah, well . . . you know . . . me and Jenny . . . we're getting to the end," Trip explained. "But Sabrina . . ."

"She got a friend for "Wonder Boy," here?" Buck asked sarcastically, pointing at Rob.

"No . . . no thanks," Rob laughed. "I'm done with girls for a while," Rob replied.

"And the girls of America thank you for that," Trip said, poking fun at Rob.

"So, the school was great?" Buck pressed.

"Oh, yeah," Trip resumed. "Everything is new . . . the gym is fantastic . . . the locker room is unreal . . . the football stadium . . . the baseball stadium . . . everything is unreal!"

"Would you play all three sports there?" Donnie asked.

"Probably . . . but the basketball coach wants me to just play basketball," Trip replied.

"Guess you'll have to get a new nickname if you do that," Rob threw out, and Trip smirked back at him.

"The basketball coach told me I would fit right in with them . . . told me he would build the program around me . . . I'd get star billing, and he said he'd make sure to get me enough time in blowouts to pad my stats," Trip said smugly.

Rob frowned and thought, *Uh, oh, Trip is going backward. He's getting selfish.*

"So, you made your decision?" Donnie asked softly . . . not liking where this conversation was heading.

"No, not yet," Trip replied. "Aunt Barb wants me to really think it over . . . but they offered me a full ride . . . no cost at all to go there . . . I can live on campus if I want . . ."

After that comment, the guys all looked sour, and Trip caught the looks.

"But I wouldn't do that," Trip said hastily. "I want to stay in the hood with you guys! Plus . . . Aunt Barb would make me stay here . . . I think . . ."

"When do you have to decide?" Rob asked.

"Not for a few weeks," Trip answered. "The coach says he wants me to sit down with him after the season . . . go over basketball stuff . . . and he wants me to hang out with the team a little bit . . . you know to make sure we mesh . . . Tony asked me to a party next weekend . . . at his folks' cabin at Colton Lake . . . he says they let him party out there with his friends all time . . . you know . . . by themselves."

It was Donnie's turn to frown and think. *Parties . . . they mean big trouble.*

"Yeah, I guess he takes girls out there . . . you know to the cabin . . . with no parents around," Trip added. "Bet the girl's parents don't know about that . . . he said Jenny and I could use it . . . or maybe . . . Sabrina!"

"Tony Russo, huh?" Rob said. "Not my favorite guy."

"Yeah, I know," Trip countered, laughing self-consciously. "But he seemed different today . . . you know . . . hate him as an opponent, love him as a teammate."

"Guy's a jerk," Donnie said flat out.

Trip gazed back at Donnie but let the remark lay there.

"But the school sounds cool," Donnie threw in, sounding upbeat and supportive. "You need to make the best decision for you . . . you know, the one that fits your Game Plan."

Trip smiled and nodded. *These guys hate the Valley Christian idea . . . but they're going to let me decide. Cool. But maybe I want them to help me decide!*

"So, which way you leaning," Rob asked with trepidation. *Not sure I want to hear this answer,* he thought. *Sure hope he decides to stay at Hillsdale.*

Trip took a long time to answer. In turn, he looked at the three guys on his porch, and all stared back with no expression or words about him staying at Hillsdale.

"You know," Trip said finally. "I'm so confused . . . I don't know yet. Pros and cons on both sides . . . I just gotta' figure out what's best for me."

A long silence followed as each boy processed the words.

He's gone, Buck Buckman thought immediately. *Just doesn't want to say it.*

At least we still have a shot, Donnie thought, hopefully.

He's staying, Rob exulted. *I know he's going to stay.*

CHAPTER 52

FEBRUARY-SOPHOMORE YEAR

THE long silence was broken by a voice coming from the street.

"Billy . . . Billy . . . is that you?"

The quartet turned toward the sound of the voice and saw a scrawny, bedraggled teenager dressed in baggy pants, a hoodie with a baseball cap turned backward underneath it, and a heavy gold necklace dangling at his chest.

"Drag? . . . Drag? . . ." Trip squinted down the walkway. "What the heck are you doing in Hillsdale?"

"Came to find you," Drag said as he approached the front porch.

"Why?" Trip demanded.

"Just thought you'd be missing your old buddy," Drag beamed. "Heard you were in L.A. a couple weeks ago . . . you didn't even come by to say hello?"

Buck, Donnie, and Rob were staring with their mouths hanging open, and when Trip saw them, he looked embarrassed.

"Oh, hey guys," Trip sputtered. "This is Drag, uh er, Dragon, uh . . . I know him from L.A. Drag, this is Rob, Buck, and Donnie."

"You know me from L.A.," Drag said in disbelief. "Know me? We were best friends, man . . . for years."

"Were best friends," Trip said with hostility. "That's the keyword, Drag. Were."

"Oh, you're still not whining about that little incident, are you?" Drag asked, looking Rob, Buck, and Donnie over as he shuffled onto the porch.

Up close, Donnie knew in a flash that this guy was bad news. *Seen it before,* he thought. *He's strung out on something.*

"That little incident is why I'm here," Trip seethed. "We're done."

"Oh, come on, man," Drag continued. "I just need a little money . . . you know . . . some cash to get by . . . you were always good to me, man . . . you took care of me."

"We're done," Trip said again.

"C'mon, man, I've got something here to sell . . . I need cash, man . . . you gotta' help me out . . . maybe give me a place to stay for a night or two . . . or a week," Drag whined.

"Ronald, you're not staying here one second longer," a voice boomed from behind the boys.

It was Aunt Barb.

She strode confidently toward Drag and thrust her finger into his chest.

"You are not welcome here . . . not now . . . not ever . . . until you go to rehab and get clean," Aunt Barb blasted at Drag.

"But, Aunt . . ." Drag began.

"But, nothing . . . out . . . away from these boys and away from my boys," Aunt Barb ordered.

"How about you guys," Drag asked, looking at the other three guys. "Maybe I could stay with one of you a few days?"

"NO!!!" Aunt Barb nearly screamed. "You turn around, get yourself out of Hillsdale, and get yourself straight. You are not welcome in their houses either."

"I got no money, Aunt Barb," Drag said with a sly grin, holding his hands out.

Aunt Barb paused and stared at Drag for a moment, deep in thought.

"I've got two choices for you, Ronald," Aunt Barb said more quietly. "Choice number one, I will buy you a bus ticket to L.A., and you will get on that bus and head home . . ."

"You'll give me cash for a bus ticket?" Drag asked.

"No," Aunt Barb replied. "I'll buy you a bus ticket, and these guys will see you get on it."

Drag's face contorted. Not what he had in mind.

"What's my second choice," Drag drawled.

"This isn't L.A., Ronald. This is a little town," Aunt Barb said. "I know the chief of police personally here . . . dated him in high school. Choice two is I give Tom a call, and he picks you up and slams you in jail."

Drag looked coldly at Aunt Barb.

"Your choice, Ronald," she spat.

Another pause.

"You want that ticket . . . or do I make that call?" Aunt Barb interrogated.

"The ticket . . ." Drag mumbled.

Aunt Barb retreated quickly to the house and bought and printed out a bus ticket ASAP. The boys were left on the porch in awkward silence.

"Man, you changed," Drag finally said accusingly to Trip.

"Yeah, I have, Drag . . . it's time for you to change now, too," Trip replied.

CHAPTER 53
FEBRUARY-SOPHOMORE YEAR

*A*UNT Barb reappeared, handed Drag the bus ticket, and turned to Trip and the guys. "Bus leaves in 20 minutes, so you have to hustle him downtown," Aunt Barb said. "You make sure he gets on that bus."

With that, she turned to Drag.

"Do yourself . . . and your poor parents a favor, Ronald, and get help before you end up dead," Aunt Barb said with emotion. "You were a good boy once . . . I know you can be again . . . give yourself that chance."

Drag looked defeated and turned toward the street with Trip, Rob, Buck, and Donnie in tow. As they walked to town, Drag seemed to regain some of his swagger. They reached the bus station with minutes to spare, as it was boarding passengers.

"So, Billy, where do you think I can sell this ticket . . . I need cash, man?" Drag implored as he looked for an escape route.

"You gotta' get on the bus, Drag," Trip said slowly. "You heard Aunt Barb . . . she'll call the cops . . . and if you're carrying . . ."

"No, man, I need your help, man . . . I need you to help me," Drag pleaded.

Trip seemed to soften . . . looked to his friends . . . started to pull out his wallet.

"NO!!!"

It was Donnie Fields.

"No!!!" Donnie repeated sternly but more quietly.

Drag recoiled and sputtered, "Hey, man . . . this is not your business . . . it's Billy's . . . if he wants to help me . . ."

"No!!!" Donnie repeated. "Get on the bus!"

Drag shook his head defiantly.

"Now!!!" Donnie shouted.

Drag backed away and looked ready to run, but the guys blocked every path to freedom.

"Listen, loser," Donnie snarled. "Your friend Trip here . . . he might bail you out . . . let you sell that ticket . . . because he is an old friend. Buck and Rob . . . they're too nice to do anything to force you on that bus . . . they could do it . . . but they're too nice."

Drag looked from Trip to Buck to Rob . . . and then back at Donnie.

"Me . . . I'm different," Donnie said with menace in his voice. "I'm strictly a football player . . . no sissy stuff like basketball or baseball . . . and it's been since October since I've been able to hit anything."

Drag recoiled again but backed into the side of the bus.

"So, I'm going to give you two choices like Aunt Barb did," Donnie continued. "One, get on that bus feeling pretty good considering the shape you're in."

"What's two?" Drag asked meekly.

"We call the cops to come get you . . ." Donnie snarled, "and you've got plenty of broken bones, and a face beat to a pulp."

Drag stared at Donnie in fear. He looked to Trip for help. Found none. Looked to Rob and Buck. Same result. Looked at Donnie to see if he was bluffing.

"I'm crazy, man . . . I'll do it!" Donnie responded to the look.

Drag moved cautiously forward, and Donnie grabbed him by the arm and escorted him to the bus door. Once at the door, Donnie guided Drag up the first step, tugged his arm, and waved him to come closer.

"You ever set foot in this town again, and you're not clean," Donnie whispered. "Choice number two happens. You can count on it!"

Drag stared at Donnie a long moment, nodded his head slightly, looked back at Trip, and boarded the bus.

The boys watched the bus pull away from the curb, wending its way through town, and disappearing into the afternoon rain.

"Would you have done that, Donnie?" Trip asked as they walked back to Trip's house.

"Nah," Donnie laughed. "I may be crazy . . . but I'm not stupid . . . they woulda' thrown me in the slammer for that."

"Hey, Donnie," Trip said, "thanks, man! You didn't have to do that."

"Hey, man, you're a Pirate . . . for now," Donnie said happily.

Trip laughed.

"We're gonna' have your back," Donnie added. "Whether you're a Pirate or not."

Trip stopped completely, stared at Donnie, and saw the nodding heads of Buck and Rob.

"He's right . . . that's what neighbors do," Buck said, acknowledging they were, in fact, next-door neighbors.

"Yeah, it's true," Rob added. "I found out it was true last year."

Trip soaked it all in. *Now, I'm more confused than ever,* Trip thought as they plopped down back on Aunt Barb's front porch.

CHAPTER 54
FEBRUARY-SOPHOMORE YEAR

"**You** had quite the dramatic day yesterday, I hear," Emily said to Trip as the "Movie Night" group sat around the kitchen table eating dinner.

"Yeah," Rob interjected before Trip could answer, "we're thinking maybe he needs a new nickname . . . "Drama King."

Trip sneered at Rob and laughed.

"One nickname is enough, there, "Wonder Boy," Trip teased. "I'm just starting to get used to "Trip!"

"Well, it did sound interesting . . . getting rid of your friend had to be hard . . . and your visit to Valley Christian sounded great," Emily said.

"Yeah . . . I was lucky to have the guys there," Trip said. "Especially, Donnie. He scared him to death." *These guys really do have my back . . . no matter what I decide,* Trip realized.

"And Valley Christian? Have you made a decision yet?" Emily asked.

Rob leaned forward in his chair to hear the answer.

"You know," Trip answered slowly. "I'm just . . . just a little undecided right now."

"Well, you've got plenty of time," Emily stated. "You said the coach at Valley Christian wanted to see you again after the season ends . . . so you've got two to three weeks to think it over."

"Yeah, the coach wants to talk about how they're going to build the offense around me next year . . . you know, give me a chance to put up good stats and get that USC scholarship," Trip said proudly.

Allison's Mom, Linda, gasped audibly as the words sunk in.

"Did you say they would build the offense around you, too?" Linda asked incredulously.

Everyone at the table swiveled their heads to Linda in surprise, as she rarely talked sports. They all waited expectantly.

"Well, I just ran into Maggie Russo a couple of days ago," Linda explained to the group. "She was laughing about the basketball coach . . . I guess the coach told Tony they would build the offense around him."

"Why was she laughing, Mom?" Allison asked.

"Well, she said she had talked with another sophomore's Mom just the day before," Linda continued. "And . . . she told Maggie the coach had just told that kid they were going to build the offense around him!"

Trip looked like he had been slapped in the face. *What's up with that?* Trip thought.

The table was silent.

"Well, that was probably before the coach knew he had a shot with you," Rob said quickly, breaking the silence.

"Yeah, yeah, that's probably it," Trip answered, trying to sound convincing.

The group nodded in agreement.

"Hey, but that's not the important thing right now," Trip said, trying to pump himself back up. "We've got Milltown and Pine Bluff to worry about!"

Minutes later, Allison and Trip sat in the living room waiting for Emily and Linda to finish up so they could start the movie. Rob was in the bathroom, and Trip seemed far away.

Allison cleared her throat, and Trip looked up to see Allison looking directly at him.

"What?" Trip asked, coming back from where he was.

"You look confused . . . or something," Allison said gently.

"I am," Trip answered. "So much of me wants to stay in Hillsdale . . . but so much of me sees Valley Christian as where I should be . . . and it's definitely where my Dad wants me to be."

"Why does your Dad want you at Valley Christian so bad?" Allison asked.

"I don't know," Trip answered. "When I first moved up, he was so gung-ho on Hillsdale . . . then after Christmas . . . he starts pushing VC or Canyon. He was really mad about Canyon!"

"What do you want to do?" Allison asked.

"I . . . I don't know . . ." Trip replied.

"What do you think I should do?" Trip asked eagerly. *Will someone just tell me what to do??? I can't make this decision alone!*

Allison paused a beat, looking at Trip for a long moment.

"I think you know what I would tell you," Allison finally answered.

"Yeah, do what's best for me," Trip said in frustration.

Allison just shook her head no.

That's right, Allison . . . good old, bold, and direct Allison. Give it to me, Trip thought.

"I think you should go where you think you're going to figure out how to be the best man you can be," Allison said.

Trip just stared at her. *More of the same old stuff,* Trip vented. *What does that even mean?*

CHAPTER 55

FEBRUARY-SOPHOMORE YEAR

*A**LLISON*** saw Trip's confusion and leaned closer.

"Think about it, Trip," Allison gently began. "This decision isn't about sports at all . . . it's about learning how to succeed in life . . . I think you know in your heart where that is."

"I don't know, Ally," Trip countered. "Valley Christian is the best pipeline to USC . . . that's what's important."

"And, there you go," Allison reasoned. "If that's really what's the most important to you, the decision should be easy . . . but it's not that easy . . . is it?"

Trip just stared at her.

"Personally, I think you're better off in a place that is going to build your character . . . your integrity. That's going to be what gets you that ride to USC. You heard Coach Wilson that morning . . . that's what will impress the USC coach."

"Ah, Allison, you don't know about sports," Trip argued.

"This comes straight from Grandpa Russell," Allison answered. "Trip's going to get that ride to USC out of Hillsdale . . . look at his stats . . . and look what he's learning about teamwork . . . he's a shoo-in."

"And you think Grandpa Russell knows it all?" Trip asked.

"I think he knows enough," Allison replied.

Trip looked skeptical.

"Your Dad got a scholarship to USC out of Hillsdale," Allison pointed out quietly. "So can you."

"But it would be easier out of Valley Christian," Trip countered.

"Maybe," Allison said coyly. "But, here's my take on it. I think you get your ride no matter where you play. The question is do you want to be happy while you do it . . . and be a better man at the end . . . or do you want to go to Valley Christian?"

Now there's the bold and direct Allison, Trip exulted.

"Why wouldn't I be happy at Valley Christian?" Trip challenged.

"Because I wouldn't be there to see you in school every day," Allison said lightly, flashing Trip an impish smile.

Trip smiled back at her. *There is something special about this girl,* Trip realized . . . again. *Something in her eyes . . .*

"Think about it," Allison continued as Trip stayed silent. "Look at the friends you've got here . . . do you think you're going to find guys like that at Valley Christian? You might find one . . . maybe two . . . but think how many real friends you already have at Hillsdale."

"They'll still be my friends . . . still have my back . . . I'll still be in the neighborhood," Trip replied.

"Granted . . . but it will be different," Allison said. "But the big difference is in becoming a better man . . ."

"What do you mean by that, Allison? You keep saying that, but I don't know what you mean," Trip said in exasperation.

"The people you surround yourself with will be the people that influence how you turn out," Allison explained softly. "So, do you want those people to be that guy from yesterday, Drag, those guys down at Canyon . . . or a coach like the guy at Valley Christian who tells at least three guys he's going to build his offense around him!"

Allison paused to let that sink in as Trip looked at her thoughtfully.

"Or, do you want to hang with guys like Donnie, Buck . . . Rob . . . that you know . . . really know . . . are true friends to you . . . friends who look out for you . . . you . . . and want what's best for you?" Allison asked.

Trip continued to look at her.

"Do you want a two-faced coach like the guy at Valley Christian?" Allison rolled on, "Or, do you want someone like Coach Bridges . . . or Coach Wilson . . . guys that teach kids how to do the right thing . . . how to be a good teammate . . . how to treat people with respect . . . how to be a good man?"

Trip looked frozen, staring almost beyond Allison, deep in thought.

"You know where I think you should go to school," Allison said quietly.

She gave Trip her best smile, and Trip smiled back. *There it is again . . . behind this geeky mask is someone very special,* Trip thought. *Lucky, Rob . . . if he's ever smart enough to figure it out!*

"More importantly," Allison finished. "When the time comes to make this decision . . . you're going to know . . . really know . . . where it is you should be for the next two years."

"Thanks, Allison . . . that really helped," Trip sputtered. "I've got a lot to think about!"

Standing in the hallway, Rob, Emily, and Linda gave each other silent high-fives, and they prepared to stop eavesdropping and make their way into the living room for the movie.

All right! Rob exclaimed in his head. *Trip has got to stay now. That just made so much sense!*

Rob looked at his Mom and smiled, and both were thinking the same thing . . . *that Allison is something special! Really special!*

CHAPTER 56
FEBRUARY-SOPHOMORE YEAR

***M**ILLTOWN* faced a do-or-die situation as the two teams squared off in the Pirate's gym on Wednesday night.

The Miners had dropped a close game to Pine Bluff last week, giving them two losses on the league season . . . a game behind both Hillsdale and Pine Bluff. A loss to Hillsdale would give the Miners three lossses . . . with Hillsdale guaranteed of no more than two losses at the end of the year . . . the result . . . championship hopes gone for Milltown.

However, if Hillsdale lost, both teams would have two losses . . . and Pine Bluff would still have just one loss. The best Hillsdale would be able to do is to share a championship . . . but only if they could beat Pine Bluff, creating a three-team tie for the title.

It was simple . . . focus on beating Milltown . . . and worry about Pine Bluff on Friday!

With the season on the line for both teams, the Hillsdale gym was bursting at the seams, with fans from everywhere crowding in to find a perch. The Danielson boys were there, along with the entire Pine Bluff coaching staff, who were scouting Hillsdale in preparation for Friday's game. No matter who won tonight, Friday's game would be a do-or-die situation for Pine Bluff.

The crowd was buzzing as the referee tossed up the ball at center court, and what happened next stunned almost every person in attendance.

The big, tough, slow Milltown Miners came out playing one-on-one, full court, pressure defense against Hillsdale . . . and the results were devastating . . . for Milltown.

Rob's eyes got big, and he actually chuckled as he saw Milltown's defense and quickly went about slicing and dicing the Miners to shreds.

It wasn't pretty . . . and after the first quarter Hillsdale had a commanding 31-7 lead . . . and Milltown was in a fix. Do they revert to their game plan of the first meeting . . . one that didn't work . . . and one that would make it very tough to launch a comeback . . . or do they continue trying to press, in hopes of getting back into the game with easy baskets off of defensive steals?

Coach Bridges was taking no chances. Even with a 24-point lead, he stuck to his game plan and kept his starters in the rotation, and the results were overwhelming. The Pirates never let up in the second quarter, the halftime score was 59-19, and the exodus leaving the building began.

Coach Bridges played his starters for four minutes to start the second half, and after a 16-2 run to open the quarter, the starters were done. Hillsdale coasted to an embarrassingly easy 98-45 stomping of a very good . . . but on this night . . . a very poorly coached Milltown squad.

***

THE *Hillsdale Express* was all over the story of this game in the next morning's edition, and Rob read portions to Emily over breakfast. Dylan Cobb wrote his entire article about the folly of Milltown's coaching staff. Dan Mercer, the "Old Grump," also had some derogatory comments . . . before heaping praise on the Pirates and a prediction for Friday's showdown with Pine Bluff.

"I've watched Milltown's coach for many years," the "Old Grump" wrote, "and I've never seen anything like it. To expect his athletes . . . who are very good at what they do . . . try to play run and gun/full-court pressure defense against a team like Hillsdale is criminal. Those kids deserve better . . . that was coaching malpractice . . . and to stick with it longer than three or four minutes . . . was inhumane treatment of children!"

"Wow, that's strong," Emily winced at the "Old Grump."

"Here's the good part," Rob continued. "The big question is, can the Pirates continue their roll Friday at Pine Bluff? This old reporter says yes . . . their loss to the Warriors earlier was a fluke . . . they were in control until that cheap shot cost them Rob Mathews. This time, barring injuries, the Pirates win. Pine Bluff will have the home-court advantage, and that has to be considered . . . it can be worth ten points or more . . . but I think Hillsdale is more than ten points better than Pine Bluff right now. The "M&M Boys" will destroy them . . . and Coach Hal Bridges will get his long-sought-after Championship Banner to hang in the gym. Question is . . . does the Coach retire after the Championship? He has said that for the last five years. I, for one, say no . . . not as long as the "M&M Boys" are together!"

"Wow!" Emily said again. "The "Old Grump" has become quite the fan."

"Do you think Coach will retire?" Rob asked, hoping the answer was a no.

"I agree with Dan Mercer," Emily answered. "As long as you and Trip are there, he'll stay. It wouldn't surprise me if he stays even if it's just you . . . but if you both are here . . . he'll be here . . . how could he miss it?"

They smiled at each other, and Rob was relieved.

"What do you think Trip's going to do, Mom?" Rob asked. "Is he staying or going to Valley Christian? I go back and forth . . . some days I think he's staying for sure and others I think he's history!"

"Good question, Rob," Emily answered, picking her words carefully. "After hearing that conversation with Allison the other night, I don't know how he could go anywhere but Hillsdale . . . but he's got a lot to consider . . . his Dad is really pushing Valley Christian."

"Well, he better stay," Rob said quietly. "I'd really miss him if he goes to VC."

Emily came forward and put her arms gently around Rob.

"You really like him, don't you?" Emily asked.

"Yeah," Rob answered. "He's kinda' like my brother."

"Yeah, he kinda' is, isn't he?" Emily said dreamily.

"So, is he nervous about the Pine Bluff game?" Emily asked playfully. "He'd have to be to be your brother."

"Aw, I'm too old for that nervous stuff, Mom," Rob scoffed.

Yeah, right, Emily thought as she beamed at her son.

✳✳✳

FRIDAY morning . . . early. Really early. Rob's eyes popped open, and it was still dark. His stomach was doing somersaults. *I guess I'm not too old,* Rob moaned. *I haven't felt the butterflies like this for a long time. But I haven't had a game like tonight's game for a long time. We have to win this championship . . . we just have to!*

Around the corner, Trip McHenry's eyes popped open about the same time. He was wide awake instantly, and he was sweating profusely. His stomach fluttered. *Am I sick? No!!! I can't be sick today. Hang on, calm down . . . OK . . . I think it's just nerves . . . but I don't usually get nervous . . .*

Trip pondered as his stomach calmed a bit, but then it kicked back into high gear. *Ah, that's it,* Trip realized. *I never cared enough to be nervous before . . . we have to beat these guys tonight . . . the whole team . . . the whole town is counting on me.*

Trip paused and considered. *The whole town is counting on US . . . not me. Us!!!* His stomach calmed again. *Yeah, it's US!*

Allison Pierce woke up at her usual time . . . and even she felt funny. *It seems like this game means more than most,* Allison thought. *Not as much as the "Pick" game . . . but almost. Maybe more in ways . . . I can't help thinking that somehow this silly game might make a huge difference to Trip and whether he stays or not. I sure hope he stays.*

Allison went about her morning but couldn't get tonight's game . . . or Rob . . . out of her mind. *Please don't let Rob get hurt tonight,* she worried. *Please let him do well . . . let the whole team do well. We just have to beat Pine Bluff!*

***

TEN hours later. The Pine Bluff gymnasium. Bedlam. Not one spare inch to be found. The place was packed! Hillsdale fans sectioned off in one-quarter of the gigantic gym. Pine Bluff rooters overwhelming in numbers and noise. A nasty, bitter feeling encompassed the whole building . . . no love lost betweens these two teams . . . between these two towns.

Teams on the floor warming up. Glaring at each other. Stomachs churning. Hard to breathe. Hard to focus. Hard to dribble . . . to shoot . . . to hear . . . to think. Tension strained every face.

Welcome to Pine Bluff-Hillsdale basketball.

Winner take all.

League Championship at stake.

Bring it on . . .

CHAPTER 57

FEBRUARY-SOPHOMORE YEAR

ROB Mathews was suddenly serene for the first time today. He looked across the team huddle at Trip McHenry. *He feels it, too,* Rob thought as he gazed over at Trip. *He knows we're better . . . he knows we're going to win.*

Rob looked over at Coach Hal Bridges. *He's not so sure,* Rob realized. *He thinks we're better . . . but he's not sure. Look at the strain on his face . . . I've never seen Coach so stressed.*

"Hey," Rob shouted over the utter chaos that was the Pine Bluff gymnasium. His teammates and Coach Bridges looked directly at him, and Rob scanned the group.

"We're better than these guys," Rob waved his hand at the Pine Bluff huddle. "Just relax . . . and focus . . . let's play our game, and everything will work out."

The faces in the huddle relaxed . . . including Coach Bridges, and Rob nodded at Trip McHenry.

"Rob's right," Trip yelled. "We've got these guys . . . and they are going down!!!"

Rob looked at Senior Captain Sam Jordan and nodded.

Sam stepped forward, put his hand in the center, and all 12 players connected hands.

"This is our time, Sam screamed. "We have waited a long time to bring a championship back to Hillsdale."

He paused and motioned to the Hillsdale crowd. "Let's take one back home for them tonight!!!"

"Let's bring this one home tonight for Coach," Trip said. Nods all around.

"All right, guys," Coach Bridges yelled hoarsely as he watched the Warriors take the floor. "Relax and do your jobs. Rob's right . . . we are the better team . . . now go show the world. Ready . . . TEAM!!!!"

The Pirates roared onto the court and were met by the surly starting five of Pine Bluff. Jeb and Clem Danielson . . . the starting guards for Pine Bluff, sneered at the Pirates as they all extended hands for a quick shake.

"You guys really think you have a chance here tonight," Jeb snarled as the teams came together at center court for the jump. "You guys are going down . . . again . . . you really think I'm letting you take away my last basketball championship? Yeah, I've got three . . . going on four . . . how many you got, chump?"

That last comment was directed at Rob. *It's true . . . we don't have a basketball championship . . . or a football championship . . . but we've got baseball,* Rob reminisced.

"We've got a baseball banner," Rob said, looking directly at Jeb. "And, tonight, we add a basketball banner . . . you've won your last championship . . ."

"Hah!!" Jeb cackled to his brother, Clem. "You hear that, bro! You'll be lucky to finish the game, chump . . . let alone win."

"Yeah, and what are you looking at, McHenry," Jeb snarled at Trip, who was watching and listening with an amused look on his face.

"You better watch your back," Jeb continued. "We haven't forgotten that morning at VC . . . you're on our list."

Trip just smirked back and pretended to yawn. Jeb and Clem shot him daggers.

The referee stepped into the center circle at mid-court, and the crowd roared in anticipation. Rob worked his way into position flanked by Clem and Jeb, and each one caught him with an elbow as they jostled for position.

It might be a long, painful night, Rob realized. *But we're going home with that banner!*

***

*A*LLISON Pierce was beside herself, scrunched into the bleachers with Emily and Grandpa Russell. Grandma Russell and Allison's Mom had stayed home... the crowd was just too big.

"I'll let someone else have my spot... we don't get too many seats at Pine Bluff," Grandma Russell had said.

It seems like every big game just gets bigger... more critical, Allison pondered, waiting for the opening tip. *Maybe it's because of Trip... one more guy I care about is playing. And, so much at stake... we just have to win!*

Allison looked over at Grandpa Russell... *he's red in the face already... and looking tense... but he has that look of confidence, too... he thinks we're going to win! I hope...*

She glanced over at Emily and could tell she was in a state. Her pretty face was strained... her brow furrowed as she watched Rob jawing with the Danielson boys near center court. Her glance went to Jake "The Snake" Gardner on the Warrior's bench. *None of you better hurt my baby,* Emily thought. *None of you.*

***

*T*HE tip went to the side, and after a short scramble, Jeb Danielson came out with the ball, dribbled to the top of the key, pulled up, and drained a three-pointer.

"In your face," he spat at Rob and Trip, moving past them to play defense.

And, so, it began. The teams clawed, scratched, and scuffled through the first quarter, with neither team able to hold more than that initial three-point lead. As in their first meeting, both teams were playing full-court, man-to-man defense that pressured every move any player tried to make. Jeb Danielson was on fire, hitting five of his first six shots and tallying 12 points on his own.

Hillsdale was playing a more balanced game, with all five starters scoring at least two points, and the quarter ended with Pine Bluff clinging to a 19-18 lead.

Rob and Trip were taking a pounding . . . and so was Josh Lee. Clem was hounding him all over the floor . . . and when Jake Gardner spelled Clem . . . he increased the dirty play, and Rob could tell the pressure on Josh was taking its toll.

Coach Bridges saw it, too, and inserted Brad Wallace to start the second quarter, along with Gabe Cantor . . . and the pressure shifted from Josh to Gabe. Pine Bluff was clearly trying to rattle the whole team . . . but figured their best chance of positive results was by attacking the two freshmen.

The second quarter saw more of the same as the teams traded baskets back and forth. The fouls were starting to mount up as the refs were determined this one not get out of hand physically. Both teams were playing physical basketball . . . the difference was Pine Bluff was playing dirty, physical basketball.

Twice Clem Danielson cut the legs out from under Josh Lee, getting caught only once, and Jake Gardner leveled Trip McHenry while Trip slammed home a dunk . . . and Trip was lucky to come out of it unhurt.

The crowd was roaring as both teams took turns dazzling their fans. Jeb Danielson continued to scorch the Pirates, adding 13 more to total 25 so far. Rob and Trip had notched 12 points apiece at the half, and the score was knotted at 41.

As the horn sounded to end the half, both teams were exhausted and straggled to their locker rooms. Both coaches were playing to win at all costs, and the substitutions had been few and far between. Hillsdale's team seemed to be eight deep tonight, while Pine

Bluff had played nine. Everybody knew this was no time to rest . . . this game was all that mattered.

The Pirates sat on benches in front of a chalkboard while Coach Bridges reviewed adjustments for the second half.

"We don't need adjustments," Coach Bridges proclaimed. "Just like the first game . . . they are going to wear down before us . . . when that happens, we'll pull away . . . only this time we aren't losing Rob to injury!"

They all grimaced, recalling Jake Gardner's dirty play that cost them the victory a few weeks ago.

"We're in better shape than they are," Coach Bridges continued. "They will run out of gas before we do . . . push the ball whenever you can . . . be aggressive. Josh, Gabe . . . I want you guys to relax and play your game . . . you're out there for a reason . . . because you deserve to be . . . you are better than these guys . . . now go prove it!!!"

CHAPTER 58

FEBRUARY-SOPHOMORE YEAR

"*COACH* is right," Rob whispered to Josh and Gabe as they headed back onto the floor.

Trip nodded and then added, "You guys are better than those guys . . . we are better than those guys . . . just relax and let it flow."

Josh and Gabe both nodded . . . but Rob was not sure they were buying it.

"We'll be fine . . . remember what Coach always says . . . perfect the process . . . build your foundation . . . and have fun playing the game," Rob said. "Let's do this! Let's have fun!"

The third-quarter pace matched the first half, but neither team seemed to be running out of gas . . . mainly because Jeb Danielson was not running out of gas.

Every time Hillsdale would build a little bit of a cushion . . . four to six points . . . Jeb would nail back-to-back threes to pull Pine Bluff even.

The pace was frantic, as Rob and Josh pushed the ball at every opportunity, resulting in good shots and a 25-point quarter for both teams. Jeb Danielson accounted for 18 of the Warrior's points and had 43 for the game.

Trip McHenry had been everywhere for the Pirates. Scoring, passing, rebounding . . . but his defense had been key . . . he was controlling the inside . . . with some help from Edgar Garcia, Sam Jordan, and Gabe Cantor . . . but he was the lynchpin . . . holding everything together . . . causing Pine Bluff to have to live and die with their outside game . . . and Jeb Danielson.

But . . . Jeb was having the game of his life . . . and it was the only thing keeping the Warriors close.

Trip was taking a pounding inside . . . and giving it back as well. As the pace quickened, it seemed the refs could not keep up, and stray elbows and knees were finding their mark on Trip and Rob more often . . . and it was wearing them down. Both had played every second of the game so far . . . and neither one was going to like it if Coach Bridges put them on the bench for a rest!

At the quarter break, Coach Bridges huddled his team close and barked out new instructions.

"Guys," he began, "we're going to go box and one . . . Jeb's killing us . . . Rob, I want you to start on him . . . you other four are the box . . . Trip, you and Edgar down low . . . Josh . . . you and Sam up top."

The guys nodded, understanding their roles.

"Josh . . . you and Rob switch jobs every two minutes . . . I want you both going full-out for those two minutes . . . don't let him get the ball . . . don't let him shoot . . . let the other guys try to beat us!!"

More nods of agreement from the exhausted troops.

In the stands, the huge crowd was also exhausted. They had been on their feet roaring for three quarters, and they wondered how they would survive another quarter.

Allison was drenched in sweat and twisted her hands together, her nerves showing. Emily's face was taut with anxiety, and her breathing was coming fast. *It's almost as if we're out there playing,* Allison thought.

Grandpa Russell, by comparison, seemed almost serene. His face was relaxed . . . a little red . . . but relaxed. His voice was hoarse from screaming . . . but he whispered something to Allison during the break before the final quarter.

"We're bringing this home," Grandpa Russell said with a smile. He turned to Emily and whispered the same thing . . . and Emily laughed nervously.

"You always say that, Dad," Emily scoffed.

"But, tonight, it's true," Grandpa Russell replied.

"Isn't that what you said about the "Pick" game," Allison reminded him, but he waved her off.

"We didn't have Rob and Trip for that game . . . this one's in the bag," Grandpa Russell chuckled.

The rest of the crowd was in a frenzy as both cheerleading squads were on the floor, willing their fans to scream louder. The fans chanted at each other, trying to find an edge.

And then it happened. A faint chant began in the far corner of the gym on the Pine Bluff side. It started in low . . . and gained volume as the rest of the Pine Bluff crowd picked up on it.

"WE'VE GOT THE "PICK!!!!" "WE'VE GOT THE "PICK!!!" they chanted until the whole Warriors side of the gym screamed it at the top of their lungs, drowning out the Hillsdale side.

Trip McHenry looked up from the huddle, smiled crookedly, and dropped his head back into the huddle.

"Let's make them regret that," Trip said passionately. "Let's get revenge for the "Pick" game . . . this Championship is ours!!!"

The team grabbed hands and shouted, "TEAM!!!!" The starters bounded back onto the floor.

CHAPTER 59

FEBRUARY-SOPHOMORE YEAR

*P**INE* Bluff had the ball and immediately noted the switch in Hillsdale's defense. But Rob had Jeb covered so tightly that they couldn't get him the ball, and Clem Danielson bricked a three as the shot clock wound down.

Trip skied for the rebound and found Rob as the outlet, and Rob pushed the ball quickly up the court. He found the middle, saw Sam Jordan filling the lane to his right, and dished a perfect pass to him for a score on a driving layup. Hillsdale was up by two.

Down came Pine Bluff again, this time able to get Jeb the ball on the inbounds pass. Rob pressured him relentlessly and forced him to waste time getting the ball across the center line. He continued his pressure, got Jeb to pass off, and then made sure he could not get the return pass.

Clem thought about another three but instead zipped a pass into the middle to one of Pine Bluff's big football type-players, who got great inside position, caught the pass, and went up for a thundering dunk.

Trip came from the weak side out of nowhere, went up with the big man, and swatted the shot down with fury.

The ball bounced crazily toward the corner, and Josh Lee won the race to the ball. He spotted Sam Jordan at half-court and fired off a pass that hit the mark. Sam turned and passed to Rob, who was in the open, and Rob cradled the pass, deked his defender, and scored on a reverse layup and a four-point lead!

Jeb again received the inbounds pass and hurried the ball upcourt... but the Pirate's defense was stifling, and Jeb launched a three that misfired badly, and Trip again corralled the rebound.

Down came the Pirates again as fast as they could, with Rob controlling the ball at the top of the key. Pine Bluff got their defense set this time, and Rob started the offense. The ball whizzed around the court... one pass, two, three, four... ball to Trip wide open... 15-footer... GOOD! Six-point lead. Time out, Pine Bluff!

"That's the way to run that defense," Coach Bridges shouted above the noise in the gym. "Josh... your turn on Jeb... Rob showed you how to do it... make it work. Trip, keep it up... you are awesome! Gabe, give me two good minutes for Edgar. Let's extend that lead!"

The Hillsdale section of the bleachers stood and cheered long and loud, trying to drown out the larger Pine Bluff contingent, while Grandpa Russell basked in the glow of those first two-plus minutes of the 4th quarter.

"You all have to learn to believe me," Grandpa Russell crowed. "I told you we were going to take control and bring this one home!"

Allison and Emily shared an eye-roll at him, laughed... and then thought they both should say silent prayers.

Back on the floor, the Warriors advanced the ball, and Jeb licked his lips, seeing he had Josh Lee guarding him. Using his veteran experience, he slipped around a screen, received the ball with just a flicker of open space, and launched a long three... nothing but net, and the lead was 72-69.

Hillsdale advanced quickly, but the Pine Bluff defense was ready, so the Pirates were content to work the ball... and the clock. Four more passes and Rob found Gabe Cantor open underneath... a perfect feed... but Gabe had trouble controlling the ball... almost lost it and looked ready to panic. But he regained control, made a nice drop-step move, cashed in off the glass, and the lead was up to five.

The Pirate's defense stiffened the next time Pine Bluff brought the ball up, erasing precious seconds from the clock. As the shot clock wound down, Jeb squirted free at the top of the key and launched a three . . . the shot clock went off . . . but the ball had already left Jeb's hands . . . a dagger . . . nothing but net . . . and the lead was cut to 74-72, with just under four minutes to play.

Rob brought the ball up again at speed and rifled a pass to Gabe Cantor, who worked it over to Sam Jordan . . . but the ball somehow slipped through Sam's fingers and out of bounds. Pine Bluff ball!

Rob and Josh switched roles again on defense, and immediately the Warrior's offense went stagnant. Pine Bluff worked hard to get Jeb open but couldn't get him the ball, and as the shot clock wound down, Josh Lee stepped in front of an errant pass, picked it off, and headed for pay dirt.

Jake Gardner was hard after him, and it was a race for the goal. Josh had a step, but he could feel Jake on his tail. Out of the corner of his eye, he also saw Gabe Cantor trailing the play, and he had an idea.

Josh increased his speed, knowing Jake would come after him. He was going too fast to have a good shot, but he went up and laid the ball up hard off the glass. Jake Gardner lunged for him, trying to push him off course and cause him to miss the layup . . . and maybe hurt Josh in the bargain.

But Gardner went flying past . . . and Gabe Cantor . . . knowing this backboard pass was coming from the many hours spent playing with Josh . . . gathered in the pass, set his feet, and skied for a resounding two-handed dunk that brought the house crashing down.

Time out, Pine Bluff!

The Hillsdale crowd was beside itself, yelling, stomping . . . cheering . . . and they continued to do that all through the Pine Bluff time out. The Warrior fans sat in confused silence . . . this was not how this game was supposed to go . . . especially at home!

Both teams were gassed as the frantic pace took its toll. Rob leaned over in the huddle, hands on his knees, gasping for air. He saw his teammates doing the same thing . . . and glanced over to see Pine Bluff's players doing it, too. *We're all gassed,* Rob thought. *But we're not letting this one get away!*

Rob glanced at the scoreboard. Just under three minutes to play. Hillsdale 76, Pine Bluff 72. Warrior's ball. The crowd is on its feet . . . no one sitting . . . no one quiet. The noise level was as high as Rob had ever heard.

"This is our time," Rob whispered to Trip as the timeout wound down.

"Lead the way, "Wonder Boy" . . . let's get it done!" Trip exclaimed.

The timeout over . . . players back on the court . . . the crowd in an absolute frenzy . . . no one in the gym was sitting. Bedlam.

Pine Bluff brings the ball down . . . tries to work their offense . . . stifled . . . desperate shot . . . miss. Hillsdale works their offense . . . gets a good shot . . . miss. Pine Bluff's turn . . . works their offense . . . Jeb smothered by Rob . . . desperate shot . . . miss . . . rebound by Trip, ripping it away from Pine Bluff's center.

Outlet to Josh . . . up the court to Rob . . . Trip running the floor. Rob to Trip in the corner. Three-pointer . . . GOOD!!!

Time out, Pine Bluff. Hillsdale 79, Pine Bluff 72. Crowd roaring. Players exhausted. Just 92 seconds to play.

Sometimes, 92 seconds can be forever.

CHAPTER 60

FEBRUARY-SOPHOMORE YEAR

*T*HE Pirates bench exploded onto the floor when Trip's shot went through, and the time out was called. They allowed the players on the floor to sit as Coach Bridges gave last-minute instructions.

Rob and Trip had played every second . . . at top speed, and the fatigue showed on their faces . . . but there was a determination there was as well.

"Josh . . . you're back onto Jeb . . . give Rob a breather . . . play him tight . . . keep the ball away from him," Coach Bridges hollered. "Use the clock on offense . . . only take good shots . . . make your free throws . . ."

Rob stared at Coach Bridges and saw in his face that the extreme strain was still there. *He knows this game isn't over,* Rob thought. *We've got a long way to go.*

The Pine Bluff fans were chanting again, "WE'VE GOT THE "PICK," while the Hillsdale fans were being led in a cheer by their cheerleaders.

Rob scanned the crowd as he stood up to return to the floor. He saw his Mom smiling warily at him . . . knowing how often they had come this far, only to see it snatched away.

He saw Allison Pierce . . . wringing her hands, with a frown on her face . . . suddenly seeing Rob . . . catching his eye . . . her killer smile . . . and Rob momentarily melted.

Back to business. Rob turned to the floor . . . caught Grandpa Russell's eye . . . *he is smiling that smile,* Rob realized. *He's thinking we're going to do it! Yeah, we got this!*

Pine Bluff put the ball in play to Jeb, and the whole world seemed to go into slow motion. The crowd is loud . . . but the players can't hear it . . . the players and the ball are moving impossibly fast . . . but it feels like the game is being played underwater.

Jeb Danielson pops free . . . receives the pass . . . squares up . . . launches a three . . . good . . . 79-75.

Hillsdale ball . . . working the ball . . . bad pass . . . loose ball . . . in Jeb's hands . . . fast break . . . pulls up from long-range . . . three-pointer . . . good . . . 79-78.

Hillsdale works the ball . . . a push not seen . . . ball squirts free . . . Jeb wins the race to the ball . . . flies up court . . . pulls up . . . three-pointer . . . an absolute dagger to the heart. GOOD!!!!

New leader . . . Pine Bluff 81, Hillsdale 79. Time out, Hillsdale. The clock shows 28 ticks left.

The scene shows Hillsdale's team with their mouths hanging open in disbelief. The body language shows a team that has just been beaten. The fans quiet . . . on the verge of tears.

Pine Bluff's team is jumping for joy, and their fans are sending down a crescendo of cheers, making it even harder to hear than before. And, then . . . the chant starts in again. "WE'VE GOT THE "PICK!!!" "WE'VE GOT THE "PICK!!!"

For the first time . . . the players were really listening to that chant . . . and they felt even lower . . . if that was possible.

***

*A*ND then there was Rob . . . and Trip McHenry . . . picking up the pieces and picking up their teammates.

"It's all right . . ." Rob barked. "Plenty of time left . . . plenty of time."

"It's all right," echoed Trip. "We got this . . . there is no way we are losing to these guys."

Heads lifted . . . spirits lifted . . . focus back.

"What's the plan, Coach?" Trip quipped to Coach Bridges, who smiled at Trip, relaxing everybody.

"How about we work the clock down . . . get the ball to you, and you make the game-winner," Coach Bridges joked.

"Done," Trip said with confidence.

Coach Bridges looked at him . . . and knew he was being serious.

"You want the ball," Coach Bridges said, "and you'll make it."

"Yes sir . . . it's done," Trip answered in all seriousness. "There is no way these guys are beating us . . . it's done!"

Coach Bridges thought fast. He pulled out his clipboard, designed a play for Trip . . . with Rob as the second option, and turned to Trip but said to the whole team. "Remember, though . . . we just need two to tie . . . if you don't get a good look at a three . . . be sure to get a basket!"

Trip just nodded, the huddle broke, and Hillsdale took the floor to find Pine Bluff already there . . . preparing to play them full court.

Jeb Danielson stood tall, with a massive grin on his face, as the Pirates took the floor.

"Losers again," Jeb celebrated. "When are you going to learn . . . Hillsdale can't win a championship . . . those belong to us."

Rob and Trip looked at each other and then back at Jeb.

"Just watch us," Rob said, brushing past Jeb.

CHAPTER 61

FEBRUARY-SOPHOMORE YEAR

*T*HE roar from the crowd as both teams took the floor was unreal. The gymnasium shook from the noise, and the fans stomping only heightened the uproar.

Allison and Emily were standing, stomping and cheering with the rest of the fans . . . except for Grandpa Russell, who stood still, peering onto the floor, a look of determination on his face.

Emily glanced over at him, and he gave her a wink, and Emily responded with a surprised look. *How can he be so calm?* Emily thought.

Allison caught the look as well. *Oh, I so hope you are right, Grandpa Russell.*

"Have faith, ladies," Grandpa Russell preached. "Rob or Trip . . . one of them is going to get it done . . . you watch now. One of them is going to do something special!"

***

*A*ND then the ball was in play, coming into Rob after a good screen by Josh Lee. The Hillsdale squad moved down the floor, and Rob brought the ball up slowly, milking the clock.

The game had reverted to slow motion . . . the noise to white noise . . . although the building was shaking.

Across half court with 20 seconds to play. Rob started the offense, working the motion offense to perfection. The ball whipped around the court. First to Sam Jordan, over to Trip, back out to Rob, over to Josh . . . off of Josh's hands . . . he struggled for control . . . two Warriors surround him . . . panic setting in . . . Josh works free. . . ten seconds left.

An outlet pass to Rob at the top of the key . . . open for a three . . . squaring up . . . Jeb and Clem Danielson both rushing him from either side . . . out of the corner of his eye spots Trip cutting around a great screen by Edgar Garcia . . . popping free at the free throw line extended.

Rob in the air to shoot . . . changes his mind and two-hands an overhead pass to Trip coming off the screen. Trip gathers in the ball and is wide open.

Rises to shoot . . .

Buries a three . . .

Hillsdale 82, Pine Bluff 81. Five seconds left. Time out, Pine Bluff.

Trip watched his shot go in, and a huge sense of relief and joy settled in. He turned to head up the floor and saw Jeb frantically calling for a time-out.

"That was for you," Trip said quietly to Jeb.

"Coming right back at you, Chump," Jeb fired back. "We are winning this game."

"We'll see about that," Trip replied.

The noise level is lower . . . only one-quarter of the bleachers is dancing, screaming, crying in joy . . . while the Pine Bluff section is dead quiet except for mumbling and grumbling and numbing disbelief.

But that was only for a few moments, as the whole building realized quickly there was an eternity left in the game . . . five seconds is plenty of time. Pine Bluff only needed a two-pointer to win . . . and Jeb Danielson was itching to get his hands on the ball.

"Rob!!!" Coach Bridges shouted as the team moved to the bench. "Guys, we're going back to man-to-man . . . Rob . . . you've got Jeb . . . stick to him like glue . . . but no fouls . . . they are in the bonus . . . play him tough."

"We got this, Coach," Trip piped in.

Coach Bridges looked and Trip and flashed a tight smile. "They only need two . . . so stick tight inside, Trip . . . don't let Jeb draw all the attention and then dump one inside for an easy one. Protect that middle!!!"

Trip nodded and looked at Rob.

"Let's do this, "Wonder Boy!!!" Trip shouted as they moved back onto the court.

Rob flashed a thumbs up and turned to find Jeb.

In the crowd, after Trip's shot went in, Emily and Allison were hugging. Grandpa Russell let out one quick "YES!!!" and then stood there with an, "I told you so" look on his face.

Sitting at home in her kitchen alone, Grandma Russell turned the volume up on her radio . . . she didn't want to miss the call of these last five seconds of the game . . . *when Keith gets home . . . I better know how the game ended,* she thought ruefully. *One way or the other, I need to know . . .*

CHAPTER 62

FEBRUARY-SOPHOMORE YEAR

"*THIS* is like déjà vu all over again . . . in reverse, Tim," play-by-play man Bob Carson said into his microphone. "Last year, Jeb Danielson hit the big shot to put Pine Bluff up, but left Hillsdale three seconds . . . and Bill Tompkins rimmed out the game-winner at the buzzer . . . the scene is set for Jeb Danielson and Pine Bluff to take a game-winner at the buzzer . . . question is . . . will he make it?"

"That's right, Bob," color man Tim Phelps answered. "What a heartbreaker that was last year . . . not sure Hal Bridges has another devastating loss like that in him . . . it might kill him."

"You see Danielson taking the shot?" Carson asked.

"Absolutely," Phelps replied," he's already got . . . what . . . 58 points . . . an amazing night . . . and that's on 20 of 26 from the floor . . . and remember a two-pointer wins it."

"Here we go, folks . . . I hope you can hear us over the bedlam inside Pine Bluff's gym . . . can hardly hear myself," Carson shouted.

"Looks like Hillsdale is going back to man-to-man coverage, Bob . . . Rob Mathews is on Jeb Danielson . . . keep an eye on those two," Phelps highlighted.

"Schmidt will inbound the ball," Carson began as the referee handed the ball to Pine Bluff. "Hillsdale playing tenacious "D" so far . . . Danielson swings around a screen and receives the ball at the free throw . . . has room . . . fires . . . tipped, THE BALL IS TIPPED BY MATHEWS . . . caught in the key by Dirk Danielson . . . he goes up from four feet out

. . . SWATTED AWAY BY . . . TRIP McHENRY . . . FROM OUT OF NOWHERE . . . THERE'S THE HORN . . . NO FOULS . . . HILLSDALE IS THE LEAGUE CHAMPION . . . FINAL SCORE, HILLSDALE 82, PINE BLUFF 81!!!!"

Then the explosion came . . . as the Hillsdale crowd erupted in cheers and rushed the court, spilling onto the floor and dancing and hugging with players and fans alike.

Allison, Emily, and Grandpa Russell also went onto the floor but stayed back from the players and stood meshed in a three-way hug.

"We need to find those guys and give them a hug," Grandpa Russell shouted.

"I think I'll wait on that until they have showered," Emily laughed, causing Allison to grin broadly.

"Good idea, Emily," Allison replied. "Good idea!"

Grandma Russell was grinning ear to ear in her kitchen as she strained to hear the announcers over the crowd noise.

"What a finish, Bob," Phelps yelled hoarsely. "Two blocks to secure the win . . . first Rob Mathews . . . fought through that double screen somehow . . . and got a piece of Danielson's shot."

"It looked like a game-winner, too," shouted Carson in reply. "Smooth as silk. The ball went directly to Dirk Danielson inside . . . and it looked like he had an easy layup . . . where did McHenry come from?"

"The weak side . . . McHenry saw the first block and moved that way immediately," Phelps answered. "He timed that jump perfectly . . . he just stuffed that shot . . . AAAAmazing!!!"

"The "M&M Boys" to the rescue," Carson laughed. "Not only do they both go for 24 points each . . . but they are there at the end on defense to save the day!"

"There's Hal Bridges, Bob . . . corralling his team and heading for the locker room . . . he's been saying for the last seven or eight years he'll retire when he wins his next championship . . . well here it is . . . does he retire?" Phelps inquired.

"Not a chance, Tim," Carson replied quickly. "I say he stays if McHenry stays put . . . and doesn't bolt for Valley Christian . . . he's a lock . . . he might stay without McHenry . . . he's a big Mathews fan . . . he's got to be dreaming about Sectionals . . . heck maybe NorCals if he keeps this team intact!"

"Agreed!!!" Phelps answered.

Grandma Russell smiled, knowing she would be up late tonight reliving the game with her husband. *And I'll be listening to the game recording with him for weeks . . .*

***

TRIP found Rob and gave him a quick hug and a high-five as they moved toward the locker room.

"We did it, "Wonder Boy" . . . we got ourselves a banner!" Trip shouted in jubilation.

"Yeah, we did," Rob replied with a huge grin.

They turned and almost bumped into a disconsolate Jeb Danielson, watching the Hillsdale celebration in confusion.

"Hey, Chump," Trip drawled with a broad smile. "You better get used to this . . . if we get you in Sectionals . . . you're going down again. You can't beat us!"

Jeb scowled at Trip and started to reply but was swept away by a large contingent of Hillsdale fans.

Trip turned to Rob and smiled, "Let's go find, Coach!"

CHAPTER 63
FEBRUARY-SOPHOMORE YEAR

INSIDE the Hillsdale locker room, the chaos continued. The team was laughing, cheering, slapping backs... and occasionally shedding a tear or two of joy.

Coach Bridges, his face finally free of strain but still red-faced, couldn't hold back a huge grin of satisfaction. He stood back... by a wall, enjoying the sight of his team celebrating the first Hillsdale Basketball title in 11 years.

Am I done? Coach Bridges pondered. His eyes fell on Trip McHenry. *What a turnaround... what a player. What if he goes?* His eyes turned to Rob Mathews. *How do I leave that kid? And, these young kids... no... whether Trip goes or not... I'm in for two more years!*

He let the team celebrate, then shower and dress before calling them together.

"Guys! Guys!" Coach Bridges finally shouted, waving them to sit in front of him.

"You just accomplished something that most people didn't expect after we lost nine seniors last year," Coach Bridges began. "Least of all, Pine Bluff!"

The team exploded in laughter and cheers.

"I'm so proud of you guys... all of you," Coach Bridges continued. "You worked hard ... and you deserve to be champions. The growth has been amazing... especially from you young guys... Josh... Gabe... you played like seniors out there tonight... you helped us get it done... just like you all did in your own way."

More cheers from the team.

"But I think we all know who carried us this year . . . who strapped us on their backs . . . and carried us to this championship," Coach Bridges said with emotion.

All eyes turned appreciatively to Rob and Trip, sitting together in the middle of the team.

Coach Bridges reached down and picked up two basketballs.

"Rob . . . Trip . . . come up here," Coach Bridges instructed.

"Not just for tonight," Coach Bridges started. "Not just tonight . . . but all season, you guys have led by example and by showing your leadership on and off the court. Tonight . . . tonight . . . you were both amazing . . . whenever we needed a score . . . a rebound . . . a pass . . . good defense . . . an encouraging word . . . a block . . . or two . . ."

The team exploded with a loud cheer.

"Anyway," Coach Bridges finished up. "Game balls for two players that deserve it!"

He handed a ball to Rob, followed by a quick hug, and did the same with Trip.

"Now, to the greatest basketball team ever at Hillsdale High . . . congratulations!!!" Coach Brides shouted.

A huge cheer.

Without missing a beat, the Coach added, "No practice Monday . . . a tough one on Tuesday . . . our first game in the Sectionals will be next Thursday."

He looked around and made sure everyone had heard that.

"OK," he shouted again, satisfied they had heard him. "Let's open up the locker room doors . . . and talk to those reporters I'm sure are out there."

Dylan Cobb and Dan Mercer, the "Old Grump," rushed in and started talking to players as quickly as possible.

Dan Mercer captured Rob and Trip and spent five minutes grilling them, while Coach Bridges stood speaking with Dylan Cobb. When Dan Mercer finished with the players, he turned to Coach Bridges.

"So, Hal," Dan Mercer began. "You got your championship . . . are you done?"

"You have never beat around the bush, have you, Dan?" Coach Bridges laughed.

Still standing close to their coach, the question caught Rob and Trip's attention, and they both turned their heads to hear the answer.

"I've always been straight with you, Dan . . ." Coach Bridges replied.

"That you have," Dan replied. "And, it's always appreciated."

"I'm not going anywhere yet," Coach Bridges replied. "I have at least two years left in me."

"Even if McHenry's gone?" Dan Mercer asked.

"Even if," Coach Bridges replied, staring first at Rob and then at Trip. "Even if . . ."

"What about it, Trip?" Dan Mercer asked, turning to Trip.

The question caught Trip off guard, and he fumbled and mumbled self-consciously.

"He's not sure yet, Dan," Coach Bridges said, stepping between the two. "And, it's not a question he's going to answer tonight . . . he's got a meeting with Valley Christian after the season . . . the season's not over."

"Got it . . . got it," Dan Mercer responded. "And, I respect that . . . great job tonight . . . all of you," Mercer yelled as he headed out the door.

"Don't let anybody pressure you, son," Coach Bridges said, thumping Trip on the back. "You make that decision when you're ready. When . . . ***you*** . . . are ready!"

"Thanks, Coach," Trip answered sincerely. "Congrats on the title."

"Congrats to you," Coach Bridges replied. "Congrats and thanks . . . to both of you!"

CHAPTER 64
FEBRUARY-SOPHOMORE YEAR

"**Hey,** a bunch of us are heading down to Pop's to get a burger . . . you coming?" Rob asked Trip as they were heading out the door.

"I'm meeting Jenny . . . ok if she comes?" Trip asked.

"I thought you were off her?" Rob asked.

"Yeah . . . she's getting a little weird . . . but we're still hanging . . ." Trip laughed.

"Yeah, bring her . . . the more, the merrier," Rob replied.

Off they went in a big group, gathering extras as they made their way through town and into Pop's, which was bulging at the seams. The counter and booths, with their chrome frames, red-upholstered bench seats, and stools, were full of happy, contented Hillsdale Pirate fans.

They saw they would have to wait, so they put in their names and hung around in the street waiting to be called.

About ten minutes later, a group of eight poured out through the front door, led by Tony Russo of Valley Christian.

"Hey, McHenry," Tony called out as he caught sight of Trip. "Heard you got by Pine Bluff tonight . . . you'll have to do it again to get to us, you know!"

Trip just nodded, embarrassed by being singled out by Russo.

"Hey, it's Rob Mathews," Tony said snidely. "The second half of the great and powerful "M&M Boys!"

"What are you doing over this way, Tony?" Rob asked icily.

"Oh, we're just slumming in Hillsdale . . . you know . . . it's not much to look at, but Pop's still has a good burger."

Rob seethed at Tony's arrogance but bit his tongue. *He's Allison's friend, be nice,* he could hear his Mom say.

"So, McHenry," Tony said, turning back to Trip. "You still coming out to the lake tomorrow? It will be great!"

Tony looked directly at Trip and then turned his head to take in the sight of Jenny standing close by Trip.

After looking her up and down, Tony said, "Hey, is she with you? She's welcome to come, too."

Trip's head snapped up in anger. *Lay off Jenny, Russo!* Trip thought immediately.

"I can't come," Trip countered. "I've got something going on."

Jenny looked disappointed, but Tony rolled on.

"Hey," Tony said, directing his comment to Jenny. "You can still come . . . you have any other friends that are hot like you?"

"Yeah," Jenny answered coyly. "I've got one friend who'd like to come . . . she's hot . . . right, Rob?"

Tony looked at Rob, laughed, and said to Jenny. "Well, both of you should come out . . . it will be a great time."

Trip was seething now . . . mad at Jenny . . . mad at Tony.

"Trip . . . can't we go out there tomorrow?" Jenny begged. "It would be fun . . . Lacy will go . . ."

"You can do whatever you want," Trip replied curtly.

Jenny flashed Trip an angry glare.

"Well, I will," Jenny snapped.

"Be my guest," Trip replied sullenly.

Jenny turned to Tony, the picture of sweetness.

"Where and when should we meet you?" Jenny asked seductively.

"Let's make it easy," Tony said smoothly, pulling Jenny by the hand toward his group. "You can come along with us now . . . call your friend and have her join us . . . and we'll figure out tomorrow's plan later tonight."

Jenny looked at Trip, expecting him to stop her, but he just shrugged.

"Do what you want," Trip said.

Jenny stomped her foot, turned, and headed off with the group.

After a few steps, Tony turned and looked at the Hillsdale group.

"Girls . . . they all just like our class," Tony said smugly. "I guess we'll see you guys on the court in a couple weeks . . . that's if you get that far . . . something I doubt very much!"

Trip's anger was about to boil over.

"McHenry . . . you know the only way to win a Sectional is going to be coming over to Valley Christian, right?" Tony asked.

Trip stood silent.

"You can't think you can ever win one at Hillsdale," Tony laughed loudly.

"You'll see the light if you ever get to us . . . but I sure can't see you beating Pine Bluff again . . . you got lucky tonight," Tony needled. "Thanks for the girl . . . er . . . girls!!!"

With that, Tony Russo and his Valley Christian crowd stalked off with Jenny, leaving the Hillsdale group deflated and angry . . . but only for a moment.

"Hey, who is ready to celebrate?" Trip asked loudly as their group was called to their booth. "We just won a championship!!! Let's party!!!"

The Hillsdale group cheered, drawing stares from patrons inside Pop's, and went into full celebration mode.

"You OK, man?" Rob whispered to Trip as they walked through the door.

"Yeah . . . I'm good," Trip replied. "Jenny and I were finished . . . remember . . . all for the best."

"You must be thinking ahead to Sabrina over at Valley Christian . . . right?" Rob quizzed.

"Yeah . . . could be," Trip grinned. "There are just so many girls for me to choose from!"

Rob snorted and they both went silent.

Silent . . . but both were thinking . . . *Tony Russo is slimy. Not my favorite guy . . . we've got to take him . . . and Valley Christian down!*

CHAPTER 65

FEBRUARY-SOPHOMORE YEAR

THE last week of February flew by, with the first two Sectional games scheduled for Thursday and Saturday.

Hillsdale's League Championship and 21-3 record earned them the #2 seed in the Sectionals... one ahead of #3 Pine Bluff... and one behind #1 seed Valley Christian. If things played out correctly, Hillsdale would face Pine Bluff in the Semifinals and Valley Christian in the Finals... if everything went right!

Their high seed earned the Pirates home games in the first two rounds... as long as they kept winning... lose one, and you're done!

The first game was against the #15 seed Avalon Aviators. Unlike last year, when Hillsdale was the #12 seed against the #5 seed, this year the Pirates were favored big... and fortunately for Hillsdale... the oddsmakers were correct.

The game was basically over by the end of the first quarter, and Hillsdale coasted to an easy 89-45 victory. Everyone on the Pirates got into the game and scored at least two points. Coach Bridges was glad to be able to get everybody on the team decent time... he would not have that luxury later in this tourney.

As expected, Union High won their game and earned the right to be Hillsdale's next victim. Union at #7 was thought to have a chance against Hillsdale, but Rob and Trip obliterated that idea in the first half.

That allowed Coach Bridges to empty the bench for the entire 4th quarter, as the Pirates coasted again . . . but this time at a more respectable score. When it was over, Hillsdale had a solid 78-57 win, which was not as close as the final score indicated.

Even with playing barely more than a half in each game, Rob and Trip each scored more than 20 in both games and had lines that looked like full games.

The significant benefit was getting the rest of the team experience in the tension-filled atmosphere that is the Sectionals. However, advancing to the Semifinals brings on a much different type of atmosphere again . . . playing in Sacramento, in a vast arena, in front of crowds three to four times bigger than the Pine Bluff game!

Pine Bluff and Valley Christian both dispatched their two opponents with ease as well, and the matchup everyone expected was reality . . . #1 Valley Christian would face #4 Claremont, while #2 Hillsdale got #3 Pine Bluff!

The bad blood between Hillsdale and Pine Bluff surfaced immediately, with both town's newspapers starting the duel early . . . both predicting their team to win.

Around the area, fans of both teams, meeting in stores and restaurants, fanned the flames with digs and snide comments . . . some joking . . . some not. But those stories got around quickly, and the whole area was talking nothing else . . . each team . . . each town . . . badly wanted the win on Wednesday in Sacramento.

***

ROB'S week was a good one . . . although he hadn't seen much of Trip, other than at basketball. Trip had seemed distant . . . like a man with a lot on his mind.

On Sunday night, Trip missed "Movie Night" for the first time.

"What's up with Trip?" Allison asked when it became apparent Trip was a no-show.

"Not sure," Rob answered. "I think he's got a lot on his mind."

"I heard he and Jenny broke up . . . do you think that's it?" Allison quizzed.

"Could be," Rob replied. "But he seemed ready to break it off anyway . . . he told her she could go up to Tony's . . . and when she went for it . . . well, that did it."

"Did you hear Jenny and Lacy got stuck out there Saturday night . . . Jenny's folks had to go get them about midnight," Allison said.

"Hmmm," Rob said, not wanting to tell Allison the truth. *I know Tony planned to get them out there . . . and keep them there,* Rob thought. *Not my favorite guy.*

"Trip seemed kind of quiet all week," Allison continued. "But he looked fine playing basketball."

"I think it could be this decision he's got coming up," Rob surmised. "His Dad is putting a lot of pressure on him to go to Valley Christian . . . I'm not sure if he knows what he wants to do."

"I know what he ought to do," Allison said softly, giving Rob a knowing smile and enlarging that smile when Rob responded.

"Me, too . . . me, too." Rob smiled grimly.

***

ON Monday morning, Trip seemed to be returning to his old self. When asked about Sunday's no-show, he just shrugged his shoulders.

"Had a big talk with Aunt Barb . . . and my Dad," Trip said.

Nothing more, nothing less. But he seemed to be himself again, so Rob didn't push.

The pair talked basketball at lunch, hashed out a plan for Pine Bluff, and agreed to get to practice a few minutes early and present it to Coach Bridges.

About 15 minutes before practice and completely ready to take the floor, Trip and Rob knocked on Coach Bridges' office door and pushed into the room after hearing a gruff, "Come in."

The Coach took one look at the pair and immediately popped to attention.

"What's up, guys?" Coach Bridges asked with a slight smile.

"Uh, er, Coach," Rob started. "Trip and I have been talking about how to beat Pine Bluff . . . well, making it a little easier than last time."

"I'm all ears," Coach Bridges laughed. "What have you got for me?"

"Well," Trip replied for them both. "Rob and I thought . . . maybe we should go box and one . . . the whole game . . . cover Jeb hard at all times . . . we think the box can handle the other guys . . . and if we can hold Jeb in check . . ."

"I see," Coach Brides replied with a satisfied smile. "I've thought that might be our plan as well. One thing though, I don't want to wear Rob out so much that he can't be effective offensively . . . uh, you, uh, saw . . . Josh wasn't quite as effective on Jeb . . . you two switching off . . . not sure I can chance that."

Rob and Trip grinned at each other, then turned back to Coach Bridges.

"Here comes the brilliant part," Rob quipped. "Sam Jordan guards Jeb!"

Coach Bridges' mouth dropped in surprise.

"Josh and I still take some turns to keep Sam fresh," Rob continued. "And Josh and I can cover the top of the box as long as Trip is down low."

Coach Bridges paused, thinking, running the idea over in his head.

"Brilliant is the word," Coach Bridges finally said, breaking into a huge grin. "It's what we'll do!"

CHAPTER 66

MARCH–SOPHOMORE YEAR

WEDNESDAY afternoon, the Hillsdale Pirates boarded their bus for the ride down the hill to Sacramento . . . and the Pine Bluff Warriors.

They were confident . . . they were stoked about their defensive plans . . . and they were ready to battle Pine Bluff!

On Pine Bluff's bus . . . they felt the same way.

As the enormous number of rooters from both schools rode down the hill, they were sure their team was going to win that night . . . and they were all ready to help their team win in any way they could.

But tonight was not a night for the fans to make a difference . . . tonight was the night for Sam Jordan to make the difference!

Sam, the team player he is, had been all over the plan. He looked at it as a way to not only help Hillsdale into the Finals . . . he also saw it as a way to shut down Jeb Danielson . . . and have the final say in a rivalry that had been going on since they started playing youth sports against each other over ten years earlier.

The plan reaped benefits immediately. Pine Bluff won the jump, and Jeb Danielson corralled the ball in the backcourt and looked up, expecting the Hillsdale pressure defense.

There was none. Jeb smiled. *You're going to make it too easy*, Jeb thought.

Jeb brought the ball up and watched as he saw Hillsdale setting up the box and one . . . *they're going to try this again? We'll kill em'!* Jeb grinned.

As Jeb moved across mid-court, he realized Sam Jordan was coming to greet him. *Uh oh,* Jeb thought frantically. *This could be trouble.*

And, so it was.

Not only was Sam an inch or so taller than Jeb, but he was also 20 pounds of hard, lean muscle heavier . . . and he was faster than Jeb.

Immediately, Sam pressured Jeb into a bad pass, picked off by Rob, who flew down the court in a two-on-one with Trip. A head fake, a reverse, the defense came to him . . . and then Rob lifted a perfect lob pass to Trip near the rim . . . and Trip slammed it home to set the tone!

The Hillsdale contingent went crazy!

The Warriors tried to get into a rhythm for four minutes, but Sam Jordan was mucking with their offense. Back and forth, the teams went at it, each with the same intensity . . . but not the same results.

Hillsdale bolted to a 14-4 lead before Pine Bluff called a time out to regroup.

When play resumed, it was Rob's turn on Jeb for two minutes, and being fresh, he badgered Jeb into a couple of bad passes, and the lead went to 14 points. Josh took his turn, and Jeb, getting more comfortable with the defense, broke free for a couple of threes and an assist, but as the quarter ended, Hillsdale had a 23-14 lead.

The second quarter started with Sam back on Jeb, and he again stifled Jeb, but Pine Bluff had made some adjustments and was finding some openings in the zone and capitalizing. However, Hillsdale was still clicking on offense, so the lead was kept in a narrow range of 8-12 points for the rest of the half.

When the halftime horn sounded, Hillsdale was on top 36-26, feeling very confident.

"Why does this feel so different tonight?" Allison wondered to Grandpa Russell in the stands.

"We're in control . . . not killing them . . . but in control," Grandpa Russell replied. "Plus, the noise is different in here . . . such a big building . . . and we haven't let the Pine Bluff fans have anything to cheer about."

Allison nodded, as did Emily, knowing her Dad was right.

"Let's not get too overconfident, Dad," Emily chided Grandpa Russell.

"I know . . . I know," Grandpa Russell replied sheepishly. "But I've got a good feeling about this one!"

In the locker room at halftime, Coach Bridges made a decision.

"Sam, you OK to take Jeb the rest of the way yourself?" Coach Bridges asked. "We'll give you a break . . . if you need one . . . but I think you're in better shape than Jeb . . . he's going to wear down before you do."

Sam just gazed directly back at Coach Bridges and nodded.

"He's mine, Coach," Sam said proudly. "I'll keep him in check."

CHAPTER 67
MARCH-SOPHOMORE YEAR

*K**EEP* him in check is what Sam Jordan did.

The second half was more of the same, except this time, Hillsdale steadily increased its lead, behind the scoring of mainly Rob and Trip, the defense and rebounding of the whole "box," and the defense of Sam Jordan.

The lead at half was ten, and it went to 12 to 14, back to ten, up to 16, back to 12, up to 18, back to 16, and as the 3rd quarter ended, the score stood at 53-36 in favor of the Pirates.

Coach Bridges took no chances in this one, and the starters stayed the course to start the 4th quarter. They were all tired . . . but none of them wanted a rest . . . they wanted to be on the floor!

Pine Bluff, though, shot out of the gates in the 4th and quickly hit a pair of threes, and the lead was down to 11 . . . and for the first time tonight, there was life in the Warriors and their fans. Jake Gardner entered the game and set two vicious screens on Sam Jordan to spring Jeb Danielson free.

On the next possession, Hillsdale's missed shot led to another score, and suddenly it was a 53-44 game, and the Pine Bluff crowd was making its presence felt as the noise level was ratcheting up.

A quick time out by Hillsdale.

"Settle down, guys . . . don't rush things," Coach Bridges advised. "I don't mean slow the offensive pace . . . just relax and focus . . . do your jobs."

Back onto the court. Hillsdale moving the ball expertly around the floor. Wide open shot. Miss. Pine Bluff rebound. Fast break. Three-pointer . . . good! 53-47.

Rob calling for the ball. *Time to take over,* he thought as he dribbled up the court.

Running the offense. Ball moving well. Back to Rob. Wide open three. Dagger. Lead back to nine.

Defense set, Sam Jordan dancing around a screen, blocks Jeb's shot. Rob hustles after it. Wins the race. Turns and fires to a streaking Trip McHenry. Dunk!!! Lead at 11 points.

Sam Jordan pressures Jeb Danielson . . . Rob double teams Jeb . . . steal. Pushing the ball up the floor quickly . . . pull up three . . . another dagger . . . up by 14 . . . Hillsdale crowd on its feet . . . noise level through the roof.

Jeb Danielson, again pressured, gets a screen from Jake Gardner, Sam Jordan on the ground, Jeb fires a three . . . no good! Trip skies for the rebound . . . bursts out the pack with the ball . . . starting the break with the dribble . . . ahead to Rob . . . back to Trip . . . pull up three . . . perfect! Up by 17.

Sam Jordan back on his feet . . . Jeb drives him into Jake's screen again . . . Gardner sticks a knee into Sam's thigh . . . Sam down in a heap . . . Jeb flies by him down the lane toward a layup . . . spots Trip McHenry . . . shoots a floater instead . . .

Trip rises and smacks the shot back where it came from! It caroms out toward half-court . . . race for the ball between Jake Gardner and Rob Mathews . . . Rob there first . . . dashes ahead . . . Jake on his heels with vengeance on his mind . . . Rob pulls up at the top of the key . . . Jake flies by . . . Rob sets, shoots . . . three-pointer . . . all net. Up by 20 points . . . time out Pine Bluff.

The crowd could scarcely breathe. Three minutes . . . a 14-0 run . . . two and half minutes to play . . . Hillsdale 67, Pine Bluff 47. Hillsdale's fans were on their feet screaming at the top of their lungs . . . Pine Bluff fans were sitting on their hands . . . in silence.

Two and a half minutes to the Sectional Finals. Two and a half minutes to savor.

Coach Bridges kept his starters in place for another minute of play . . . enough time to tack another score, after another Trip McHenry block . . . and then he started emptying his bench one by one.

First, out came Josh Lee, then Edgar Garcia. Rob and Trip were next, coming out together. All received great ovations.

With a minute left and Hillsdale up 69-53, Sam Jordan was tapped out of the game to a standing ovation from the entire team . . . and the Hillsdale crowd.

Sam, the unsung Senior Captain . . . team player . . . MVP of the game . . . had held Jeb Danielson to 11 points . . . and disrupted the Pine Bluff offense . . . and led his team to the Sectional Finals!

The final horn sounded, and the Hillsdale Pirates . . . now 24-3 on the year, were victorious by the count of 71-55 . . . and they were able to watch Jeb Danielson walk off the court for the last time as a Pine Bluff basketball player . . . in agony . . . as a loser.

***

*I*T only took a matter of moments to know that the Finals would also be a grudge match. The Pirates knew Valley Christian had won their Semifinal game, and as they walked toward the locker room, Tony Russo and several Valley Christian players were waiting for them.

"You better enjoy tonight, McHenry," Tony said to Trip as they got close. "Saturday, you go back to being a loser . . . until you come play with us, of course . . ."

Trip glared at Tony and the others and started walking around them.

"Hey, Trip . . . come on, man," Tony said, trying to smooth things over. "We're going to be buds when you get over here next year . . . you know Hillsdale has never beat Valley

Christian at any sport . . . ever . . . you know you've got to play with us to get a Sectional title."

Trip continued to glare at Tony, and Rob quickly grabbed Trip by the shoulder and pushed him toward the locker room before Trip did something he'd be sorry for.

"Hey, by the way . . . thanks for letting us use your girls last weekend," Tony said sarcastically. "Yeah . . . thanks for nothing . . . they almost got me in trouble . . . why didn't you tell me they were just freshmen!"

Trip stopped and turned, now glowering with hatred at Tony Russo.

"Not that we didn't have fun with them before they called their parents," Tony laughed.

"You are a real sleaze-bucket, Russo!" Trip snarled as he started toward Tony.

Rob pushed Trip harder and got him into the doorway to the locker room.

"Not now, Trip . . . take it out on him Saturday night . . . when we beat Valley Christian!" Rob pleaded.

Trip grunted . . . turned at waved his hand at Tony Russo in disgust . . . and let Rob push the door closed behind him.

CHAPTER 68

MARCH–SOPHOMORE YEAR

*F**RIDAY* night found Rob, Trip, Buck, and Donnie watching basketball, playing video games, and eating pizza . . . on the eve of the first Sectional Championship games for Hillsdale in years.

Close by sat Emily and Allison, doing some dorky project about the environment. *Geez,* Rob thought, *doesn't Allison ever give that stuff a rest?*

Rob berated himself immediately. *Allison could say the same thing about me . . . don't you ever give "spooorts" a rest?* He looked over at her and smiled . . . *what a geek! What a great geek!*

"You guys nervous about tomorrow?" Buck asked as the evening wound down, bringing Rob back into the moment. "This is a pretty big deal . . . maybe not the "Pick" . . . but pretty close!"

"Nah," Trip answered first. "In ways . . . you know how it is . . . it's just another game. We have to go out and do the job!"

"Just another game?!!!" Donnie exclaimed. "I mean, it's not the "Pick" game . . . but it's a big deal."

"Yeah, but you know how it is, Donnie," Rob replied. "Once the game starts . . . you just kinda' go on auto mode . . . you know . . . you forget about the crowd and stuff . . . and focus on the game."

The other guys nodded in agreement.

"I don't know how that's possible," Allison said quietly to Emily. "I get so nervous just watching... I can't take it!"

Emily laughed softly.

"I agree," Emily replied. "But they seem to know how to do it and I have watched them do it over and over..."

"Well, how about for you, Trip?" Donnie asked. "This may be your last game of basketball at Hillsdale... that make it any tougher?"

That question got the attention of everyone in the house.

"Nah," Trip replied without missing a beat. "A game's a game."

"So," Allison blurted out, "is tomorrow your last basketball game for Hillsdale?"

The room suddenly grew quiet. The elephant in the room had just been acknowledged.

Trip looked over at Allison, not sure if he was perturbed at her or not. *I'm not ready to talk about this,* he thought. *Good, old bold, and direct, Allison!*

"Too early to tell," Trip said at last. "Still have my meeting with the Valley Christian coach next week. Might need to meet up with Sabrina again, too... she might make a difference!"

"Right," Allison mumbled in disbelief.

Trip glared at her across the room... but softened and gave her a slow smile. *You know she's not going to give this up,* Trip thought.

"You know I'm meeting him next week," Trip continued. "Talking about how I'll fit into their offensive and defensive schemes... you know, Allison... all that basketball stuff."

"I know more than you think," Allison spouted with her big, wide, tin grin. "I've been sitting next to Grandpa Russell for two years now... and I've learned a lot!!!"

"Right," Trip answered, letting the word linger on his lips. "Little Miss Know-it-all."

"I know enough to know where you ought to be going to school next year," Allison said, looking directly at Trip. "And . . . you know it, too!"

Trip paused, letting the words sink in.

Allison was staring at him . . . defiantly . . . but with compassion . . . and a playful glint in her eyes.

This girl is great, Trip thought. *I hate her for putting me on the spot like this . . . but she is really something!*

"You know I'm meeting him next week," Trip repeated slowly as if speaking to a child. "Talking about how I'll fit into their offensive and defensive schemes . . . you know, Allison . . . all that basketball stuff."

The answer defused the tension in the room. Allison softened, then laughed, and Trip did the same. She flashed him her best smile . . . the one usually reserved for Rob . . . and he smiled back.

And Rob, watching the smile, felt a little jealous. *Trip and Allison . . . no way,* Rob thought.

***

*T*HE bus ride down the hill Saturday morning was a little subdued. *Maybe this is a little more than just another game,* Rob mused.

Coach Dave Wilson had joined the team for the bus ride. As Athletic Director, he needed to be on hand, and Coach Bridges had offered him a seat.

The two coaches sat in the front seats of the bus, chatting away like they were going for a drive in the country.

Rob had butterflies floating up and down his insides but knew they would be gone come game time.

Trip was listening to music and seemed calm and relaxed. Sam Jordan was listening to music, too, and seemed almost asleep.

Josh Lee and Gabe Cantor seemed to be tense. They sat together, fidgeting, laughing, joking . . . but it all seemed a little forced.

Those two played so well against Valley Christian the first time, Rob remembered. *They need to do that again.*

The team filed off the bus at the arena, headed for the locker room, and made final preparations.

Rob looked around the room and realized, *I've gotten close to this bunch. We only lose Sam . . . and maybe Trip. I hope not. If he comes back next year we could be here again . . . and again. But I don't want to lose the day-to-day stuff . . . hanging in the halls . . . after school . . . all that stuff, either. He needs to stay at Hillsdale High!*

Rob looked around at the guys and saw Coach Bridges getting ready to call them together. He took a deep breath and thought, *I've got to stop thinking about it now . . . it's time to focus on the game!*

***

*A*FTER going over the game plan, Coach Bridges took a deep breath and cleared his throat.

"OK, guys, listen up," Coach Bridges began. "Short and sweet. We're here because we deserve it. We can beat that team out there. We nearly did it back in November . . . and I think you will all agree we are a much stronger TEAM . . . now . . . than we were in November."

The team murmured their agreement.

"Sectional Champions has a nice ring to it," Coach Bridges continued. "It would be great ... but the important thing is you play to your potential tonight ... be the best team you can be, and everything else takes care of itself!"

The team yelled out their agreement as one.

"Finally," Coach Bridges added. "Thank you, guys, for this year ... it has been one of the best years of my career, and the things you have accomplished as players have been impressive."

Coach Bridges paused and gazed around the room, making eye contact with each and every player. He found Trip's eyes and then added, "But the things you have accomplished in becoming fine young men ... are even more impressive!"

Trip locked eyes with Coach Bridges, and the pair looked deep into each other's eyes for a few seconds. The connection complete, Trip and Coach Bridges both gave an almost imperceptible nod, and the moment was done.

"Now, men," Coach Bridges finished, "let's get out there and kick some Valley Christian butt!"

CHAPTER 69
MARCH-SOPHOMORE YEAR

*T*HIS was, of course, not just another game. This was a Sectional Championship game . . . and both teams wanted very much to win.

Valley Christian and its fans came into this game much like last spring's Sectional Championship baseball game. They knew they would win . . . it was just a matter of by how much.

The attitude expressed was, "They have never beaten us before . . . why would that change?"

But deep down, those knowledgeable fans on the Knights' side knew that Hillsdale had a shot. They had nearly won the baseball game . . . and the last two basketball games had been anything but a sure thing.

The fans knew they had been in control of those games . . . and that Valley Christian was a better team . . . but in a game that close, anything can happen.

For Hillsdale, their fans were hoping . . . hoping for that one miracle. It had not happened last fall in the "Pick" game . . . but they had finally beat Pine Bluff to capture a League Championship . . . so why not Sectionals? Valley Christian was why . . . and they stood in the Pirate's way. But there was that sliver of hope.

We need to play perfectly, fans like Grandpa Russell thought as the ref tossed the ball high in the air at mid-court to start the game.

They got their wish to start the game.

Rob Mathews scrambled to get the opening tap, brought the ball quickly up the court, found himself wide open, and buried a three.

Two stops and a steal later, the Pirates had hit three straight shots, and Valley Christian found itself with a bloodied nose and a 9-0 deficit!

Valley Christian had come out lazy. . . thinking all they had to do was show up. A quick time out. An attitude adjustment. A different Valley Christian squad.

Trip watched closely as the Knights took the court. *These guys are real jerks. I didn't notice that the first game . . . thinking just about myself. But these guys . . . the arrogance . . . they're all like Tony Russo . . . not my favorite guy!*

The Knights became more focused, started clamping down defensively, and began running their offense with purpose. It didn't all come back in one gigantic run, but the Valley Christian talent started to show, and little by little, they fought their way back.

By the end of the quarter Hillsdale still had the lead . . . but it was down to two points at 20-18.

To start quarter number two, Valley Christian went to their bench with five new players, including Tony Russo. Coach Bridges countered by sticking with his starters, except he gave Josh Lee and Edgar Garcia a quick break. Brad Wallace came in for a brief two-minute stint, while Gabe Cantor played four solid minutes.

During that time, the talent factor changed . . . it now favored Hillsdale slightly . . . and they took advantage, stretching the lead back to six at 32-26.

At the four-minute mark, it was back to the starters for both teams, and they traded buckets back and forth until a minute remained, with Hillsdale still holding the lead at 41-36.

For Hillsdale, the starters had been magnificent, especially Rob Mathews and Trip McHenry. Together they had combined for 28 points, 12 assists, 15 rebounds, three blocks, and three steals, with just one turnover between them.

Trip was doing it all. Scoring almost at will, dishing passes, controlling the boards, and anchoring a stiff defense that was routinely limiting Valley Christian to one shot . . . unfortunately, the Knights were shooting at a high percentage.

After a 30-second time out, Valley Christian came out a nailed a long three to draw within two . . . and then, for the first time of the night, slapped a full-court press on the Pirates.

Josh Lee, surprised, panicked and made a bad pass, which was picked off at half-court. Three dribbles later, a pull-up three. Good! Valley Christian by one.

Another press . . . another steal . . . another three . . . horn sounds ending the half. Valley Christian 45, Hillsdale 41.

The 9-0 run completely washed away Hillsdale's great beginning . . . and they now faced a four-point deficit.

Nobody said it would be easy.

***

THE whole arena had a feeling of uneasiness.

On the Valley Christian side, their fans had lost the air of invincibility . . . but they were still cocky. The late run had restored that cockiness to a degree . . . but there was doubt . . . and the worry that this might be the time Hillsdale pulled a win out of its hat.

For Hillsdale, the beginning run had won over new believers in a miracle . . . in fact, the whole first half had done that . . . until the fateful last minute, when Valley Christian had caught fire.

Emily and Allison watched the teams warm up for the second half, both dreading what might happen.

"Do you think we can do it?" Allison asked fretfully. "Valley Christian is just so good."

"I know," agreed Emily. "They are so good . . . I'm afraid we're going to get worn out."

Allison nodded knowingly, spouting out something Grandpa Russell had said just before the end of the half.

"Yeah, Valley Christian has so much more depth." Allison echoed. "I'm afraid that could hurt us in the 4th quarter . . . our guys are going to be tired."

Grandpa Russell overheard the exchange and smiled at Allison.

"You're right, young lady," he said. "The thing to watch out for now is the press . . . it was effective . . . but more importantly, it will make our guys have to work harder . . . they can wear us down."

***

THAT is just what Valley Christian did. Fortunately, Coach Bridges had figured that, too . . . and he at least had the team prepared for the press.

The result was that while it had the effect of wearing down the Pirates . . . their ball handlers were ready, and the press did not lead to turnovers.

In fact, early on in the 3rd quarter, it led to a couple of easy baskets that helped Hillsdale forge a tie midway through the quarter at 55 apiece.

With two minutes left in the quarter and the game still tied, Valley Christian subbed in a new five and let them go at the Pirates until the end of the quarter. Tony Russo forced a turnover and hit a big bucket, but Trip made a long three and slammed home a vicious dunk that just beat the horn . . . leaving the Pirates with a slim 63-62 lead.

Coach Bridges herded his players to the bench and sat them down. He had a huge decision to make. *Do I stick with these guys the full 32-minutes . . . or do I give them a quick blow?*

He gazed over at his players . . . *Sam, Rob, and Trip had played every second so far . . . but how can I take them out?*

His gaze went to the scorer's table. The starting five for Valley Christian was checking back in. *No room for error,* Coach Bridges thought. *They have to stay in . . . with them out . . . the game could get away from us real fast!*

"OK, guys," Coach Bridges said decisively. "We go back to the starters."

Coach Bridges looked his starters over. *Tired, but no hint of not wanting to be out there. Good! They have to give it their all.*

"I know you guys are getting a little tired . . . but we've got just eight minutes left . . . eight minutes . . . you have played your hearts out so far . . . keep doing that . . . that's all we can do," Coach Bridges said passionately.

The team huddled up, looked at the floor, and back at each other.

Coach Bridges thrust his hand into the middle. The whole team joined hands.

"All right, on three," Coach Bridges shouted. "NEVER QUIT!!! TEAM!!! One, two, three . . ."

"NEVER QUIT!!! TEAM!!!" the team yelled.

CHAPTER 70

MARCH-SOPHOMORE YEAR

THE crowd was noisy but nothing like the Pine Bluff championship game.

As they waited for the 4th quarter to start, Rob made his way first to Gabe Cantor, who would be on the bench to start the quarter. "You be ready," Rob whispered. "When the time comes . . . you are going to come through . . . just be ready."

Gabe smiled, inspired by Rob's confidence in him.

"I'll be ready," Gabe replied.

Next, Rob went to Josh Lee and swatted him on the back.

"You and me, Josh . . ." Rob said calmly. "We've got three time outs . . . you get in trouble, use them. Stay cool. We know these guys . . . you can play with them. Do your job."

"Got it," Josh replied quietly, feeling stronger.

Next, Rob moved to Sam and Trip, standing together at mid-court.

"We got this one, guys . . ." Rob said, slapping hands as he made his way to Edgar Garcia.

"Remember that first day of football practice last year, man," Rob said to Edgar.

Edgar nodded at the memory of doing a crab walk at the end of a grueling practice.

"This is nothing compared to that," Rob shouted above the din. "We got this."

"That's right, man," Edgar grunted.

Suddenly the noise dropped away . . . the fans were gone . . . the exhaustion was gone . . . the ref put the ball in play, and the Sectional Championship was within reach.

Valley Christian came out and expertly worked their offense for a score. Hillsdale bounced back with a three-pointer and a two-point lead. The Knights got a quick score, a steal, and another score, and they were up by two.

Back and forth, with neither team able to stretch the lead beyond two points. At the four-minute mark, Brad Wallace came in for Josh Lee, but only for a quick one-minute blow. Gabe Cantor came in for Edgar for two minutes and had a block, a rebound, and a huge basket that tied the score at 74 with two minutes to play.

The strain started showing on the Pirates as the minutes ticked off. They were outgunned here . . . exhausted . . . but there were only two minutes to play. Suck it up!

The crowd had now built themselves into a frenzy. Gone were the ideas of a sure win on the Valley Christian side, while hope was sprouting everywhere a Pirate fan sat.

They might do this! Allison thought, standing like everyone else around her.

Please, please, please, Emily pleaded.

We got this! We got this! Grandpa Russell knew. *But I can't say that out loud . . . not tonight . . . not against this team.*

Coach Bridges gave his instructions. "One time out left. Good shots. Tough Defense!"

He looked over the sweat-soaked faces of his players. *They have played their hearts out tonight . . . win or lose . . . doesn't matter.*

Coach Bridges saw Rob and Trip together . . . smiling through their fatigue.

They're enjoying this, Coach Bridges thought. *They aren't stressed . . . they love it.*

Allison poked Emily and motioned to look at the court . . . she saw the same thing.

"How can they both look so relaxed?" Allison shouted.

Emily followed her gaze and just smiled.

"Teenage boys . . . they're just brain dead!" Emily joked.

"I can't understand how they can do that with so much pressure?" Allison continued.

"They're good stock," Grandpa Russell bellowed. "Both of them. Not any kid can do that . . . those two are special!"

***

VALLEY Christian ball. Milk the clock. Get a good shot. Bingo. Two-point lead.

Hillsdale does the same. Pass from Mathews to McHenry. Boom. Two-pointer. Tie game. Just 72 seconds remain.

Valley Christian, quicker this time. Three-pointer. Swish. Three-point lead.

Hillsdale breaks the press. Works the offense. Outlet back to Rob. Wide open. Three-pointer. Nailed it. Tie game. . . . 79-79 . . . 42 seconds to go.

Time out, Valley Christian.

Valley Christian ball. In play. Two exhausted teams working hard. Running the offense. Playing defense. Loose ball. Mad scramble. Ball pops loose. Tapped underneath.

Shot clock winding down. Scooped up by Valley Christian. Shot. Shot-clock horn blares. Ball goes through. Count the basket. Seven seconds left. Time out, Hillsdale.

Valley Christian 81, Hillsdale 79.

Bedlam in the arena.

CHAPTER 71
MARCH–SOPHOMORE YEAR

*T*HERE was no real decision to make. Hal Bridges looked at his team... his valiant team... on the brink of a Sectional Championship... on the verge of a win over Valley Christian.

The ball is going to Rob or Trip. Everyone in the arena knows it... I do... Valley Christian knows... the fans know.

He made his decision and barked at his team.

"No need to recreate the world here," Coach Bridges shouted. "We run the same thing we ran against Pine Bluff. Rob, if you're open, shoot it... if not, look to Trip... we only need a two... but if you get a good look... a three's even better."

Rob and Trip both smiled... they looked like they were in a pickup game in the streets or Rob's driveway.

"One of us is doing this," Trip laughed. "Nail it, partner!"

"You, too," Rob called back to Trip.

"Seven more seconds, guys," Rob continued, turning to Sam, Edgar, and Josh. "Relax and make these the best seven seconds of the night!"

"Bring it in," Coach Bridges announced gruffly. "DO IT!!!"

"DO IT!!!" the team echoed, taking the floor.

The crowd collectively held their breath and said their prayers.

Allison and Emily's hands were each steepled together at their chins in prayer.

Grandpa Russell stood straight, a peaceful look on his face.

"They got this," Grandpa Russell muttered over and over.

Grandma Russell, by his side, knew the next seven seconds would determine her husband's happiness for the next seven days . . . or weeks . . . was in silent prayer as well.

The Pirates inbounded the ball, and the crowd started to roar. The defensive pressure by Valley Christian was intense . . . their arrogance almost gone . . . but their determination to win . . . to beat back these nothings . . . was at its peak.

Rob started the play . . . gave up the ball to Josh . . . a double team by Valley Christian. Josh squirts the ball through to Sam, back to Rob . . . open . . . but not much . . . Trip breaking free off Edgar's excellent screen. Pass rifled to Trip.

The crowd gasped as Valley Christian frantically played defense. Three seconds left . . . two . . . one . . . Trip gathers in the ball. Goes up in one motion. Beyond the three-point line. Horn sounds. Trip releases.

Nothing but net!

Ref wildly waving his arms.

No shot.

After the horn sounded.

Basket no good.

Valley Christian wins 81-79.

In the Hillsdale section, there was immediate elation when Trip's shot zipped through the net. A three-pointer . . . 82-81 Hillsdale . . . a Sectional Championship. A trip to NorCals!

But Grandpa Russell knew right away that it was a dream. He had heard the horn . . . had seen the ref start waving the shot off even before Trip released. *Milliseconds . . . we lost this championship to milliseconds,* he groused, as the crowd around him suddenly realized the Pirates had lost.

Rob and Trip stood across the court from each other in stunned silence. *We had this game,* they both thought. *We had it.*

They found each other's eyes and shared a long, anguished look . . . looked at the ref . . . at the scoreboard . . . at the Valley Christian fans streaming onto the floor in wild celebration . . . and they knew it was over.

Rob shrugged, feeling the hurt welling up inside. *At least I know I'm going to live through this,* Rob thought. *I'm not going to like it, but I'm not dying from it. But this might have been our best chance . . . if Trip leaves . . . we'll have no chance at Sectionals again . . . ah, it's not going to kill me.*

Trip moved across the court toward Rob, and he could see that Trip was hurting . . . fighting to control his emotions.

So close, Rob thought. *So close. Just like the "Pick" game two years in a row. This is getting really OLD!!!!*

"Sorry, Rob," Trip said, almost breaking down. "I hesitated just . . . I just didn't get it off . . . in time . . . I'm sorry."

"Are you kidding," Rob protested. "Not your fault, man. Slow pass . . . should have got it to you sooner. I'm sorry."

They reached out for a quick hug, and both could feel the sweat-drenched jersey of the other.

"We did our best, man," Rob said sincerely, remembering what Coach Wilson had told him long ago that sometimes your best wasn't good enough. "Days done."

"Yeah, we'll get em' next year," Trip proclaimed.

Rob's face broke into a huge grin.

"We'll get them next year?" Rob asked.

"Yeah, we'll get them next year," Trip answered softly.

"As in we'll . . . you and me . . . us . . ." Rob replied excitedly, waving toward the rest of the team across the floor.

"Yeah," Trip said, quietly looking down.

"So, that means . . . you are staying at Hillsdale?" Rob asked excitedly. "You're not going to Valley Christian?"

"No, I'm not going to Valley Christian," Trip grinned. "I don't belong over there . . . those guys are jerks . . . no class at all . . . I belong with you guys . . . that's where I belong."

"Jerks, huh? You loser . . . staying at Hillsdale . . . you'll always be a loser."

It was Tony Russo.

"Staying there means no Sectionals . . . and probably no USC, hotshot . . . what a loser!" Tony growled.

Trip just stared at him.

"Nothing to say, loser!" Tony smirked.

"Yeah, I got something to say, jerk," Trip replied darkly. "Write it down . . . this is the last game Valley Christian beats Hillsdale in basketball until after I graduate from Hillsdale in two years."

"Hah," Tony laughed hard. "You have one lucky game, and now you really think you can beat us?"

"Not think . . . know," Trip responded with the hint of a smile. "You guys lose your whole starting five . . . our whole team is back . . . you're going down next year and the year after."

Tony laughed again . . . but not as hard . . . and with a little less confidence.

Trip caught his look and was caught up in the moment.

"You a baseball player, too?" Trip asked, taking Tony off guard.

"Yeah, I'll start at short this year on the Varsity," Tony answered.

"Great!" Trip said. "Then we'll include baseball, too . . . you . . . and I mean you . . . won't ever beat Hillsdale again . . . at anything!"

Although not very convincingly, Tony Russo laughed again, got swept up in his team and their fans, and carried away from Rob and Trip.

"Not sure I should have opened my mouth like that," Trip said apologetically to Rob. "Kinda' puts us in a bind . . . locker room wall fodder . . . you know."

"I'll take the chance," Rob crowed. "If we've got you, I think we can make it work."

The pair laughed. "Course, we better let Coach Bridges know . . . and Coach Wilson know," Rob said.

"Yeah, probably better," Trip said sheepishly.

"Hey, Rob," Trip said softly. "Can you keep this decision quiet today . . . not tell anyone . . . I think I kinda' want to get a few people together at one time and tell them all . . . can you help me set that up?"

"With pleasure," Rob said as they turned and headed for the locker room.

CHAPTER 72
MARCH-SOPHOMORE YEAR

SUNDAY morning, Rob awoke to the familiar smells of coffee brewing and bacon frying. He stretched himself out . . . remembered yesterday's game . . . got sad . . . but immediately snapped out of it when he remembered Trip's announcement.

Rob glanced at the clock, hopped out of bed, popped in the shower, and headed downstairs just as he heard the front doorbell ring.

He headed toward the door, but his Mom beat him to it and opened the door to see Dave Wilson standing there.

"Well, good morning, Dave," Emily said, a little flustered. "How are you this morning?"

"Good," Coach Wilson said with a shy smile. "Good. How about you?"

"Great!" Emily replied, a little puzzled. *What is he doing here?* she wondered.

"Uh, last night on the bus trip home, Rob, uh, asked me to stop by this morning," Coach Wilson began, stopping as he could see Emily had no clue what he was talking about.

"Hey, Coach," Rob called out as he hit the bottom of the stairs.

Emily turned to Rob with a look that said, *What's up?*

"Oh, I forgot to tell you, I asked a few folks over this morning," Rob continued to the door, shaking Coach Wilson's hand.

"For . . . for . . . breakfast," Emily said in a panic.

"No, no, just for a few minutes," Rob laughed, drawing Coach Wilson inside. As he did, he saw Coach Bridges walking up the porch steps.

"Hi, Coach," Rob said, welcoming his coach, and shaking his hand, as Emily looked on in confusion.

Both coaches walked in, and Emily led them to the kitchen area where Grandma and Grandpa Russell were perched, Grandpa Russell poring over the *Hillsdale Express*.

"Oh, hi, Hal," Grandpa Russell said, rising in surprise and shaking hands. "Hi, Dave. What's up?"

"Not sure," Coach Bridges responded, just as there was a knock on the kitchen door.

Emily looked at Rob in surprise and opened the door to find Buck, Donnie, and Allison.

"Good morning," Emily said, clearly bewildered by her burgeoning party at 9:00 am on a Sunday morning. "Come on in and join the crowd."

They all piled in, and the front doorbell rang . . . Emily looked at Rob in panic.

"How many are showing up here this morning, Rob?" Emily asked, with a concerned look on her face.

"This should be it," as Rob ran for the door to let in Trip, Aunt Barb, and Trip's two nephews.

They all crowded into the kitchen, with some spilling into the great room area . . . with no one but Rob and Trip having any clue of what was going on.

Finally, as everyone settled in, Rob cleared his throat and announced, "Thanks for coming over, everyone . . . Trip asked that I get everyone together . . . everyone who has really helped him sort out where to go to school next year . . . and I think . . . I think he has some things to tell you."

CHAPTER 73
MARCH-SOPHOMORE YEAR

*T*HE room hushed immediately, and Trip walked to where everyone could see and hear him. The faces looking back were all concerned... concerned that what Trip had to say might ruin their day.

Allison felt sick to her stomach. *Rob and Trip don't look happy,* she thought, searching their faces. *They don't look really sad... but they don't look happy. I hope you're staying Trip. I hope you're staying.*

Around the room, everybody had a sense of what was coming... Trip has made his decision... but nobody knew what Trip had decided... except Rob and Trip... and they weren't giving anything away.

"Thanks, everybody, for coming over... I didn't want to make this a big deal... but I only wanted to do it once," Trip began. "I'm not comfortable with this kind of thing, so I'll try to keep it short."

Uh, oh, Allison thought, sharing that feeling with Emily by quickly glancing her way.

"You all had the most impact on my decision on where to be for the next couple of years," Trip continued. "You all... well, all but one of you... were very careful to let me make up my own mind... and I know you all had my best interests at heart."

Allison felt her face go bright red with embarrassment. *I know he's talking about me... when will I learn to shut up and mind my own business? If I'm the one to cause Trip to leave, I'll just die,* Allison wailed.

"You all have had a tremendous influence on me since I've been here," Trip went on slowly. "Coach Wilson . . . you got me up here . . . and have taught me about being smart . . . doing the right thing . . . how to start looking at things like an adult . . . well, kinda' like an adult . . . I'll never forget that . . . thank you."

Oh, that sounds like he's leaving, Allison cringed. *You can't leave!*

"Emily, you . . . and you, Grandma and Grandpa Russell, have welcomed me into your family . . . made me feel like I belong here . . . taught me how a real family acts . . . you have all been huge . . . thank you!" Trip went on.

The trio mumbled in return, and Emily gave him a big smile . . . but a smile tinged in uncertainty.

"Buck and Donnie . . . you guys taught me what it's like to be a real friend . . . and what it's like to have real friends," Trip added sincerely. "You have had my back since the first day . . . no pressure . . . no opinions . . . just support. Thank you, guys!"

Buck and Donnie smiled back and nodded but stayed quiet.

Allison stiffened in fear. *All he's talking about is how everyone else let him make up his mind . . . and I just told him what to do. He must hate me! Please don't leave because of me, Trip . . . please.*

"Aunt Barb, what can I say . . . you being willing to move up here . . . take me in after all that happened in SoCal . . . tell me I have a real home to live in . . . no matter where I go to school . . . I mean . . . I just can't thank you enough," Trip sputtered out, near tears.

Aunt Barb, standing close, reached out and stroked Trip's arm as he struggled for control. His head bowed, he bit his lip, struggled to regain his composure, and turned to Coach Bridges.

"Coach Bridges," Trip choked out, teeming with emotion now. "You taught me how to play the game . . . how to be a team player . . . how to grow up. I appreciate it so much. These are lessons I'll never forget . . . long after I'm gone. Thank you!"

NO!!!! Allison screamed in her head as her face went ghostly white. *You can't be leaving!!!*

Coach Bridges grunted . . . as he fought to retain control . . . something almost everyone in the room was struggling to do.

"Wonder Boy," Trip said, turning to face Rob. "Wonder Boy" . . . let's just say you were a little too perfect for me when I first got here . . . but once I got to know you . . . I realized you aren't perfect at all."

Rob laughed the hardest as the whole room erupted in laughter . . . except Allison.

"But really," Trip continued. "You're the best man . . . the best friend I've ever had . . . you've helped me in so many ways . . . on the court . . . off the court . . . I couldn't have made this decision without you . . . without you being yourself . . . guiding me . . . but not telling me what to do . . . telling me to do what's best for me. Thanks, bro!"

Rob nodded, choking up . . . and not very successfully trying to hide it.

Trip looked at Rob for a long time before he looked down at the floor . . . and back up as he faced the group, his face betraying his emotion . . . and how hard this was for him.

He looked the group over slowly, took a deep breath, and turned to face Allison.

"And . . . then . . . there's . . . Allison Pierce," Trip announced, flourishing his arm toward her . . .

Allison felt like she was going to be sick . . .

CHAPTER 74
MARCH-SOPHOMORE YEAR

*A***LLISON** turned red again, choked back tears, and fought to keep the vomit rising up her throat from spewing onto the floor at her feet!

Trip faced the group again, sighed heavily, and began speaking softly.

"Allison flat told me that I'd be an idiot for leaving Hillsdale High. And, of course . . . she knows best . . . just ask her," Trip quipped, drawing nervous laughter.

"She looked at all the pros and cons and decided Hillsdale was the right decision. Not because she wanted me on the teams . . . not because it was my best chance to get into USC . . . and it isn't . . . but it was my best chance to be a good man," Trip added emotionally.

Trip choked up again and paused. "I'm sorry," he said after a moment. "Nobody can tell anyone about this crying stuff, right," he said, wiping his eyes through a smile.

Allison looked at Trip and cautiously gave him a smile . . . the one she loved to give Rob.

Trip saw that smile, returned it, and then took a deep breath.

"Allison said . . ." Trip stammered, "that the best way for me to become a good man was to stay at Hillsdale . . . and watch . . . watch and learn from great role models like Coach Bridges . . . Coach Wilson . . . Grandpa Russell . . . Rob . . . guys that live life the right way . . . try to do the right thing . . ."

Trip was crying again, trying hard to hold it back.

"Allison convinced me . . . in her own special way . . ." Trip said, trying to lighten the mood. "Convinced me in her own special way . . . to stay at Hillsdale!"

A loud gasp rose from everybody in the room. They had seen it coming as Trip got closer to the end . . . but the tension released to hear him say the actual words was wonderful.

Immediately, it was a party, and everyone shook hands or hugged Trip fondly, and after a short while the gathering began to break up.

"Son, I'm proud of you," Coach Bridges said. "You took your time . . . thought it through . . . and you arrived . . . arrived at the right decision. I'm so glad you're staying."

"Me, too, Coach," Trip said. "Me, too."

As the rest of the group peeled off, Trip found himself alone with Emily, Rob . . . and Allison, who had finally recovered from her worry about Trip heading to Valley Christian . . . and it being her fault.

"Well, I've got to roll, guys," Trip said, coming closer to Emily.

"Can I give you a hug, Emily?" Trip asked.

Emily just smiled and moved in to give him a big hug.

"You're really like a Mom to me, you know," Trip choked out. "Thank you!"

Emily, her eyes misted over, just smiled, nodded, and hugged him tighter.

"Bro!" Trip said more brightly, turning to Rob. "See you at the ballpark tomorrow . . . can't wait . . . don't be expecting me to have the same skill level as you in baseball . . . you'll see . . . your "Wonder Boy" name will come back . . . basketball's my main game!"

Rob laughed and replied, "Yeah, well, you better be awesome. You told the world we're never losing to Valley Christian again . . . you better help me back that up!"

Trip laughed while Emily and Allison looked at each other quizzically.

"A long story . . . I'll tell you all about later," Rob said, seeing the confusion on their faces.

"And, Allison," Trip said, moving closer and looking her directly into her eyes. "You, my dear . . . you are simply amazing!"

Allison blushed deeply and didn't know quite how to react. "Uh, thanks, uh, Trip," she finally managed.

"You are always there to say the right thing," Trip began, pausing as he saw doubt in Allison's eyes. "Always there to say things the right way to get me to understand."

Allison's blush deepened.

Emily and Rob exchanged glances, and both started to well up.

"I'm so lucky to have a friend like you," Trip continued, reaching out and grabbing her by both shoulders. "You make me a better person . . . you make Rob a better person . . ."

Now, Allison was welling up.

"Besides, Rob . . . you know you're my best friend," Trip said quietly.

Now, Allison sobbed.

"Thank you, Allison," Trip said, hugging her close. "Thanks for being you . . . you're amazing . . . and you're very special."

Allison hugged him back, pushed him away, stepped back, and dazzled him with a smile.

Trip returned the smile, walked to the door, and said, "Later!"

"I think Trip has arrived," Emily said softly, turning to see Rob and Allison smiling broadly at each other.

That smile, Rob thought. *That smile is amazing . . . and so is Allison!*

END OF BOOK FIVE

About Author

A sports fanatic since early childhood, Mac grew up watching the great San Francisco Giants teams of Willie Mays, among others. Also on the watchlist; the San Francisco (now Golden State) Warriors, the San Francisco 49ers, and Oakland Raiders. A decent athlete, he played basketball for Pacific Grove High and spent 10 years playing men's open-division fastpitch softball. In his 30s, he began his coaching career, which spanned over 40 teams with kids as young as six all the way up through high school girls softball at Carmel High, where he headed the program from 1997-2006. After retiring from active coaching, Mac spent several years giving coaching clinics on topics including fundamentals, philosophy, practice organization, and team building for high school and youth league coaches. The insights into high school kids and coaching proved invaluable for these books. Add to that six children and 13 grandchildren, and he definitely knows kids!

Mac's writing "career" began in high school as the editor of his school newspaper during his senior year. The idea of writing a series like this stemmed from reading the classic Chip Hilton books written by Clair Bee, mostly in the 1950s. From start to finish, the 12-book Rob Mathews Sports Series project "only" took 28 years to complete . . . family, coaching, and work kept getting in the way!

A native of California's Bay Area and Central Coast, Mac and his wife Suzanne (Suzy) have a home in the Sierra Nevada Foothills east of Sacramento, the setting for the series. Ironically, this area was chosen as a setting for the series 25 years before acquiring the home.

Also By

The Rob Mathews Sports Series

FRESHMAN YEAR

1. FRESH START 2. GAME PLAN 3. TEAM PLAYERS

SOPHOMORE YEAR

4. LAST CHANCE 5. TRIP ARRIVES 6. MISSED CHANCES

JUNIOR YEAR

7. ALMOST PERFECT 8. NEW NORMAL 9. BEST CASE

SENIOR YEAR

10. SUDDEN DEATH 11. FINALLY RIGHT 12. DECISION TIME

ALL BOOKS AVAILABLE IN E-BOOK, PAPERBACK & HARDBACK FORMATS

REVIEWS WELCOMED AND APPRECIATED ON BOOKSELLER WEBSITE

Made in United States
Troutdale, OR
11/24/2024